SCOTTY

SCOTTY

JAMES B. RESTON AND THE RISE AND FALL OF AMERICAN JOURNALISM

JOHN F. STACKS

Little, Brown and Company
Boston New York London

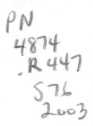

First Edition

Library of Congress Cataloging-in-Publication Data
Stacks, John F.
    Scotty : James B. Reston and the rise and fall of American journalism /
John F. Stacks. – 1st ed.
       p.   cm.
    Includes bibliographical references.
    ISBN 0-316-80985-3
    1. Reston, James, 1909– 2. Journalists – United States – Biography. I. Title.

PN4874.R447 S76 2003
070.92 – dc21
[B]   2002020776

10 9 8 7 6 5 4 3 2 1

Designed by Interrobang Design Studio

Q-FF

Printed in the United States of America

For Carol

AND

Ben, Kim, Hannah, and Kate

AND

Nicole and Andrew

AND IN MEMORY OF

John F. Stacks, Jr.

CONTENTS

ACKNOWLEDGMENTS

THIS IS NOT an authorized biography in any sense, but Scotty Reston's family was generous and cooperative over the years it took me to research and write about his life. Until her death in 2001, his wife, Sally Reston, was most helpful through hours of interviews, as were Scotty's three sons, Richard, James B. Jr., and Thomas, and their spouses. Without their help, this book would not have been possible.

The New York Times Company, with the special assistance of Susan Dryfoos, opened its archives without restriction. Those files provided enormous amounts of material illuminating the relationship between the Reston and the Sulzberger families and between Reston and the editors in New York. I am also grateful to Mai Pan, who, first as a guide to the *Times* archives and then as an independent researcher tracking down old *New York Times* stories in the microfilm libraries, provided crucial assistance.

Barbara Gamarekian, who once worked in the *Times* Washington bureau, spent hours and hours interviewing her former colleagues and other sources in the capital. Their remembrances of working with Reston form a key part of this book. I thank as well all the present and past executives, correspondents, and columnists from the *Times* who shared their thoughts and recollections with me.

After his death in 1995, Scotty willed his papers to the University of Illinois, his alma mater. The Reston collection in Champaign-Urbana is large and rich, and I thank archivist William Maher and his wife, Terry, for helping me to navigate it.

Geoff Shandler at Little, Brown became the third editor to have a role in shepherding this project. His editorial guidance was superb. The first editor, Jim Silberman, deserves special appreciation for commissioning the book in the first place. Bill Phillips was the second editor and applied the welcome pressure to move the book into high gear. And my thanks to my agent, Amanda Urban.

When I had finished the first draft of this book, I asked Johanna McGeary, my friend and colleague at *Time* magazine, to give it a quick read. Instead, she devoted uncounted hours to editing it, quite rigorously. I can't thank her enough for the much-needed scrubbing she gave the manuscript. My thanks too for the painstaking copyediting of DeAnna Satre.

Finally, I have to thank all my family, friends, and even squash partners, who endured years of my talking about this book. Some have read it already, but the rest don't have to; they've heard it all before.

JOHN F. STACKS
NEW YORK CITY

SCOTTY

CHAPTER 1

THE REPORTER AND THE PRESIDENT

JOHN FITZGERALD KENNEDY arrived in Vienna on June 3, 1961. As he drove through the streets, tens of thousands of Austrians lined the roadway to cheer the young American president. Kennedy had just come from a triumphal meeting in Paris with the crusty president of France, Charles de Gaulle. He was full of confidence and hope that his upcoming summit meeting with the leader of the Soviet Union would serve to ease tensions between the two nuclear superpowers. But Chairman Nikita Khrushchev surprised Kennedy. Taking advantage of Kennedy's youth and his recent embarrassment in the Bay of Pigs fiasco, in Cuba, Khrushchev spent the next two days denouncing American imperialism. And he demanded that the Soviet Union be given the right to control access to West Berlin in divided Germany, something he knew Kennedy could not concede.

In fact, the Vienna summit meeting went so badly from the American point of view that Kennedy asked for a final, private session with Khrushchev to try to salvage some mutual understanding between the two nations. With only their translators present, Kennedy began by reminding the Soviet leader that each country had the ability to destroy the other. He then asked Khrushchev to back off his demands on Berlin. The bombastic Khrushchev did no such thing, warning Kennedy that "force would be met by force," adding that "if the U.S. wants war, that's its problem." Kennedy was stunned.

"Then, Mr. Chairman, there will be war," Kennedy concluded. "It will be a cold winter."

The first person with whom Kennedy discussed this bleak, frightening encounter was not his secretary of state nor any member of his administration. Astonishingly, it was a journalist, James Barrett Reston, Washington bureau chief and columnist for the *New York Times*. By prior arrangement, Reston had slipped into the American embassy and was waiting, with curtains drawn to conceal his presence, to interview Kennedy. The president arrived ten minutes after leaving his last meeting with Khrushchev.

Reston, older than the young president, had recently been on the cover of *Time* magazine, which called him, quite accurately, the most powerful journalist in Washington. He had been covering the nation's capital since the early 1940s. Shorter than Kennedy, Reston generally dressed in a casually tweedy way, often with a bow tie and almost always with a briar pipe and a pouch of tobacco in his pocket. Reston had a full head of brown hair now graying slightly on the sides and a round, open face that invited confidence but disguised a good deal of cunning and ambition. He was quite accustomed to dealing with powerful men.

"How was it?" Reston asked casually.

"Worst thing in my life. He savaged me," Kennedy responded. The president seemed to Reston to be almost in shock, repeating himself and speaking with astonishing candor to the journalist. "Not the usual bullshit," Reston wrote in his notepad. "There is a look a man has when he has to tell the truth." Kennedy went on to say that to counter the battering by Khrushchev, which he attributed to the Soviet leader's underestimation of Kennedy's resolve, the United States would have to stand more firmly against the Soviets' demands in Berlin and against the mounting Communist insurgency in South Vietnam. Reston wrote later that he was "speechless" when Kennedy mentioned Vietnam, since that troubled country was at that point nowhere near the heart of the Cold War conflict and, in Reston's estimation, did not carry much weight in the superpower tug-of-war. Ever afterward, Kennedy's remark to Reston was seen by historians and by Reston himself as the moment marking the beginning of America's long slide into the tragedy of Vietnam.

From the perspective of our own time, that Reston was with Kennedy at this critical moment in American history is almost unimaginable. No reporter, no matter how famous his face or his byline, would have this sort of access today, would be trusted to hear an American president reacting honestly and without pretense to a frightening failure that could have presaged nuclear war – and then, without stated rules or restrictions, would be able to write carefully and subtly about that encounter. The relationship between journalists and politicians in America is today most often a distant and hostile one, marked by distrust and anger and cynicism.

James "Scotty" Reston was the best journalist of his time, and perhaps the best of any time. He was a reporter of amazing skill, able to relieve powerful men of their most important secrets. He was a writer of easy, graceful prose who revolutionized the style in which American newspapers are written. As a columnist, he was a shaper of public opinion, an explicator of the byzantine politics of Washington and the world. In his heyday, he was read by more Americans than any other single writer on public affairs. As a newspaper executive, he recruited men of enormous talent into the previously rather shabby career of journalism and inspired an entire later generation to join the trade. Together they raised the quality of journalism beyond what it had ever been. He was skeptical without ever lapsing into the current disease of American journalism: unrelieved cynicism.

Working at the reporter's trade is an odd way to make a living. The pay at the beginning is barely above minimum wage, and even at the end of a career, except at the very upper reaches of the craft, the compensation is barely enough to achieve entry into the middle class, no matter how loosely that category is defined. There is little status attached to the work; most people view reporters as parasites, taking their sustenance from tragedy, misfortune, misdeeds, and the public humiliation attendant to failure and illegality. Bad news is usually good news for the reporter, since the worse the tragedy, the more egregious the misbehavior, the more alarming the threat, the more avidly the story will be consumed.

There is nothing glamorous about most of the work. Almost as a matter of ritual inauguration, the neophyte reporter is sent to cover the police department, where the stories are raw, the cops are contemptuous, and unless there is a spectacular crime involving socially prominent people, the stories wind up deep inside the newspaper. There is not much pleasure in interviewing, say, the widow of a cab-driver shot by a robber, or the parents of a boy tragically drowned the night before, or, as I once did, a father numb with grief after his two little boys had been killed by a pack of feral dogs.

After a period of apprenticeship, the reporter moves indoors to cover the tedium of civic lunches and canned speeches. Then, with some luck, there might come the chance to write, even with a bit of the edge of discovery and outrage, about the chronically miserable public schools. The best reporters throw their energies into the beat, but often as not, nothing changes.

Covering election politics is frequently the next step up the career ladder. Here the reporter is often viewed as a pariah, seen by the candidate and the campaign as a potential debunker of the glowing self-portraits they wish to paint for the public. And rarely is the reporter seen as a pillar of the broader community. At a social gathering, admitting that one is a reporter is roughly like saying one is a mortician: necessary perhaps, but not welcome.

In the days when James B. Reston was entering the trade, men and a few bold women became reporters (the appellation "journalist" was widely adopted later in an effort to dignify the trade, which also began calling itself, with absolutely no justification, a "profession") in part because there were low barriers to entry. A high school degree was an asset, as was a certain facility with formulaic English. A college education was certainly not required. The smartest and most able might finally reach the position of editor, and there, at the top of the masthead, there was respectability, some measure of community prestige, and on the biggest and best newspapers in the largest cities, even a certain prosperity.

"Journalism" may not be a profession, like the law or medicine, but the craft of reporting does require skill. As in the manual trades, there is a continuum in newspapering, from competence to mastery to superior craftsmanship, even to art. The best reporters have a few qualities in abundance that set them above the rest of their trade. Curiosity is foremost. The desire to learn how the world works, how people live their lives, to understand what is really happening below the surface of appearances – this is what drives the best reporters. It is a cliché in the trade that reporting is like being paid to go to a graduate school that lasts a lifetime. That cliché is true. For the reporter who succeeds – who moves from cop shop, as we always called it, to school board, city hall, Washington, a presidential campaign, the White House, exotic foreign assignments – the trade is an unending education. It is, after all, the *news* business, and so the work is about discovering what is *new*, what is different, what is actually the case as opposed to what seems to be the case. The best reporting is not just about what happened but about why it happened and what may happen next. It is about discovery, not of some profound scientific truth, but of how human beings go about their lives, how they do their jobs, how their businesses operate, about what kinds of people public figures really are. The reporter is the curious amateur, poking into unfamiliar worlds for others too busy with their own lives to follow their own curiosity. The joy of discovery for the curious reporter can be found in the mundane or the profoundly important. I can still remember the pleasure of finding out, when I was twenty-two years old, how an artificial cattle-breeding cooperative worked, how the bulls were rated, and how, with amazing precision, they were induced to deliver their creamy product. I can remember the pleasure, almost two decades later, in finding out exactly how Ronald Reagan operated inside his own White House.

Reporting is not academic work. To find out the reality of things, leaving aside the problem of knowing the *entire* reality, the reporter has to find the people who really know what is going on and then get them to explain what they are doing and why. The reporter plays consciously on the fact that simply having someone pay attention is mildly intoxicating for the object of that attention. But the more secret the information, the more carefully it is guarded, the more difficult is the transaction between reporter and source. To accomplish that exchange – that is, to get another person to divulge information sometimes against self-interest – is the high art of reporting. So the second quality of the great reporter is the ability to establish a trusting relationship with the people who have the information. The relationship between reporter and source can take various forms. It can be simple and direct: the source has information he or she wants made public, and the reporter can provide that service. It can be more complicated: the source has information he or she wants made public but does not want to be identified as the person who made it public, becoming an anonymous source. Or more complicated still:

the source does not want to make the information public but does not want to lie to the reporter, fearing his or her reputation for honesty will be damaged. So the source divulges the information and trusts that the reporter will treat the material as "background" for further reporting. The trust inherent in these transactions goes both ways; the source must trust the reporter, and the reporter must, to some extent, believe in the essential truthfulness of the source. There are gradations and variations: the reporter may trust the source up to a point but understand the limit of the source's knowledge and bear in mind the self-interest of the source. Good reporters have the ability to make sources willing to talk to them. Great reporters make sources *want* to talk to them.

The source not only needs to trust the basic integrity of the reporter but also must trust the intelligence and understanding the reporter has about the subject at hand and believe that ignorance will not distort the resulting story. That is the third important asset of the great reporter: he or she understands the subject at hand nearly as well as the source. It is not enough for the reporter to be curious; he must also be informed enough to place the new information in context, to weigh its value, to explain how it changes the known body of information about that subject. The good reporter must bring context to what has been learned. The good reporter needs to read more than he writes, to learn the antecedents of the story at hand. The reporter needs to be a striver, a person who wants to raise himself up, if not to the high status and accomplishment of top experts, at least high enough to reduce the gap of information and understanding between source and reporter.

A master reporter must stay outside the story, independent enough to make judgments about the truth of the matter, the wisdom of the participants, the likely consequences of events being reported. At the same time, he must be far enough inside the process to be known by knowledgeable sources, to be trusted, to have access to those who know the story. This is the most delicate of straddles, an outsider who can penetrate to the inside of a story. Success in the trade, especially success at the top of a trade in which the subject matter often includes the most urgent and important issues facing the nation and even the world, requires a rare combination of ambition and restraint, of inquisitiveness and discretion, of the burning desire to expose and explain along with the good sense to know what must remain private.

For the reporter, there is always danger lurking. Writing a story that is factually wrong can be damaging. Being seen as a propagandist for a particular source or a particular point of view is likewise extremely destructive to the journalist's reputation. The combination of error and special pleading for a source is ruinous. These dangers increase in direct proportion to the fame and status of the reporter. Fame will of course attract attention to the reportorial failure. And that very fame, the record and accomplishments and scoops accumulated through the years, can dull the reporter's skepticism. It can seem to the famous reporter, after a lifetime of excellence in his craft, that no one would dare lie to him. But no reporter is ever immune to that danger. Journalism is a craft in which one's mistakes and misjudgments are visible to all. It is truly a highwire act, often performed before a very large audience.

James Reston came to America with his family early in the twentieth century from Scotland and was naturally called Scotty from the day he arrived. Rather than shed the childhood nickname, he kept it all his life, both as a way of not putting on airs and as a reminder to himself that he was from somewhere else, that he was by definition an outsider. As an immigrant child, he had felt that apartness keenly and painfully. In the memoir completed late in his life, he still recalled that feeling vividly. It was, he wrote, the thing he "hated the most – the fear of being rejected, of being ridiculed as an outsider, different, even absurd." An exemplary marriage to a smart, beautiful, and graceful woman he met in college helped soften that anxiety. But the feeling was always there, making him very determined to succeed, very competitive, eager to be among the powerful and to have the secondhand power that was once enjoyed by the most eminent of America's print journalists.

At the middle of the twentieth century, Reston was the model of what a young journalist wanted to become: wise, fair, able to speak in his own voice, and most of all, so well respected by those in power that he could find out and tell his readers what was really going on in the world he covered. He had access to the corridors of power because he was trusted to report and write with a sense of balance and humanity; he was often critical of policies and policy makers but rarely harsh in these judgments. He got to know the powerful as human beings, as people with strengths and weaknesses. He usually thought they were trying to do their difficult jobs as well as they could and in what they saw as in the best interests of the nation. There was, at the heart of Reston's style of journalism, a sense of common purpose with the government and political leaders. He felt that journalism and government were integral parts of the fabric of the country, working in different ways toward the same goal: helping the country deal with threats to its health and survival from abroad and at home. The press and the government, although with different interests and different priorities, were seen by Reston as collaborators in one enterprise, the preservation of the United States of America.

Reston had a deep antipathy toward those in government who wanted to keep secret important matters of public concern. He believed strongly that an informed public was the prerequisite of a self-governing society. In Reston, the impulse of the outsider to become an insider was expressed as the desire to know what the insiders knew. He wasn't content with discovering big secrets, which he did with stunning regularity; he liked little secrets as well and urged his reporters to work hard at finding out such relative trivia as, say, the name of an ambassador whose appointment would become public knowledge the next day. He believed that by publishing even the small secrets of government, he could create the illusion that he and his staff were almost as inside as the real insiders, and that it was futile for officials to try to keep information from him and his colleagues.

For more than three decades, nearly all his professional life, Scotty Reston successfully walked this thin and difficult line, an outsider-insider, trusting and being trusted, close to power but not seduced by it.

But then, near the end of his career, some of Reston's greatest virtues became liabilities. He trusted the untrustworthy, apparently believing he was too important to be lied to. His commentary and reporting became suspect. He was seen as toadying during a very tense and dramatic time. Rather than the very model of what young reporters wanted to be, Reston became a symbol of what they didn't want to be: a shill and an apologist. The reputation he had built and sustained throughout a stellar career was sadly tarnished. His own colleagues, men whose careers Reston had nourished and supported, turned on him in public. He became in some circles, even among colleagues still working on the newspaper he helped make great, the personification of what the true journalist should not be.

The story of Scotty Reston's life runs parallel to the story of the United States, from the Great Depression through World War II, the Cold War, Vietnam, and the scandals that fundamentally changed the way we understand – or more commonly misunderstand – our leaders and their policies and the choices they face. The story of how Scotty Reston got to the top of his trade, how he worked when he was the most powerful journalist in America and possibly in the world, can perhaps help transform the relationship between journalism and politics into something more than a game of lies and confrontation.

CHAPTER 2

THE OUTSIDER

IF EVER THERE was a born outsider, it was James Barrett Reston. And if ever there was a child raised from birth by a mother who was determined that he escape from that status by way of seriousness and hard work, it was that same boy.

Reston was born November 3, 1909, the second of two children. His mother, Johanna, was twenty-six years old when he was born. Johanna's mother had been a hotel manager at age nineteen. Her father styled himself a sculptor, but his highest accomplishment was the carving of gravestones. Johanna was the third of nine children, eight of whom were girls. Reston's father, also named James but always called Jimmy, or even "Wee Jimmy" because he stood only five feet, two inches tall, was the son of a woman named Elizabeth Barrett and a father who had been a fishmonger before becoming permanently disabled after being hit on the head by a barrel of salt herring. James B. Reston never met any of his grandparents.

The family lived in a flat in Clydebank, just outside Glasgow.

They had enough money for simple food and plain clothing but almost nothing extra. Scarcity of money combined with a harsh code of self-denial, sacrifice, and rigid religiosity imposed by his mother created a household almost entirely devoid of fun.

Wee Jimmy Reston was a machinist by trade and worked in the famous Glasgow shipyards, where luxury yachts and the various *Queen* ocean liners were built. Like many turn-of-the-century workmen, he was employed on an as-needed basis, with no ancillary benefits and no guarantees of full-time work. And like millions of other struggling working people across Europe, Jimmy Reston came to believe that real opportunity could be found only in America. Eighteen months after their only son was born, Jimmy and Johanna Reston had scraped together enough money for passage to the United States.

Wee Jimmy went first and moved in with his brother David and sister-in-law Alice in Dayton, Ohio. Then he sent for Johanna, young Jimmy, and their daughter, Joanna. The two families lived together, but within months the arrangement unraveled. Johanna Reston, who certainly was no fashion plate herself but was always busy finding ways to believe she and her family were not at the bottom of the ladder, was overheard one day criticizing the meagerness of her sister-in-law's wardrobe, a clear case of the pot calling the kettle black. She concluded that brother-in-law David must be cheap. The argument that followed led the newly arrived Reston family to decamp to a boardinghouse. Then the angry Johanna and the homesick and acquiescent Jimmy quickly moved back to Scotland, as if moving to another part of town or even to another city could not provide sufficient separation between her and her in-laws. Although too young to understand what was going on around him, James Reston later described the failed attempt to settle in America as "a disaster." It was also an enduring embarrassment; he once explained to one of his own sons that "illness" had driven his mother to yank the family back to Scotland. "As soon as she got back and got well again, she realized she had made a very expensive mistake," Reston told his son. In his memoirs, Reston recalled the accurate version of those traumatic events. "I never forgot this incident all my life," Reston wrote, blaming his mother's anger for the reverse migration, "and lived in dread in my own house of ever saying anything that might cause a break in my own family." The adult James Reston could be blunt and sarcastic, like his mother, but his anger and his tongue would always be held in check.*

Less than a year after they had finally realized their dream of moving to America, the Restons were back in Scotland, their savings gone, living in a tenement house outside Clydebank. They eventually settled in Alexandria, this time in a red stone tenement, on the banks of the River Leven. And there they remained for another decade, trapped by poverty and then by the outbreak of World War I, their hopes for a better life shattered by Johanna's sharp tongue.

She ran the household by her own rigid rules. She confiscated Wee Jimmy's paycheck when he got one and enforced a strict prohibition on whiskey, tobacco, movies, and dirty boots that might sully her spotless home. "'Take your shoes off, Jim.' That was always her greeting to him," Reston recalled. The fear of God was her constant companion, along with her firm belief that life on earth was but a "vale of tears," which, with proper conduct in this life, would be rewarded when the time came to pass on to the "other world." On Sundays the family would make two separate two-mile round trips on foot to attend church services. The midday meal on the Sabbath was served cold, since no cooking was permitted. All meals and

---

*None of his three sons could recall their father ever raising his voice to them or to their mother, although he himself recorded having once spanked the daylights out of his eldest son.

bedtime were preceded by prayer, and in the evenings Jimmy Reston would frequently read to his family from the Bible.

Little James especially pleased his parents when at age six or seven he was asked what he was going to do when he was grown up. "Preach the gospel to the heathen," he replied brightly. That story was repeated endlessly, by the family and by the adult James, who delighted in saying that preaching to the nonbelievers was not that different from his work as a newspaper columnist. When she was an elderly woman, his mother bragged to an interviewer that the key to her son's success lay in the fact that "he was raised in a Christian family." Her son the columnist, she added, "could go into a pulpit and preach."*

Life in Alexandria, Reston remembered, was one of "intimidating piety, austerity, and authority, respectful of religion, education, and hard work." The home itself was modest in the extreme: two rooms, one a large kitchen with an open fireplace that provided the only heat, and a parlor reserved for guests who never came. The flat had running water, but the toilet was outside, at the back of the house. Cooking was done on a hob over the coal grate, and the meals were simple and basic. Breakfast was always porridge, which young James hated. "Stop your boking," his mother would scold when he gagged on the gray mass. The family bed was in an alcove on one wall in the kitchen, and Reston remembered the family sleeping together at night, the children at the foot of the bed, the parents at the head.

His mother, speaking when she was nearing eighty, was indignant at the notion that they were very poor. Jimmy was at work slightly more than he was out of work, for a time at a munitions factory, and

---

*Reston would write later that he could never muster the faith of his parents, but he didn't make much of that fact to them. His mother's aggressive Presbyterianism spilled into a profound dislike for Catholics. She taught her son a triumphalist song celebrating the victory of King William over the Catholic James in 1690, at the Battle of the Boyne, a victory that still roils hatred in Northern Ireland. When her eldest grandson decided to marry a Catholic girl in the Catholic Church, Johanna declined to attend, telling her son, "I wouldnie hold ma tongue."

they lived on what he made. Johanna said they certainly didn't all sleep in one bed, although she didn't specify how many beds there were. "We would not be designated as poverty stricken," she insisted. "In fifty years of marriage we have never been dunned for a bill. We always had a little reserve."

The circumstances were nonetheless severe. "My first memory of Christmas," James Reston once wrote in an on-again, off-again attempt at a personal diary, "is as a boy in Scotland, where Christmas is regarded as a Holy Day and Santa Claus as a sort of an old commercial fraud. When we were children, my sister Joanna and I walked two miles obediently to church on Christmas morning and back again to a cold dinner, for it was forbidden by the Presbyterians to cook on such a sacred occasion. So when I hear the big bands playing 'Should Auld Acquaintance Be Forgot,' I am inclined to answer 'Yes!'"

But his adult memories of his childhood in Scotland were, he insisted unconvincingly, pleasant. "I have the happiest memories of our life in that village," he wrote. Even the strict mother was recalled kindly in the son's memoirs. "She was canny, shrewd, sometimes witty, but always true and always kind," he claimed. "My mother often threatened to box my ears, but never laid a hand on me, nor did my father, but if I argued with her, she would take me by the shoulders. 'You're downright cheeky,' she would say."

In a conversation with his middle son in the 1970s, Reston told a different version: "My father never licked me," Reston said, "but my mother licked me all the time. She would give me a clout on the side of the head. She was not brutal. There was usually a good reason. I had terrible trouble as a boy telling the truth, and they were always after me about that. I would lie about why I was late getting home. I was usually playing football [soccer] or fishing, not doing anything wrong. Sometimes she would turn me over and hit me on the backside."

He also remembered a horrible accident that took place in the kitchen. He managed to knock a pot of boiling water off the hob, badly scalding his arm and shoulder. The injury was apparently mistreated by a local physician, who bound up the burn instead of letting it breathe. His mother was furious at the doctor, Reston told his son years later. But "she was mad at everybody, just naturally mad at everybody," he said.

Despite the ascetic existence, there was a constancy in his home. "Above all," Reston wrote, "there was a sense of security in this Spartan routine. If I came home late, my mother was always there demanding an account of the day's activities and wanting to know if I had got into any mischief. When I disobeyed, she predicted that I would end up in 'the bad fire' if I didn't mend my ways." His uneducated father managed to be, as his son later described him, "contentedly unhappy." The father was a member of the church choir and had a habit of constantly humming to himself "as if he had no cares." His son remembered him clowning in the kitchen by walking on his hands, until his wife made him stop that "nonsense." He relieved the frequent tension in the family kitchen when he was jobless by going on long walks, often hauling his son along until the boy cried with fatigue. Even his hikes were not exempt from spousal criticism; Johanna would complain that he was wearing out his boots. He solved that problem by getting free hand-me-downs from the Salvation Army, soaking his feet in water with the new boots on, and then walking in them to achieve a rough fit.

Jimmy Reston grew vegetables and flowers in a community garden and would often save a few seeds from the packets and plant them randomly along the path of his long walks, taking delight in imagining the surprise their unpredicted presence would provide for passersby. In addition to the long, escapist walks, he would absent himself from the household by spending hours in the public library, underscoring his favorite passages in red ink in his Bible. Years later, in his retirement in America, he had a variant on that escape. He would go to the public library and find a newspaper that carried his son's syndicated column. Then, in a meticulous and tiny hand, he would copy his son's words into composition books. It was both a diversion and an homage to the success his son had achieved, an affirmation, perhaps, that his own difficult life had been worthwhile. He stored the composition books in a battered old suitcase. His son, unaware of his father's labors, found the suitcase and the composition books after Jimmy died.

Throughout the years of World War I, and in the face of periodic unemployment and the expense of two children, the family scraped together enough for another passage out of Scotland. "How they ever saved enough money on my father's salary to get back to America, I'll never know," Reston said. In 1920 Jimmy Reston again went off to America. Months later, Johanna, James, and Joanna sailed in steerage to make another try at success. In New York they were immediately put into quarantine as a precaution against smallpox, and young James worked in a kitchen at the quarantine facility to, as his mother put it later, "get more food for his family." When they finally arrived again in Dayton, Jimmy met them at the train station, running happily down the platform. He had found a job and had rented space in a gloomy rooming house along the railroad tracks. The good news was that there were electric lights and an indoor toilet. Jimmy resumed his friendship with his brother and sister-in-law, but Johanna never did; that relationship remained a point of contention with her husband, and she openly resented his Sunday-afternoon visits to his brother's home.

Dressed in her Sunday-best black dress, Johanna packed her son off to grade school in Dayton. The boy was decked out in English kit: starched white shirt and tie, jacket and short pants, long stockings and bare knees. Right away the American kids roughed him up on the playground and laughed derisively at his getup. Back home and in tears, he threatened a boycott of the school unless he got a pair of proper knickers, which he soon did, but the hurt remained. Six decades later, he quoted his childhood lament at being made to feel different, complete with his own italics: "But you don't understand, they *laughed* at me!"

The American language was a bit alien as well. Asked to spell "been," which was pronounced "bean" at home, the boy wrote out *b-i-n*. His sister remembered her brother coming home, pounding his fist, and declaring, "I'm going to be an American if it kills me." He was instantly nicknamed Scotty because of the brogue with which he spoke. Though he would never use the nickname as his newspaper byline, he was happy enough to be called Scotty all his life, and always signed his informal correspondence with that moniker. It was as if he wanted to remind himself and the world at large of how far he had come.

In Dayton he and his father quickly found jobs caddying at the Dayton Country Club, making one dollar for lugging clubs around eighteen holes. On weekends the boy started at six in the morning weeding greens and pocketed another couple of dollars. He benefited from the kindnesses of the golfing members, including the gift of his first bicycle, which his parents could not afford. Some weeks the lad brought home as much as fifteen dollars, not an unimportant addition to his mother's coffers. His sister was going to night school to learn shorthand and typing, with the goal of finding work as soon as possible. The Restons eventually rented a house in the east end of Dayton, where the two children finally had their own bedrooms. Still, Scotty remembered his early years as "stressful." There was never enough money, nor enough work for his father, and his mother complained constantly about Jimmy's lack of ambition. Johanna cleaned the homes of wealthy families in Dayton, and

Jimmy did some gardening for the same families. To keep everyone warm at night, the carpets were taken off the floor and laid across the beds.

To save money, the boy was sent for his haircuts to a barber college, where they cost only fifteen cents. But the shop had a big glass window where the patrons sat while being shorn, and to the young Reston this seemed a public admission of poverty. He soon figured out that by skipping one fifteen-cent school lunch, he could afford a proper haircut at a proper barbershop.

Reston's boyhood was not filled with joy; it was filled with effort to make bits of money, to Americanize his speech patterns, to avoid the embarrassment of being poor. He began his later schooling at Stivers High School, a trade school where, in addition to normal classes, he was taught tailoring. It was a skill he never forgot, often sewing on his own buttons even when he was a very successful newspaperman. In off hours he worked variously as a soda jerk, a movie usher, an attendant at a roller-skating rink, and a newspaper delivery boy. This last occupation was apparently done without his mother's knowledge. "He was not made for all weathers, and I wouldn't have let him if I knew," she explained. He later transferred to Oakwood High School, where the student body was decidedly more middle class and the family had to pay $175 a year in tuition because the school was out of their neighborhood. The snooty, richer kids made the young Reston uncomfortable, and one day he played hooky to look for a job, apparently intending to drop out. As punishment, principal Arthur Clagett decided to expel him, which Reston's mother resented all her life. "It [Oakwood High School] was attended by ritzy, rich men's children," his mother recalled decades later. "They tried to expel him, but now they claim him."

The expulsion never happened, not because he was a stellar student – he got mostly B's – but because he had become an exceptional golfer. The assistant principal at Oakwood talked Clagett out of his decision by reminding him that he was about to toss away the state schoolboy golf champion. At the Dayton Country Club, the Scottish pro, in a gesture of national solidarity, had made young Reston the caddie for James Middleton Cox, the publisher of the *Dayton Daily News* and a former governor of Ohio. In 1920, just as the Reston family was arriving in America, Cox had been the failed Democratic candidate for president of the United States (running with Franklin Delano Roosevelt as his vice presidential choice). Cox had taken a liking to Scotty and had given him some old clubs and a lesson with the club pro. Scotty practiced until his hands blistered. His father encouraged the game, over his mother's strong feeling that all games were a waste of time. In his last year of high school he won not just the state high school championship but also the Dayton men's tournament and the Ohio Public Links title. He accumulated a roomful of trophies, so many that they were once displayed in the window of a downtown department store. His father was proud and delighted, but his mother characteristically cautioned, "Don't get all puffed up." Nevertheless, Scotty was so good that he began to contemplate moving to Florida, to play the game full-time and professionally. "All foolishness," his mother told him. Asked how she blocked Scotty's professional golf career, his mother explained: "Prayer and argument."

Being a championship golfer did have important career implications. His local golf fame led him into a friendship with the sports editor of the Dayton newspaper. Scotty would spend winter afternoons in the newsroom after school, doubtless intoxicated by the gritty urgency of those wonderful places. Before the antiseptic age of computers, newsrooms were fabulously filthy shops with oiled wood floors, grungy paste pots with dark collars of old glue around their tops, carbon paper to make copies of the typewritten stories, and the acrid smell and insistent noise of hot-lead Linotype machines. The news wires' clanging bells alerted editors to breaking news coming from around the globe, giving a local office the sense of being in touch with the wider world beyond. The reporters often worked with their fedoras tilted back on their heads, shouting into two-piece telephones with the receiver in one hand and the mouthpiece and dial mechanism in the other. Scotty was permitted to write short accounts of high school basketball games, which would appear in the paper, he remembered, exactly as he wrote them. The editor, Si Burick, described him as "all ambition, a kid with tremendous guts and courage." Jimmy Reston encouraged his son's venture into newspapering. He collected Scotty's meager little clippings and kept them all his life. His mother, on the other hand, attempted to counter the twin evils of golf and newspapering by demanding strict church and Sunday school attendance, supplemented by visits to revival meetings as the evangelists who wandered into small-town America came through Dayton.

After his high school graduation, with golf ruled out and money in short supply, Scotty followed his mother's admonition to "get a job and get an education." Parlaying his little bit of journalistic experience on the *Daily News,* he became editor of the company newsletter at the Delco Remy Corporation, where Jimmy Reston was then working. For a year after high school, he wrote the stories, took the pictures, made up the pages, and even had a company car at his disposal. Although having a white-collar job in the same company where his father was a machinist must have provided some sense of generational progress, it was the most modest of beginnings for the man who would become the preeminent journalist in America, and he quickly realized that *Delco Doings* was a rather limiting enterprise.

A good high school friend had gone off to the University of Illinois and promised Scotty a room in the Sigma Pi fraternity house and a job at another frat house washing dishes to pay for his meals if he would join him in Champaign-Urbana. The school had what amounted to an open enrollment policy, so in 1928 Scotty packed his clothes and his golfing gear and hitchhiked west to go to college, the first in his family to reach that level of education. He enrolled in the school of journalism (tuition: twenty-five dollars a semester) and got a second job at the university's sports publicity department, which gave him just enough money to pay tuition and room rent.

Scotty Reston was now truly on his own. His parents were not able to help him financially, and, worse, the tensions between the two of them had grown intolerable. Some months earlier, Jimmy Reston had packed up and fled back to Scotland. Johanna had immediately sought, and been granted, a divorce. When Jimmy found this out, he had returned to protest to the court. The divorce was annulled, and he moved back into their home in Dayton just as Scotty was leaving for Illinois. The dollar cost of this attempted escape is not known, but it surely exacerbated the family's financial struggle. The marriage then settled into a sullen, unhappy stalemate, with Johanna's contempt for her husband, and Jimmy's stoic forbearance, always obvious. Scotty said the separation and divorce were never mentioned again in his presence, and he later described being "amazed and desolate" at this incident. Desolate indeed. Here was a nineteen-year-old boy, off to a strange town, a strange experience, with no money and now a family held together by no more than the hardened resignation of two unhappy people.

He had, at least, escaped that home. But he was, in his own mind, still an immigrant kid who carried, despite his enormous efforts to expunge it, a bit of Scots burr on his tongue. To combat the accent, he developed the habit of speaking slowly and carefully, a mannerism he retained all his life, which in later years sometimes lent an air of pomposity to his conversational style. His academic preparation was meager. His major skill was golf, with a lesser but still impressive ability at soccer, like many European kids who kicked a ball at every opportunity. He was rather short of stature but quite handsome, especially in a photograph the university sports publicity department took of him in a golf getup of white plus fours and matching sweater. But he remembered himself as a "skinny little guy, maybe 130 pounds, a bit out of place in those boozy Prohibition days." He thought his nose too large and "didn't particularly like what I saw in the mirror."

Whatever the external appearance, inside he had a fierce determination to make something of himself. The insecurity of his youth, from the double immigration to America to the difficulty of assimilating into a new culture and constant concerns about money, and the fragility of his parents' marriage, made him a very serious young man. And he carried with him a veritable encyclopedia of tough, Scots nostrums supplied by his mother. "It's no sin to be poor, but it's a shame to remain that way" was one of her favorites. She exhorted her son to "make something of yourself." She hated pretense and frequently exclaimed: "No nonsense, boy." She demanded honesty and insisted that "every lie will be punished and every good deed rewarded." She would forecast a long and uncomfortable eternity in hell if the boy misbehaved. She counseled frugality ("a little money put by is a great comfort") and patience ("you can get used to anything but hanging").

But for all her hectoring and severity, she loved the boy, and he loved her in return, once describing her ambivalently as "good and unyielding." Scotty's sister once complained that she had gotten little of her mother's affection: "Jimmy got all the love. If he hadn't been marvelous, I would indeed hate him. I never got the love I should have." Scotty, clearly the favored child, understood the travails his sister had with their mother. Later in his life he wrote to Joanna:

I am well aware of the struggles you had with our Mother, and the reasons you had for resenting her strong and dominant character. . . . They believed in the family, and stuck together for you and me, even when at times their differences seemed intolerable. Alas, this is not the habit of these selfish days. It seems to me that we should forget the differences of the past, and thank the Lord for our good fortune, and particularly for the fidelity of our Mother and Father. Particularly I have to say this, because you, rather than I did so much to hold them together.

He signed it: "Love, Jimmy."

When his mother was in her nineties, Scotty was in California to make a speech. He rented a car and visited her at the nursing home in which she lived. He took her out for a drive around Santa Cruz and, either by accident or with the intention of preserving their conversation, let his tape recorder run.

It was early evening and they were driving along the seashore. He pointed out the boats moving in the water. She commented that he was a good driver. "Do you have your own car?" she asked, her voice still thick with the accent of Scotland. He explained he had a car provided by the *New York Times*, omitting the fact that it was a Mercedes-Benz with a driver. She must have been impressed at the frugality of his having a car for which he didn't pay.

"Did you expect to see me looking so good, Jimmy?" she asked.

"No, I didn't, Mother. But I'm just delighted."

"I may live till I'm a hundred. But I'm ready when the Lord calls me. I've been ready for many, many years."

"I know that's right, Mother," he replied.

"Are you ready?" she inquired, but Scotty didn't answer.

"You are, too," she replied for him. "That's the only way to be."

They drove by the hospital where Scotty's father had been treated for cancer before his death.

"He went away very, very quietly. Not a murmur," she remembered.

"Well, that's because he was ready," Scotty commented.

"Oh, he was ready. A great many people are afraid to die. You're not afraid to die, are you, Jimmy?"

Again Scotty didn't answer, but she reassured him that his ultimate fate would be good, that he would avoid the bad fires of which she had warned.

"You never did anything wrong in all your life," she declared. Then after a moment of thought, she wanted to be sure.

"You ne'er were drunk, were you?"

"Oh, yes, I've been drunk," he admitted with a chuckle.

She laughed and then summoned the requisite disapproval.

"Disgraceful, something that your father never was."

"You know," Scotty said, "I remember once I took him out to the cabin and I mixed him a drink. And it was like a lemonade but it had gin in it. He just took it and gulped it down."

"Yes, he was great at that gulping thing," his mother said.

"And right away he slapped his knee and he said: 'It's a good thing I could nee afford that stuff when I was a young man.'"

"I didn't know about that," she said.

"What a wonderful man he was," Scotty said wistfully.

"He was awfully fond of you, Jimmy. He thought there was never anything like ye."

Near the end of his life and from the vantage point of his own success, Scotty Reston wrote affectionately about both his parents. His mother lived until she was ninety-eight and in her final years became more and more concerned with religion and death, repeatedly and unpleasantly warning Scotty's wife, Sally, that she would go to hell unless she paid more attention to church. "If she were a man, you'd say she's not the kind of person you give your hat to very easily," Sally Reston once said of her mother-in-law. "But she was very, very intelligent." Scotty absorbed his mother's preachments about success but turned away from her harder side, tending more to the geniality of his father. He was grateful for her love and for his parents' striving, especially in bringing him to America. But like many men whose success carries them far beyond the boundaries of what their parents knew, he saw their lives as limited. He once confessed to an interviewer, "I'm ashamed of the fact that I was a little bit ashamed of my parents."

CHAPTER 3

SCOTTY AND SALLY

WHEN SCOTTY RESTON arrived in Champaign-Urbana in the autumn of 1928, the university's main distinction was the fact that Red Grange had been a football star there. The school sat on the edge of the Illinois cornfields and the great American plains. While it was a solid and commendably inexpensive place of opportunity, it was hardly the most rigorous academic institution in the state, let alone the nation. But it was the perfect place for a scantily prepared young man like Reston to earn a college degree. He was away from home for the first time in his life, one insecure boy in a sea of some twelve thousand undergraduate students. He came to college powered by the twin engines of insecurity and ambition, but with no firm direction in mind. He signed up with the Department of Journalism, where his rudimentary jottings for the Dayton sports pages and for *Delco Doings* gave him at least a hint of what was required. He was also attracted to the journalism program because it had no foreign-language requirement.

It was, however, his athletic ability that gave him a sense of identity in the huge student body. His European facility with a soccer ball got him onto first the freshman and then the varsity soccer teams, where he played with distinction. Of more importance was his high skill on the golf links. He became captain of the team in his senior year, and while this was not nearly as prestigious as being a gridiron star, the Illini did win the Big Ten golf championship his junior year. He became a member of the Sigma Pi fraternity soon after arriving at college, and the frat house was the focus of his social life throughout his college years. He ended up as president of Sigma Pi and was a member of the interfraternity council.

But while he made a place for himself in the school, Reston remained deeply insecure about his differences from the other students. He still had the same fear of being laughed at that had made his first days in the Dayton public schools so difficult. He barely endured the fraternity hazing and, for example, often took the paddle rather than make a fool of himself as entertainment for the older brothers. He learned some basic social graces at his fraternity, such as the proper use of various eating utensils and the correct way to introduce guests visiting the house. But he never mastered the rudiments of dancing and he did not like doing things at which he was not good. Interestingly, he recalled in his memoirs being labeled as "the cocky kid from Ohio." In addition to the insecurity that he remembered so well for so long, he must also have affected a certain swagger and sureness to mask his anxieties. One can assume from his gift for golf, a sport that punishes insecurity with swift and awful failure, that the immigrant kid had at least a powerful streak of self-confidence to balance his sense of inferiority.

He saved money by mailing his laundry home to his mother and he made extra money washing dishes at another fraternity house with Fuzzy Evans, the friend from Dayton who had urged him to come to Illinois. The work was performed with a touch of resentment at his servitude. Evans remembered one occasion in the kitchen when he tossed a dish to Scotty, who fumbled the pass and dropped the plate on the floor. The cook came up to Reston and asked him angrily how it happened. Scotty had another plate in his hands at the time. "He just looked at her and then dropped the plate on the floor, where it shattered, and said, 'That's how it happened,'" Evans said. Scotty took a second job in the sports publicity department crafting flattering profiles of the university's athletes. The sports job earned him a seat in the press box for football games, and he watched in awe as the great sportswriters like Grantland Rice sent their stories in Morse code.

The epic stock market crash of 1929 occurred during his second year in school, but the onset of the Great Depression made little difference initially because Scotty had so little to begin with. He did take notice in the middle of his senior year when his $100 tuition check bounced because the Ohio bank on which it was drawn had failed. He was promptly threatened with expulsion, only months from graduation.

Reston quite naturally never forgot the embarrassment and the fear associated with the incident. Here he was, a few months from actually having a college degree to call his own, when, through no fault of his own, it appeared as if he were to be sent packing. When Scotty pleaded his case to the dean of men, one Tommy Arkle Clark, saying he was sure the bank would reopen before graduation, Clark told him that the university could not operate on such assumptions. When Scotty then argued that it was not fair to punish him for circumstances beyond his control, Clark gave him a little lecture, which Reston remembered verbatim: "The University of Illinois is maintained by the taxpayers of the state of Illinois, primarily for students who live in Illinois. I understand that the taxpayers do the same in Ohio and have an excellent university in Columbus. Perhaps you could finish your senior year there." Reston then pleaded that he was the golf captain and felt an obligation to the team. Clark answered that he was more concerned about the university than about the golf team and showed the young man the door. Decades later, in a speech to the university's incoming class of 1969, Reston said that the dean looked like Mr. Chips and acted like J. Edgar Hoover.

Reston recalled that he didn't even return to his room at the fraternity. Instead, he walked out of the dean's office and promptly hitchhiked back to Dayton. He went straight to the *Dayton Daily News* offices and told Governor Cox his story. Cox wrote out a check, which he said was a loan, and told Reston that when he finished school he might have a job for him on one of his newspapers. The loan, and later the newspaper job, enabled Scotty to pay his tuition, and he was deeply grateful to Cox. But his mother, remembering the event decades later, felt less obliged to the former presidential candidate. She claimed that after her son became famous, Cox bragged that he had put Scotty through college. "He went to his grave with that lie," she said, adding that Cox was "the best-hated man in Dayton." The idea that her son needed outside help to pay his way was not to her liking. "The Scots are a proud people," she explained.

Scotty was an indifferent student by his own admission, largely ignoring what did not seem immediately useful to him. He picked up one D in a journalism class and failed a philosophy course. Classmate and fellow journalism student Bertha Enger remembered him as unremarkable in college. "Nobody ever thought he was outstanding then. If you picked people whom you'd thought most likely to succeed, you wouldn't have picked Scotty." One of his professors, Bruce Weirick, had a similar recollection. "No one would have guessed where he was going. I had no idea he had this in him. Neither did anyone else. Neither did he."

Reston's own recollections of college, as produced in his memoirs, are notable only for the clarity of his account of the financial

embarrassment and for one little item he remembered from a literature course. The course's professor was an admirer of a popular New
York journalist's self-improvement aphorisms and passed them on to
his students. Scotty still remembered one sixty years later. "Say each
day: This day is my opportunity to do something which will count
for improvement in the lives I touch. This day throw your weight
heartily against the wheel in the mud. This day speak with increased
precision and force. This day give a lift or an encouraging word to
somebody. There are 365 long days in the year when something
might be done." He added this to the list his mother instilled in
him, the bottom line always being, "Make something of yourself."

College for Scotty Reston was not for fun and not for the glorious
exploration of new ideas. His aim was to get a degree and to find a
way to make a living, hardly surprising given the times and where
and what he had come from. Ten years after graduation, he wrote a
kind of confessional about his college years: "As I recall our midnight sessions at the University of Illinois in 1932, what most of us
were really doing there was trying to figure out some way to make a
lot of money. The motto of the University of Illinois was, 'Learning
and Labor,' but we didn't let that get in our way; what we were
doing was trying to 'get by' in the naive belief that, depression or no
depression . . . a diploma in itself was a guarantee of the economic
security which was our main goal."

It was in December of his senior year that Scotty first met Sally Fulton. He was double-dating with a fraternity brother: Scotty's girl was
named Winnie Haslam, and Freddie Lindall was with Sally. "By the
end of the first Coke," Scotty recalled, "I could tell we had the
wrong partners. After the melted cheese sandwiches, I had reached
the firm conclusion that Sally Fulton was the prettiest and brightest

girl on campus. . . . By the end of the evening, I had developed an intense dislike for Freddie Lindall."

For the first – and only – time in his life, Scotty Reston was crazy in love. He and Sally would meet in the library to "study" and walk together between classes. But as president of his fraternity, Reston, stiff moralist that he was and always would be, had insisted that all the brothers pledge not to steal another member's girlfriend. By Christmastime he wrote to Sally, who was home for the holidays, that because of the pledge they could not go on seeing each other. Back on campus, Scotty began to regret his "false nobility" and started to haunt the streets outside Sally's sorority, hoping for a chance encounter. His despair mounted until one day she sat down beside him in the library and remarked on his elegant penmanship. She had dumped Freddie Lindall.

Looking at the pictures of Sally Fulton in the college yearbook, it's easy to imagine the effect she had on Scotty Reston. She was three years younger and two years behind him in college. She was stunningly beautiful, with dark hair and a luminous smile that was to light up his soul the rest of his life. She would eventually graduate Phi Beta Kappa, with a double major in English and philosophy. Compared with the Restons, her family was aristocracy, at least Illinois aristocracy. She came from Sycamore, where her father was a lawyer, then later a judge, and finally chief justice of the Illinois Supreme Court. She was sparkling and charming and through her paternal grandfather had a common connection to the town in Scotland where Scotty's mother had grown up. Scotty and Sally also shared a connection with the hard-hearted Dean Clark. The dean had thrown her brother Bill out of the University of Illinois for driving their father's car on campus. Bill, however, probably in light of the prominence of the Fultons and their Illinois residence, was permitted to complete his studies from home.

Sally grew up in a big house – if not Sycamore's biggest, still quite large. She had fond memories of an annual charity dance held in a ballroom at the top of the building that housed her father's law office. Her mother danced in white gloves and her father held his handkerchief in his hand to shield his wife from his perspiration. The ball was a family affair, and Sally remembered dancing there with her father. It was a far cry from the Calvinist austerity of the Reston household.

Her grandmother on her mother's side was named Mary Busey. The Buseys were farm folk in central Illinois and owned eight farms. They eventually moved into the town of Urbana, where the university is located, and built a big house with a cupola. They owned an entire city block, had a street named after them, and gave land for a town park. Sally's mother went to the university for two years; there she met Sally's father, the future judge, and they married when he got out of law school. Both of Sally's older brothers had graduated from the University of Illinois. Compared with Scotty's own parents and grandparents, none of whom had much education and who kept house and worked with their hands all their lives, the Buseys and the Fultons were indeed upper class.

To Scotty, Sally was almost beyond his imagination. Her beauty was only the beginning. "It was not my family that gave me any sense of the importance of ideas," he explained to one of his sons years later. "It was Sally and my love for this girl. Her friends were all intellectuals. My friends were jocks. She and Bruce Weirick [his journalism professor] just changed my whole life. The only ideas I had were from the Bible. I was a lousy student, but she was of a totally different intellectual class. She was not only a very beautiful girl, she was kind of the top girl on campus. I couldn't even dance. I could only go in one direction. She was a beautiful dancer." William Maxwell, later an editor at the *New Yorker* magazine, lived in the old Busey house in Champaign. A kind of literary salon developed around him, and Sally took Scotty along to the meetings. "I had never heard anything like this," Scotty said.

Sally found Scotty different from the other boys at school, more "purposeful." "I thought he was much more adult really than most of us were," Sally remembered. "His humor was interesting. He wasn't funny, he was witty. For instance, he had a sense of pride. He didn't like games where you got up and made fun of yourself. He wouldn't do that sort of thing. He had too much pride or grown-upness to him. He was a serious guy, more serious than most. We never had fun and games or anything like that. He had a kind of Scottish, stiff-necked pride to him. He wouldn't make a fool of himself."

Sally recalled that one of the intimacies he permitted himself with her was the occasional use of a Scottish word or phrase, something he would never do in public. "He was, as the Scots would say, ca' canny, careful with other people," she said. Sally believed that caution about saying the wrong thing was rooted in having seen all the trouble his mother's sharp tongue had caused.

In the spring of his senior year, Sally took him home to Sycamore to meet her family. He was a big hit. Scotty beat her father at golf and went swimming with her brothers, impressing them by jumping off a bridge into a river. They talked of marriage and decided that when he finally earned fifty dollars a week they would wed. But she still had two years of college left when he graduated and they worried together about how they would keep the relationship going during that separation. There would not be enough money to be visiting back and forth or to be making expensive long-distance phone calls. Even Sally's family had been hit by the depression. Her father had been a director of a bank that failed, taking his stake and savings with it. A law partner had committed suicide because of financial ruin. Sally remembered her father returning home from a downstate business trip and stopping to see her in Champaign. He was so broke that he asked her if she could spare him some money.

Scotty gave Sally his fraternity pin, a kind of preliminary engagement in those days, that bound each partner to date no one else. And off he went to make his way in the world. Governor Cox made good on his promise of a newspaper job and Reston was hired in Springfield, Ohio. He considered himself fortunate to find any work at all, since millions of Americans had none. The ten dollars a week he earned wasn't quite sufficient, so he did some publicity work for a hotel in return for a room. When, not long after, the newspaper's sports editor retired, Reston took his place, earning now the princely sum of twenty dollars a week. The managing editor suggested that his new responsibilities obliged him to wear a hat to work and so he did. He put out a sports section seven days a week and wrote his own column, lamely titled "Rest On This." All the while, he pined for Sally, penning silly notes and serious letters. "Oh Sally," he wrote, "I had not known it was possible for me to miss anyone as I have missed you. . . . Only now am I beginning to realize how alone I would be without you. I have no desire to be with anyone else." And, as far as is known, he never was.

It wasn't long after Sally got back to college for her junior year that she realized that the pledge of nondating wasn't going to work. She wrote to him telling how miserable it was sitting in the sorority house while all her friends were out having fun. They agreed that she could date other boys but that she would keep his pin as a symbol of their love and intention to be together eventually. He said that if he ever changed his mind about her, he would ask for it back. "That's what saved us," she recalled. "The pin was a promise of a sort. I think that is what really held us together. Promises meant a lot in those days." And there was nothing casual about this arrangement in his mind. He recalled in his memoirs that he was "afraid, constantly, almost morbidly afraid, that I would lose the one thing that meant more to me than anything else in life." She was already much more than a girlfriend; she helped him feel complete. That would never change.

The sports editor's job on the tiny Springfield newspaper wasn't really much of a job, even for a novice journalist. In charge of making up the page, Reston at first used every font in the type box, making it look, in the words of the publisher, "like a Boston store ad." His salary was nowhere near the fifty dollars a week that was his marriage benchmark. He tried to get transferred to another of the Cox papers, was turned down, but then became telegraph editor in Springfield. This suited him better, since he was in charge of selecting and editing national and international news as it was delivered by the wire services. His ambition was showing through. The publisher in Springfield remembered him as "an egotistical son of a gun." He and the top editors at the paper "rode him hard," the publisher said, "but with a purpose." Reston, a bit unsure and in search of perfection, found it difficult to write on tight deadlines, something he struggled with throughout his newspaper career. "We're not getting out a weekly paper," the editor would scold, or, when things were really tense, "What do you think this is, a quarterly?" However, there was another man under Scotty's direction, and that was enough for his mother to recall this position as a triumph. "He was put over the older gentleman," she crowed decades later. "Think of it."

The young Reston was by no means yet committed to journalism as a way of life. He was, however, committed to increasing his income. With the help of his old boss at the University of Illinois sports publicity department, he took a job as director of sports publicity at Ohio State University. The salary was forty dollars a week, and Scotty moved to Columbus in the summer of 1933.

Shortly after the move, he ran into Leland Stanford MacPhail. Reston had first met MacPhail during the Ohio Amateur Golf Tournament in Canton, when MacPhail was secretary of the Ohio Golf Association. A dispute had arisen between public-course golfers and private-club players over domination of the tournament by the public-links players, with the private-club players arrogantly insisting that the others should be excluded. Scotty was competing from Dayton's Community Country Club, a municipal course, and he argued fervently for the rights of any amateur to play. MacPhail agreed with him. Now, in 1933 MacPhail was in the bidding to buy the Cincinnati Reds baseball team, which like most other major-league clubs was struggling through the depression. MacPhail wanted Reston to become the club's traveling secretary at seventy-five dollars a week — more than the marriage minimum, but it made no difference, since Sally was still in college.

However, MacPhail wound up as the club's general manager when Powell Crosley, who owned a home appliance and radio company, bought the team. According to Reston, Crosley had wanted to save the hometown ball team but couldn't see how it would help his business. Reston says he suggested to Crosley that he put his own name on the ballfield so that every time the place was mentioned on radio, there would be publicity for the Crosley brand. Crosley took his advice and gave Reston the job MacPhail had offered. This was, of course, a half century before major-league teams began selling branding rights for their arenas to large corporations.

Baseball was not Reston's first sports love and his job consisted mostly of endless travel and playing nursemaid to players (and MacPhail) who liked to live a less-than-saintly lifestyle. But the baseball job did get Scotty to major-league cities across America, where he pounded on the doors of the big newspapers trying to get hired. He haunted the *New York Times* building off and on through the summer of 1934, but never succeeded in getting past the lobby. The travel did not take him to Champaign, and Sally, restless because of the lack of contact from Scotty, seemed to be drifting away. Reston wrote to his friend and mentor Professor Fred Siebert back at the University of Illinois, asking if he had seen Sally at all. He was heartbroken, he said, but tried to console himself. "When one wishes for the moon and the stars, he must be prepared for disappointment."

Not long afterward, Reston was in New York again and looked up his old friend Milt Caniff, with whom he had gone to Stivers High School in Dayton. Caniff was a cartoonist, working for the Associated Press, doing a daily cartoon called "Dickie Dare" (he later invented the comic strip "Terry and the Pirates"). Caniff introduced Scotty to Wilson Hicks, head of the AP's feature service. "I didn't know it, but they were looking for someone. Some sort of chemistry took place between Scotty and Hicks and he was hired," Caniff said. His beginning salary at the AP was forty-five dollars a month, a big step down financially but a big step up from being nursemaid to drunken ballplayers. He reported to work the following Monday to write sports feature stories. His editor, Herb Barker, thought Reston a nice writer but "so damned slow." "He'd try one lead and then rip it out of the typewriter, over and over," Barker recalled. "After about ten days of this, I had a little talk with him and made a deal that as soon as he had a lead, regardless of whether he liked it or not, he'd turn it over to me. Once he finally got over that hurdle, he did fine." It was a modest debut, but Reston was now in the big city, if not in the big time.

CHAPTER 4

BIG CITIES

ALTHOUGH RESTON COULD not have known it, 1934 was a year full of portent for him. Franklin Roosevelt had been president for two years and the United States was still in the grip of the Great Depression. Roosevelt would remake the American government so that Washington would become the news capital of the world and the place where Scotty Reston would become the dominant journalist of his time. At the same time, in Europe, Adolf Hitler was consolidating his hold on Germany; the war that he would start would be the first big story Reston would cover.

In New York, John D. Rockefeller Jr. had begun work on his namesake development in the middle of Manhattan. The centerpiece of that complex was to be Radio City, with tenants like RCA and NBC. Eventually, the new broadcast journalism would winnow away the weakest newspapers and would change the way print journalists did their jobs. No longer able to be first with the news, print would eventually be forced to refine its mission beyond recording *what* happened to explaining *why* it happened. Reston, one day, would be an important pioneer in that effort. And over in Times Square, the *New York Times* was being run day-to-day by Arthur Hays Sulzberger, the son-in-law of the founder of the modern paper, whose health was failing. Sulzberger would, upon the death of Adolph Ochs a year later, become publisher and turn the *Times* into the best newspaper in America. It would be Sulzberger's eventual patronage that would make Reston's career.

Yet the journalistic world the twenty-four-year-old young man entered in the early 1930s was still very much of the old sort, and so was the work that he did. Reston, like all the other reporters, lived in terror of his bosses, who could fire reporters at will (the Newspaper Guild had just been founded by Heywood Broun but still had only a few members). His early assignments included covering boxing matches, which he detested. "This involved," he recalled in his memoirs, "sitting within arm's reach of the ropes and dictating to a Morse code operator blow-by-blow descriptions of two sweaty pugs beating each other bloody just above my head."*

More appealing was the job of heading out into New York harbor on a cutter to greet the incoming steamers from Europe. The trip took him past Ellis Island and the Statue of Liberty, two landmarks he had seen twice before as his family began their life in America. Reporters would interview arriving dignitaries, scribble their reports on lightweight paper, and send them to the city on the legs of homing pigeons. Reston remembered interviewing the arriving Somerset Maugham, who at the time was embroiled in a minor controversy over a short story he had written about a young twenty-something

---

*Foreshadowing the kind of access to news-making figures that would one day make him famous, he caused a big fuss among sportswriters once when covering the meeting of the National League baseball-team owners. As the meeting convened, he simply fell in with his old colleagues from the Cincinnati Reds and joined the meeting. But before he could get a scoop, other owners recognized him and threw him out.

man who was a virgin. Maugham had been criticized for imagining such an unrealistic situation. "So, I didn't interview him; he interviewed me," Reston said. "I told him I thought he had it right. I was in my twenties and thought I had lived a normal life and I was still a virgin." Reston also claimed that he had never taken a drink of alcohol until he was working in the sports publicity department at Ohio State. Such deprivations make sense when one thinks about the moral climate his mother imposed on her household. "There was no sex education in our home," Scotty once said. "In fact, I think there was damned little sex."

His evenings were often spent with Milt Caniff and his wife. Scotty often read as Milt drew his cartoons. Of Reston, Caniff said years later, "He was a lot brighter than the rest of us, but we weren't bright enough to know how bright he was."

Reston's mother had of course been suspicious of his moving to New York, as she had been of all his moves farther from home and from her strict influence. She had heard, she once warned her son, that the baseball players he worked with in Cincinnati drank alcohol. New York, in her view, was the capital of sin. "We've brought you up in the ways of the Lord," he quoted her as having reminded him at the time, "and now you'll be led into temptation wherever you go." And there was still Sally, who graduated from the University of Illinois in the spring of 1934, just before he got his job with the AP. Unable to afford the trip, Scotty did not return to Champaign for her graduation.

He wrote to her regularly as he explored the big city, but he was still running out of money at the end of each week and was not pressing marriage. "Whenever I let myself think of all this in relation to my life as a whole, I miss you very much, Sally," he wrote about the time of her graduation. "But you are so much an illusion most of the time that I cannot rid myself of little pangs of despair. I do love you, Sally, only please, please let me know your plans. We must get together." He had Milt Caniff design a bookplate that he gave to Sally.

Sally went to work doing publicity for the Chicago World's Fair and Scotty did make his way to the fair while she was working there. But once there he ignored her. Sally found out from some mutual friends that he had been in the city without even calling. She wrote to him in New York saying she was returning his fraternity pin. Scotty explained years later that he had come to imagine her dating and having a great time with other young men and his pride prevented him from calling her. But when he got her letter, he picked up the phone, finally, and in what they both recalled as a very emotional conversation, she agreed to come to New York. It took her months to save enough money for the train fare.

It wasn't until the fall, on his twenty-fifth birthday to be exact, that they were finally reunited after a separation of more than two years. She stayed with her brother Bob and his wife, who lived in the Westchester County suburbs, where Bob was president of Anaconda Wire and Cable Company. The trip accomplished two things: it gave Sally her first glimpse of the ocean and it reminded her how much she loved Scotty. After she went back to Chicago, she wrote tenderly: "Oh, Scotty, I didn't want to leave you, to see you walk one way and I go the other. How little I thought before going to New York that those ten days would bring such beauty and happiness. I hate to give them up. Write to me as often as you find time. . . . I don't want to remain out here a thousand miles away, hanging indefinitely aloof." They both always believed it was this trip that saved their relationship. Afterward, there was no doubt they would eventually marry.

Still, it was another year before they saw each other again. Scotty's work at the Associated Press became a bit more interesting when he was given his first nationally syndicated column writing about what he later called "all the wonderful nonsense of New York." The column was somewhat misleadingly titled "A New Yorker at Large," since the now twenty-five-year-old young man could hardly qualify as a sophisticated urbanite. He didn't much like New York, and he never did come to appreciate its density and vitality. But the column was a free ticket to a good deal of fun, like the theater and restaurants, where he freeloaded in return for publicity. The column itself was printed in cities all across the country and its chatty style was perfect for small-town consumption.

In 1935 Sally found work in New York, and the long wait to be together was over. She became an editor at the *Junior League Magazine*, which appropriately had offices in the Waldorf Astoria Hotel on Park Avenue. There she edited and wrote and helped with production of the magazine, although she herself had never been a debutante. She took a single room near Gramercy Park, while Scotty shared a room farther uptown with an AP buddy. They went out almost every night, taking advantage of his "At Large" entrée. He asked for his fraternity pin back and gave Sally his mother's old engagement ring. The wedding was set for December 24, Sally explained, because neither of them could get time off from work, and to give up their jobs would have meant economic disaster; Christmas Day would be their twenty-four-hour honeymoon. Milt Caniff remembered taking a boat ride up the Hudson River with Reston before the wedding and there witnessing one of the occasional dour Scots moods into which Reston would fall. "He kept saying how the hell can a guy afford to get married on an AP salary," Caniff said.

Before the wedding, Sally went back to Sycamore for a visit with her family. She wrote to Scotty that she had gone walking alone in the fields outside of town. "After racing the wind down the creek, I lay for a time under the trees, not so much myself but more an integral part of the familiar world around me. When you grow up in the simplicity and modesty of a place like this, your spirit remains colored by its skies forever, with the cool shadows of the trees, and with the sunlit green of the sloping fields. Therefore, I suppose I shouldn't really regret leaving these surroundings, for I'll carry them with me wherever I go. . . . My love remains and will always remain the compelling force in my life. We've had through all these months natural doubts and discouragements. We've walked precariously on the brink of misunderstanding at times. That we've won our way through isn't the end, I know. Nevertheless, I'm confident in this love tonight, for I've seen it grow stronger with the threatening winds that have sometimes blown between us."

"It was a big step for me, leaving the Midwest," she recalled years later. "I didn't know New York very well. I came from a little town, nothing like Dayton, which I regarded as the big city. Our house was at the end of this little town, this little county seat. I remember reading in somebody's book that she could look out the window and see nothing forever. That was what I could see. We were at the end of town and I could look out over these fields and then the railroad tracks about a mile away, which were built up higher than the fields. There were forty-five hundred people. I'd grown up there. The sky's so big out there. It was a big, big step for me. I was a little nervous and sorry to leave my family. I had a deep feeling about the Middle West." But she added, "I don't think there was ever any doubt about the marriage, from him or from me." Whatever "threatening winds" had blown during their long separations, her memory in later life was of the solidness and certainty of her relationship with Scotty Reston.

They were married in the evening at the Larchmont Presbyterian Church, with Scotty's old Dayton and University of Illinois friend Fuzzy Evans as best man. Sally wore her mother's wedding dress, and to spare her sister-in-law from having to buy a bridesmaid's dress, Sally loaned her a long dress she had in college. Her parents came from Sycamore and Scotty's father came from Dayton; his mother stayed home. (Sally's memory was that she was needed to attend to the birth of Scotty's sister Joanna's baby. But even the tough Johanna could see the wisdom in Scotty's choice of Sally. "I also think," she wrote in a note to the bride, "he has been most fortunate in finding such a dear girl for his life's partner.")

The bride and groom had a small reception at the little gatehouse they had rented at 9 Shadow Lane in Larchmont. Their first home sat at the edge of an estate but was quite modest: two bedrooms upstairs, a sitting room and a living room, kitchen, and bath on the first floor, with a garage attached. Each day they commuted together to the city on the train, coming and going through Grand Central Station. They couldn't afford a car but on weekends would go on long walks together. "We didn't have any money, so we did it all on the cheap," Sally remembered. "But it was all very nice." Scotty's salary had soared to $85 a week; Sally remembered making maybe $100 a month at the *Junior League Magazine*.

By the spring of 1937, Sally was pregnant. "We were using contraceptives," she recounted years later, "but things don't always work out the way you plan." She intended to go right on working, but just then Scotty was offered an assignment in London by the AP. He was to cover the big English sporting events, the British Open, Wimbledon, the Derby, and the like. His boss decided that Reston should sail in June with the U.S. Ryder Cup team so that he could cover the biannual competition between the best golfers America and the British Isles could muster. Reston explained that with Sally expecting, the timing might be inconvenient. As Reston later described it, his boss "in the kindly manner of news executives of those days," told him to take the offer or leave it. He took it and sent Sally ahead in May, aboard the *Queen Mary*, to find lodging and a doctor to assist with the birth. (When he did sail to England with the team, his cabin mate was none other than Sam Snead.)

Scotty and Sally, finally married, were separated again, although this time briefly, and the burden of relocating in a foreign land fell on her. She had never been out of the United States but handled the challenge well. She wrote letters almost daily to Scotty, with wide-eyed descriptions of England. She remarked on the later setting of the sun and on the verdant and unspoiled countryside. This little passage describing the train ride after the *Queen Mary* docked is one of many demonstrations that she was at least as good a writer as Scotty. "I got into the funniest little train I ever saw. It chuckled over the rails all the way from Southampton to London, and so did I." As delighted as she was by England, she was also seized by bouts of tears she blamed on the pregnancy.

After staying a couple of weeks in Oxford, she rented an apartment on Upper Berkeley Street near Hyde Park Corner in London, a one-bedroom walkup with, as Sally remembered it, "a closet for a kitchen and one or two radiators that helped a little. We froze in the winter." When she discovered they couldn't afford the price of the fancy doctor recommended to them by friends in New York, Sally found a young physician named John Peel who agreed to attend the delivery. (Years later, Dr. Peel was knighted for having provided obstetrical services to the queen.) Scotty arrived in London just before the baby; Richard Fulton Reston was born on July 14.

Scotty's first major story was the Grand National steeplechase. Because of the large betting interest in the event, the Associated Press racing editor in New York (Reston called him "Hoofbeats" Robertson) wanted quick results, so Scotty left nothing to chance. He steeped himself in the legends and history of the race and recruited another young AP reporter, Ralph McGill, to be his legman at the race. This was probably the heaviest journalistic firepower, or at least future firepower, ever to cover a horse race; McGill went on to become a crusading antisegregation editor of the *Atlanta Constitution*. Reston arranged with the Western Union office in Liverpool to have a message, with a blank left for the name of the winning horse, waiting to be sent as soon as Scotty called from the special phone he had had installed in the grandstand. Then, according to McGill, Reston walked the entire four-mile course.

Scotty recalled that his heart was in his throat as the horses approached the wire, with two horses, one Irish and one American, neck and neck. From his vantage point slightly off the finish line, Reston decided the Irish horse had won and sent the flash report back to Hoofbeats Robertson. But the official posting, some minutes later, gave the race to the American horse, which was sensational news, since until then no American horse had ever won. Flash, again, with the correction. Reston imagined bells ringing on the wire machines in newsrooms everywhere, alerting editors far and wide that James B. Reston had screwed it up. He later attributed his error to the fact that he was poorly positioned to see the finish line. But McGill's version was that the horses were so splattered with mud that it was impossible to tell which was which.

Reston and McGill also went off to Scotland together to cover the Walker Cup, an amateur competition between golf teams from America and Britain. It was 1938. Reston played a practice round with two of the British players and beat them, a fact that was recorded in the news dispatches from other reporters at the scene. When the British won the cup, some twenty-five thousand Scots flooded onto the eighteenth fairway at Saint Andrews and, linking arms, sang "Auld Lang Syne." One would think this outpouring would have stirred some residual Scots pride in Reston. But he remembered in his memoirs that he didn't really feel at home, despite reminders of his parents in the burr of the native tongue. "I went back to London feeling vaguely sad," he wrote, "and wondering why that should be so." Perhaps it was the realization that he was really on his own, a husband, a father, scratching away at his trade in a foreign land and, as a mere sports reporter, not really setting the journalistic world on fire.

CHAPTER 5

WAR

IN AUGUST 1938 Reston wrote to Fred Siebert in Champaign-Urbana saying he was loving England, dividing his year between covering sports in the summertime and the foreign office in the off-season. "International politics, for sheer impertinence, trickery and graft," he wrote, "is the only thing in my experience to surpass sports. The only difference actually is that at a given time and at a given place the sports principals are made to account in action for their claims and promises. In politics, this is not true." His coverage of the diplomatic beat did not consist of highbrow foreign policy analyses but rather a dogged pursuit of diplomats in hopes of catching a good quote. Reston later compared it to nothing more than prosaic police reporting: "We just gumshoed those people," he said. Indeed, the wire service reporting out of Britain was largely informed by reading the *Times* of London and summarizing the debates in Parliament. Even with the threat of war increasing on the Continent, the British government, the British press, and the British people, still traumatized by the agony of the Great War, were in deep denial of the Nazi threat, concerned lest they provoke Hitler. Prime Minister Neville Chamberlain's efforts to appease Hitler were greeted, at least initially, with great relief in Britain. Press magnate Lord Beaverbrook had his tabloid, the *Daily Express,* take an optimistic view of the gathering storm, advising in one headline that Reston always remembered: "Go Take Your Holidays: There Will Be No War."

Reston was confused by much of this. He would frequently stop at the Marble Arch on his way home and listen to the debaters flailing away, some urging peace, others war, none helping the sportswriter from Dayton figure out the puzzle of the impending conflagration. "We lived in London," he wrote, "at the mercy of events beyond our understanding or control. Sometimes Europe seemed, in the words of Harold Nicholson, 'a foul world of lunatics.'...I was bewildered."

The flashy arrival of the new U.S. ambassador to the Court of Saint James's, Joseph P. Kennedy, "did not dispel my confusion," Reston recalled. The young correspondent met Kennedy when he first fetched up in England and reported on his noisy isolationist proclamations, which were, at best, undiplomatic. Kennedy, Reston concluded, had a talent for "strong opinions and weak judgments." And as the Nazi machine strengthened and as he listened to Kennedy's rantings, Reston was gradually persuaded that appeasement was not working. He was influenced by his conversations with the charismatic Czech ambassador in London, Jan Masaryk, who resigned his ambassadorial post to protest the 1938 British agreements with the Germans at Munich. (Ten years later Masaryk died after he either jumped or was pushed out of a window in Prague as his country tried to resist Soviet domination.)

"Sometimes it takes a major surgical operation to get an idea into a Scotchman's head," Reston wrote in his memoirs, "but even I began to realize that this was no sporting event I was covering." He noticed that some journalistic big hitters such as Edward R. Murrow had started to arrive in England and that war was definitely coming. He and Sally decided to move out of London, first taking a row house in Temple Fortune Hill near Hampstead, later migrating progressively farther from the city to a timbered cottage in Kent, heated only by fireplaces ("very charming," in Sally's recollection), then to Buckinghamshire, and finally to Cornwall. They were still young and he was not well paid, but they managed to hire a cook named Annie who insisted, to the Restons' severe discomfort, on calling them "madame" and "sir."

In late August 1939, Scotty and other journalists met with Ambassador Kennedy, who told them flatly that war was coming and they should get their families out of England. Kennedy was still urging the British government to roll over for Germany and told the American reporters, Reston recalled in his memoir, that he was for appeasement "one-thousand percent." He also confided, off the record, that there were six German submarines lurking in the North Atlantic. It was a threat that would soon be real enough for the Reston family.

Almost from the beginning of his posting in London, Reston had been courting the *New York Times* bureau chief, Ferdinand Kuhn, in hopes of finally getting hired there. In 1938 Kuhn had asked his New York bosses for permission to hire Reston, but *Times* managing editor Jimmy James had instead proposed transferring another staff correspondent to London. Kuhn had objected, and as was frequently the case at the paper, the clash of executive wills led to inaction. But as war became imminent, Kuhn renewed his request for Reston. After six weeks of cabling back and forth, James relented, according to Kuhn, largely to save the cost in money and time of transferring another reporter. Kuhn also recalled that when he got back to New York a while later, the indifference had evaporated and he was congratulated on having hired Reston. "Where'd you get that fellow?

He's wonderful!" his colleagues said. Two days after the meeting with Kennedy, Kuhn told Reston to report to the *Times* bureau on September 1, 1939. Scotty and Sally were ecstatic. Seven years after his graduation and four years after making it to New York, James B. Reston was now a full-fledged correspondent for one of the most important and powerful newspapers in America. Two days after Reston joined the *Times*, the British foreign office notified Kennedy that it was declaring a state of war with Germany. Reston was in the House of Commons when Chamberlain, belatedly admitting the obvious, pledged British support for the Poles after the Germans invaded their eastern neighbor.

For all his striving, and for all his joy at finally getting to the *Times*, Scotty was not without his doubts about his ability to deal with covering a war. He and Sally worried about baby Richard and about themselves. They had gotten what they had wished for, but this very success had put them all in peril. As London braced itself for war, Reston roamed the city to write a mood piece. "I wasn't scared," he remembered, "I was terrified." The city was blacked out, the railroad stations were filled with people fleeing the expected bombardment. Giant balloons floated above the streets to deter or destroy dive bombers. Reston heard an air raid siren and jumped into a doorway to seek shelter, but it was only a test. He returned to the *Times* office, which was in the building that housed the *Times* of London, and began writing.

"The world's largest city folded up tonight, just like London, Ohio. After a week of war there is not a single play or movie in town; there is not a chink of light in Piccadilly Circus; the big restaurants are deserted, and the boys didn't even play football in London today." In a piece that ran more than one thousand words in length, he painted a brilliantly vivid picture of the British capital getting ready to be bombed. The writing was luminous, full of clever images, yet relaxed, even casual. It was not like anything else that was appearing in the *Times* of that era.

Reston asked his readers to imagine their hometown in a similar situation:

> If you can possibly imagine all the youngsters from the lower East Side and Hell's Kitchen and Brooklyn and the Bronx suddenly thrown into every corner of every safe mansion in Westchester and upper New York State and New Jersey you will have a vague idea of what the evacuation was like. . . .
>
> If you could watch Manhattan suddenly fill up with thousands of young boys in uniform, young lads of 20 running for trains in Grand Central Station and manning anti-aircraft guns and digging trenches in Central Park you would understand what London is doing right now. . . .
>
> If you saw, like some fabulous picture on a popular science magazine cover, silver anti-aircraft balloons floating night and day above the skyscrapers . . .
>
> And if at 9:30 o'clock it had got darker than you had ever seen Manhattan and every light on the Great White Way went out and every movie and every single show closed, and cars crept along dark streets in second gear with only vague blue lights showing on the ground, you would have a glimmer of an idea of what a London blackout is like. . . .
>
> For all these things are happening in London tonight and the people in the city are grim and strained.

The dateline was London, September 9, 1939. The byline was James B. Reston.

The piece still reads as if he had spoken the lines, not whittled them painfully out of the raw material of his reporting. But his writing habits had not changed much from his first days in Springfield and then at the Associated Press in New York. Even with a five-hour lead on New York deadlines, Reston still gave his bosses anxiety attacks because of his meticulous slowness. After Kuhn was replaced by Raymond Daniell as bureau chief, Daniell advised Reston to treat his reporting as a sort of letter to a friend at home, which was the perfect advice for a naturally informal writer. Still, Daniell recalled years later, Reston would litter the floor with crumpled copy paper filled with false starts. His desk would be covered with reference books as he tried to educate himself while on the job and to find apt quotations and citations to dress up his reportage.

As the country braced for war and British nerves frayed waiting for the expected onslaught, the government decided on a bombing run over Germany, hoping for a propaganda boost. The *Times* was offered a seat on the mission and Reston says he volunteered eagerly. But a more senior correspondent, Bob Post, was sent instead. He died when the plane was shot down over the North Sea.

Wartime censorship was imposed by the British government and all news dispatches leaving London were vetted. Thus when a German submarine sneaked into the naval base at Scapa Flow in Scotland and sank a British battleship, the news was suppressed. The *Times* bureau complained to the government, arguing that the enemy already knew about their success. The government's position was that the incident was demoralizing for the country and that the national interest was being served by censorship. Not long afterward, another German sub slipped into the Firth of Forth in Scotland and torpedoed the British cruiser *Belfast*. This time Daniell and the bureau vowed to get the news to America. The British Admiralty confirmed the story to the *Times* but refused to overrule the censors and permit the story to be sent to New York. Daniell then tried telephoning *Times* correspondents on the Continent to have them relay the information to New York. When that failed, a rather obvious code was devised in which the last word of each sentence was to be the one that was taken seriously. They divided their messages between two cable companies to further disguise their ploy and sent one set to the managing editor, Jimmy James, and one to a friend of Daniell's at the *Times*, telling him in the first message: "If you and James will get together we may get somewhere tonight." The messages followed:

"Yes, we're sending story about submarine."

"Please tell Harvard I want my son entered."

"As ordered, am setting forth."

"No government was not attacked."

"If you persist somebody's reputation will be damaged."

"Smith covers Dublin not Belfast."

"Untrue that any prisoners escaped."

Then they sent a follow-up message: "James don't miss the boat consult Baldwin's Bible and that no credit extended anyone here." The point was to make sure the story was not traced to the London bureau. The story made the paper and was printed before the attack was known about in London.

The Admiralty, under the direction of Winston Churchill, was furious, as was the British press, which criticized the *Times* for its violation. An investigation was begun, but it wasn't until eight weeks later that an intelligence agent approached Reston in a Fleet Street pub, flashed his ID card, and said sternly: "We know exactly what happened. But it isn't done here. Understand? Never again!" Churchill, not eager for more publicity about the country's feeble defenses, let Daniell, whom the *Times* feared would be expelled or imprisoned, off with a warning. Churchill was also angry that it had taken his spooks so long to figure out a schoolboy code. Reston recounted later that his editors were also upset about the little adventure, judging it to be a high risk for a small reward. "Looking backward," he told an interviewer, "I am inclined to agree, but it was the first real beat of the war, and it was a sort of declaration of independence of a sometimes silly censorship." Over the years, his opinion hardened against this little piece of journalistic derring-do. "A newspaper gathers more news by trust than by tricks," he concluded.

As London waited for war, Reston toured the city, writing features on topics like the quaint Home Guard, made up mostly of World War I veterans in tin, soup-bowl hats, or a court proceeding against a conscientious objector who had lost most of the males in his family in the first war and refused to join the army; he was permitted to stay on air-raid-warden duty. He also interviewed the aging writer H. G. Wells, telling one of the Reston sons years later that because of the limits of his own education, he didn't have any idea what to ask him. He talked with the cranky Irish playwright George Bernard Shaw, who, Reston reported, wanted the prime minister to either bomb Berlin or stop the war and negotiate with the Germans. If a peace conference failed, Shaw observed, "we must, I suppose, fight it out, but as I am a born coward and dislike extremely all this blackout business and ruinous taxation and all the rest of it, I will still want to know what I am fighting for."

In April 1940 the German army smashed into Norway and whipped the British army troops posted there to defend Scandinavia. In May and June more than 300,000 Allied troops were evacuated across the English Channel from Dunkirk, when France fell and the Germans extended their dominion across the Continent. In early June, too, the Restons got word that the time had come for the evacuation of Americans who did not want to stay for the duration of the war.

Transport boats were sent from the United States and Scotty and Sally and Dick made their way to Dublin, bound for Galway on the west coast of Ireland. The boat that Sally and Dick were to take home was torpedoed and sunk by the Germans on its way to Ireland. She and the little boy boarded its replacement, the liner *Washington*, and sailed anxiously for New York. Scotty was alone again, and so was Sally, with Dick in tow. As they were leaving London,

Scotty and Sally decided they would try for another child, since they didn't really know what was to become of them during the war. They took advantage of the night in Dublin on their way to Sally's boat, remembering with great amusement that the brand name of the mattress upon which they slept in Dublin was "Restonia." There Scotty sired his namesake, James Barrett Reston Jr., although Scotty did not learn that fact until later, when Sally wrote from the States.

Before that good news arrived, Scotty fell into a lonely funk. "I returned from Ireland depressed," he remembered. "What was I doing here waiting for the slaughter, frightened and ashamed of my fear, amputated without Sally while my own government was standing aside? I felt sure the Germans would then turn on London. I didn't have long to wait." As the bombing began, the *Times* of London office was damaged and the *New York Times* bureau moved into the headquarters of the Reuters news service at 85 Fleet Street. Daniell joked to the staff that they now had the choice of being killed by a bomb on the roof, suffocated in the fumes of a very bad first-floor kitchen in the building, or buried under the steeple of a neighboring church.

The office had a view of the City of London, the city's business district and a prime bombing target for the Germans. Wrote Reston:

> With uncanny regularity, the German bombers would come over just about ten minutes after blackout and start dropping incendiary bombs all over the section. About an hour later, before we could see the flames, we would begin to hear the steady throb of scores of engines along the bank of the Thames; these were the pumps, driving the muddy water from the river up through miles of new hose that covered the waterfront streets every night for months. A little later, the sky would begin to change in color from midnight blue to a reddish glow, and soon the great dome of St. Paul's Cathedral would stand out in silhouette against the flames of perhaps a dozen raging

fires. Night after night we watched this incredible scene, and morning after morning we marveled at the fact that the fires were somehow put out.

Later the bureau moved into the swank Savoy Hotel, partly because it had deep and strong basements to serve as shelters, and partly to have rooms for the staff to sleep when not on duty. Commuting back and forth from home to office was impossible as parts of London began to be reduced to rubble. The main stories were being written by bureau chief Daniell, with Reston and the others doing backup feature material. Because of increasingly tough censorship, the journalists were not learning much of large significance, but they were able to see and hear the horror of war. Reston wrote years later of hearing the "unbearable" screams of children during the night raids, but also remembered the stoic English women busily sweeping away rubble to make things tidy again. He recalled the randomness of the bombs' destruction, one house leveled, the next spared. He recounted lying on the ground near the coast of the English Channel, watching duels between the Royal Air Force and the Luftwaffe. He told the story of visiting with British air marshal Arthur "Bomber" Harris, who showed him aerial reconnaissance pictures after British attacks on Dusseldorf factories. Reston said he commented that the workers' homes seemed to have been destroyed as well as the factories. Replied Harris, "Yes, they burn beautifully."

There was, Reston remembered, a certain "bogus lighthearted bravery" among the other correspondents like Ed Murrow and Eric Severeid. There was teasing back and forth: Reston accused Murrow of inventing Hitler to give drama to his broadcasts, while Murrow taunted the *Times*men for residing in a "fancy bunker" at the Savoy. But it was a horrible time for everyone, the swashbuckling correspondents included, and it was especially hard for Reston. None of his memories of the time were anything but melancholy. There was no bravado about the risks he took or nostalgia for the camaraderie many war reporters develop with their colleagues. Nor was he satisfied with his work. Censorship kept him from writing about the real horror that he saw, the tens of thousands killed in the blitz. He wrote to Sally, "We are not reporting what is happening over here. . . . There are times when I feel so cut away from everyone I love that I lose all sense of proportion. If the pride in one's work is destroyed by censorship, sometimes it doesn't seem worth the sacrifice." They were working and sleeping in the bunkers under the hotel and there was really no place to go and nothing to do but work. The bureau chief, Daniell, recalled coming upon Reston one day in the lobby of the Savoy wearing "sun-tans" with his shirt open at the collar. "This is my day off," Reston explained, "and I'm wearing my country clothes to remind me of it."

In fact, the war was making him sick. He developed what he thought was an ulcer and began drinking milk to soothe his stomach or ordering finnan haddie boiled in milk for dinner. He'd venture an occasional sherry, while the others were belting down scotch whiskey. Doctors had trouble diagnosing the problem, and he dragged around London fearing the worst. He composed a simple will and wrote a letter to Dick in case he didn't live long enough to ever speak with him again. Almost as if his mother were guiding his hand, he advised the young boy that he should "live simply and accept your responsibilities." Finally, he was diagnosed as having undulant fever, contracted by drinking raw, impure milk. It gave him high night fevers, weakness, and chills.

The doctors told him to go home, and he did. William L. Shirer had fled from Germany and was in London when it was time for Scotty to leave. Shirer asked Reston to take the manuscript of his book *Berlin Diary* with him to the States, and Reston obliged, flying first to Lisbon, then taking a boat to Bermuda, helping Shirer get his manuscript past the British censors. When he got back to New York, Scotty was forbidden from being close to Sally for fear she and the unborn baby would be infected, but he was plainly relieved to be back. Unlike the time twenty years before when he had made his second trip with his family to the United States, this time, he wrote later, "I knew where home was and what it meant."

CHAPTER 6

THE SULZBERGER ADOPTION

ON CHRISTMAS DAY, 1940, Scotty and Sally celebrated their fifth wedding anniversary in the city where they had wed. They were looking forward to the birth of their second son, who was due in the spring. Reston had no real assignment at the *Times*, and in fact, upon his return he had made his first trip above the lobby of the building on West Forty-third Street. He was thirty-one years old, still a young man to be sure, if not exactly a star in the *Times* firmament. Yet his writing from London, despite the constraints of wartime censorship, had been noticed, not just by his editors, but also by the proprietors of the newspaper. The very fact that he was back from London with firsthand accounts of what he had seen made him interesting to the newspaper's publisher, Arthur Hays Sulzberger, and to the publisher's wife, Iphigene Ochs Sulzberger. Soon Reston would meet, for the first time, the person who was to be the most important man in his life, far more influential and paternal than his own father. And if one were to rank in order of importance the women in Scotty's life, first would be Sally, second his mother, and a very close third, Iphigene Sulzberger.

Mrs. Sulzberger was the daughter of Adolph Ochs, the founder of the modern *New York Times*, who had died only five years earlier. Arthur Hays Sulzberger had become publisher of the paper shortly before his father-in-law died and established a line of family succession that continues even today, with Ochs's great-grandson Arthur Ochs Sulzberger Jr., who now runs the paper. The notion of a female member of the family's ascending to the publisher's chair was not, and has never been, seriously considered.

The Ochses and the Sulzbergers and their extended families were exemplars of the assimilationist, secularized, German Jewish families who had risen to social prominence in the second and third generations after their immigration to America. And Adolph was determined that the *Times* not be seen as particularly Jewish. As a result, the paper's coverage of the rise of anti-Semitic fascism was bland and restrained, and remained that way even after the extent of Nazi genocide began to be known.

Still, the Sulzbergers were keenly interested in what was going on in Europe. Iphigene had been in Switzerland in 1934 and had met a German Jewish couple and their children. The husband had been thrown into prison by the German government but released after the intercession of a high-ranking army official. The couple told Iphigene of others less fortunate who were still in jail. Iphigene's father's cousin, a wealthy toy manufacturer, was imprisoned in the same year. He too was eventually released, but the trauma was blamed for his death soon afterward. By 1935 one of that uncle's nieces wrote to Iphigene saying conditions for Jews had worsened and asking for her sponsorship to immigrate to America. The Sulzbergers signed the papers and eventually endorsed immigration for as many as thirty other relatives escaping Nazism. Over time, Iphigene recalled, they were flooded by letters from people they didn't even know asking for their support. The Sulzbergers refused these strangers, wanting to believe that the situation wasn't as bad as the supplicants described. Late in her life, she expressed her deep regret for having refused anyone. "I wish I had signed for them all – I wish to God I had," she wrote.

Scotty Reston came home from London believing that only American intervention would save Britain and defeat Hitler. He was shocked to find that his countrymen didn't exactly share that view. Shortly after Christmas the Sulzbergers invited the Restons to their Manhattan home for dinner. It was the most important social invitation of their lives, and they sensed that fact right away. Sally went to Macy's and bought what Scotty later and ungraciously described as a "maternity tent" for the event. The two of them must have been awestruck by the building they entered at 5 East 80th Street. The five-story town house had been bought by Adolph Ochs and deeded to Iphigene. The previous owner was a Rothschild. It was furnished in a classic English style, full of Persian carpets, painted screens, and plenty of chintz. There were ten servants, among them a live-in cook, a laundress, a chauffeur, a nurse for the children, and a parlor maid. Appropriate to the setting was one of the dinner guests that evening, Thomas Lamont, a partner and soon-to-be chairman of the banking firm J. P. Morgan. It was Lamont's opinion, apparently expressed with a certain disdain for the young newspaperman, that it was foolish to think that Britain would not survive the German onslaught without American help. Reston disagreed, with some vehemence, despite his triple disadvantage in status, age, and social class.

Whatever Lamont thought of the cheeky young man, Iphigene Sulzberger was taken with his charm and with what she considered his sound judgment. She weighed in against Lamont as well, denouncing Neville Chamberlain. "It's not only that I hated his arrangements with Hitler," Scotty later quoted her as saying that evening, "but what he has done to the word 'appeasement.' It used to be a beautiful word. It meant to pacify, to soothe, to try to understand and heal. That's what most women do all their lives, and now he has made the word shameful."

Reston recalled that he "took a liking to that lady then and there." And the sentiment was returned, although Arthur Hays must have been less impressed by Reston; when he encountered him a few years later, he failed to recognize him. Iphigene, however, came to see Reston and his Presbyterian morality as a Protestant echo of some of her father's own values. In time she would come to think of him nearly as a member of the family. Reston did not then imagine how much he would eventually owe to her, but would, in fact, soon join a large company of people who owed much to Adolph Ochs's daughter. In many ways it was her strength, her forbearance of her husband's shortcomings, her progressive politics, her support for her young son when he succeeded Arthur Hays as publisher, and her devotion to the newspaper her father had built that made the *New York Times* what it was and is. The eventual bond between the publisher's family and the young Scots immigrant, who was roughly the same age as the older Sulzberger children, grew so strong that he would come to be called "the adopted Sulzberger" by those who resented his access to the top of the *Times* family.

Jimmy James, the managing editor of the *Times,* was a man without much imagination or particular brilliance, but his dandyish wardrobe earned him the nickname Dressy James. He had not wanted to hire Reston in London and now had no idea what to do with the returning war correspondent. He suggested that perhaps the Boston bureau might be open, but Reston had another, grander idea. He asked to be sent to the Washington bureau so that he might continue to cover the war by way of the diplomatic beat. It was not an especially original idea, since other foreign correspondents, displaced as the countries to which they were assigned fell to the Nazis, had also been congregating in Washington. Arthur Krock, the *Times'* crusty and turf-conscious bureau chief in the nation's capital, strenuously resisted accepting Reston. His hostility might have been based on some vague premonition of the threat Reston was to become to Krock's own position in Washington, but Scotty was still a small figure at the paper. Krock instead complained that he was "just running a displaced persons' office" in the capital. Reston used his new Sulzberger connection immediately, and Arthur Hays personally asked Krock to relent. Reston went to Washington, the city that he would come to dominate as no journalist before or since.

The Restons arrived in January 1941, and it was the first time either Scotty or Sally had been to the U.S. capital. Its monuments and its cleanliness, after the rubble of wartime London, made them believe it was "the most beautiful city we had ever seen." The thrill of coming to Washington was not unique to Reston. Journalists measure their own importance by a simple formula: take the power and fame of the people one covers, discount heavily for being an observer, not a real participant, then multiply by the amount of access to those people. As America prepared to go to war, it was obvious that Washington and the people who ran it would be even more powerful than they had been before. This fact was not lost on Scotty Reston. He was about to cover the personalities and the institutions that would determine the very survival of his adopted nation. What could have been more important or more exciting?

Though a beautiful city, Washington was far from the most cosmopolitan place the Restons had been. The city was still very much a small town, deeply segregated, a company town that rolled up its streets when the bureaucrats went home. It was a town, as John Kennedy famously cracked years later, of "southern efficiency and northern charm." Georgetown, which was to become the posh residence for rich white folks, was only beginning to gentrify, with young couples like the Restons displacing the resident African-American population. Scotty and Sally rented a townhouse there for fifty dollars a month and in March added James B. Reston Jr. to their family. The house was soon offered to them for $11,000. The notion of borrowing the money was alien to the parsimonious Scotsman and they passed on the deal. "My first mistake in Washington," he recalled.

His second came when he was dispatched to fill in for the vacationing *Times* Senate correspondent. Covering the Senate chamber's proceedings, he failed to notice an announcement that Adolph Ochs's cousin, the vainglorious Colonel Julius Adler, who also happened to be the general manager of the *New York Times,* was being promoted to general in the U.S. Army Reserve. The paper the next day was of course silent on this piece of news and Adler took the oversight quite seriously. Reston was forced to phone Adler and deliver a personal apology for his inexcusable failure.

Despite that error and his inexperience in Washington's ways, Reston was not really outclassed by his competitors. The press corps in those days, even as the New Deal and the war were making Washington the news hub of America, was a clubby little band of rather uneducated hacks. They mostly fawned on the politicians they covered. In return, the reporters had easy access to the men who ran the country, even to President Roosevelt, who treated them like begging children, chastising them for any critical stories, joking at the expense of one or another of the reporters, bantering amiably, but keeping most of what he said strictly off the record. The press largely accepted what was told them, reporting it as fact. The notion of investigative reporting was quite alien to that culture. It was not a hard game to play. Reston himself attended some of Roosevelt's Oval Office press conferences and was thrilled to be there, covering the president.

Similarly, Secretary of State Cordell Hull convened regular chat sessions with a mere dozen reporters, often including Reston. Hull was obsessed with his rival, Undersecretary Sumner Welles, and shared gossipy dirt about the man with the reporters. Welles was eventually dismissed, and Reston wrote a sympathetic piece about the departing diplomat. Reston was promptly summoned to a private session with Hull. The secretary of state handed Reston a dossier from the Federal Bureau of Investigation purporting to show that Welles was a homosexual. Reston said he asked Hull if he was willing to be cited as the source of the report. The secretary, of course, declined. Reston gave the file to Arthur Krock, and, observing the unwritten rules that prevailed, Krock decided no story about Welles's sexual preferences would appear in the *Times*. That refusal to report on the personal lives of public figures was an important lesson for Reston, one that he applied repeatedly over the long stretch of his career.

The intoxication of journalism often comes from the sort of proximity to power Reston enjoyed early in his career in London and in Washington. For him the idea of an immigrant kid from Dayton conversing with presidents and diplomats and senators was overwhelmingly exciting, and for good reason. The chance to be witness and critic, the opportunity to learn and write about the great events of one's time, is a wonderful experience. It was heady stuff. Five decades later, Reston still remembered with wonder going to the U.S. Senate lobby and being able to send a note summoning a member of that august body for a chat. He recalled meeting Ohio's Republican senator Robert Taft and being taken into the man's confidence, partly, he insisted, because Taft had heard of him when he was traveling secretary to the Cincinnati baseball team. Taft introduced him to Alice Roosevelt Longworth, Teddy Roosevelt's daughter, a central figure then and for decades after in what passed for Washington society. Soon Sally and Scotty were guests at the gossipy, and very anti-FDR, soirees she held in her mansion near Dupont Circle.

Reston was a good deal smarter and a good deal more ambitious than the average Washington reporter, but he had not yet developed the instincts and intuitions that set the great journalists apart from the run-of-the-mill. He worked hard, combing the embassies and talking to the foreign ambassadors to whom no one else was paying much attention. In the summer of 1941, shortly after FDR imposed an embargo on shipments of oil and scrap iron to Japan, Reston had an interview with the Japanese ambassador. The diplomat told him Japan took the embargo as "an act of war," strong words indeed, especially as the Japanese war machine was rolling in Asia. Reston reported back to Krock and phoned his sources at the Department of State to get their reaction to what the ambassador had said. When Krock and the State Department wrote off the incendiary words as mere propaganda, so did Reston. In early December, three days before the attack at Pearl Harbor, the same ambassador assured Reston that he thought war could be avoided. Reston took careful notes, believing the ambassador's assurances. It was only after the attack occurred, Reston said later, that he realized the ambassador must have known Japanese ships were steaming toward Hawaii. He had been gulled, but then so had most of the American military and civilian hierarchy.

What he lacked in judgment and savvy at that point, he made up for with ambition. But Reston had not fully recovered from the illness that sent him home from London. In April 1941 the bureau chief, Krock, wrote to the managing editor, "After a painstaking investigation I have concluded that it is essential to Mr. Reston's full recovery that he be separated from work for the daily [newspaper], even the light work he has been doing, for a month or so. . . . So I am willing, beginning next Monday, to turn him over to Mr. Markel [who ran the Sunday edition of the *Times*]." Reston had been surprised in his first year in Washington at the widespread and deepseated isolationism and antiwar sentiment, not just in the capital, but across much of America. He had seen the bombing of London firsthand and understood the power of the Axis as against the lesser power of Britain. So he believed firmly that Hitler could not be defeated without American help. While seconded to the Sunday department of the paper, he wrote a highly opinionated piece with the headline "Are We Awake?" making the case for a full American commitment. After the United States did enter the war, Reston expanded his argument into a book called *Prelude to Victory*, for the prestigious publisher Alfred A. Knopf, who narrowly outbid competitor Viking's $1,000 advance. The book was personally edited by Knopf's wife, Blanche.

The main point of the book, published the next spring, was that America needed to pull together to win the war. Its language is often florid, even racist by today's standards, and its message seems rather obvious in retrospect. But it was still a powerful call to arms at a time when the country was most reluctant to go to war to save Europe and Asia from aggression. The conventional wisdom still held that the United States was geographically invulnerable to any serious threat. Given Reston's relative youth and inexperience in American politics, it was a bold polemic. It began:

> It is necessary now that we admit the facts: many of the things we have laughed at, or taken for granted, or minimized, or despised in the last few years have risen up to plague us. The man with the Charlie Chaplin mustache who merely wanted living space for the Germans and could not attack even if he wanted to is the master of Europe whose submarines are taking pot shots at our East Coast. The little grinning yellow men, the

growers of our vegetables, the makers of our cheap toys, the imitators of the West whom we brought into the modern world and could vanquish in three months, are the conquerors of the East.

In the book he criticized greedy capitalists, selfish unions, the power of the "farm bloc," shortsighted politicians, including a gaggle of powerful congressional committee chairmen whom it might have been better not to offend, and even the newspaper business — but not the *Times* — for putting profits ahead of the need to keep their readers fully informed about the urgency of the war. He slammed editorial writers for not being clear about the problem and bemoaned the reliance of many newspapers on "canned" opinion and the "craze for syndicated columnists," a view he wisely abandoned when he himself came to dominate the genre a couple of decades later.

While the book was hardly a work of stunning philosophical merit, it was well received. In the *New Yorker*, Clifton Fadiman, then the magazine's book editor, snidely called Reston a latter-day Paul Revere, telling us the Nazis are coming. But Fadiman added:

He feels, thinks and writes with warmth and precision, and is clearly fashioned by nature and experience to carry the torch when the hands of the older newspaper columnists begin to fail. . . . Mr. Reston is a valuable propagandist not only because what he says is true but because he cannot be accused of party hackwork. He is very far from being entirely pro-Administration, and much of his sharpest, though never malicious, criticism is directed not at you and me but at Washington.

The *Times'* own review of *Prelude* called the book "brilliant and altogether admirable," adding that "time may even decide it is a great book." The review took up three-quarters of a page, with a three-column-wide picture of Reston. It was a big sendoff for the new author, though time has decided it was not a great book.

In any case, the *Times* review and Clifton Fadiman's prediction of the rise of Reston were enough to alarm Arthur Krock, who by now must have clearly seen what was coming. Reston had been careful to praise and quote some of Krock's editorial opinions in his book. Nonetheless, Krock "was not amused," Reston remembered, "by a new boy in the office blowing off about the big issues of the war." Nor could Reston's growing relationship with Lester Markel have made Krock happy. Markel ran his Sunday department as a totally independent barony, outside the supervision of the managing editor and, of course, Krock. Markel was thus another important patron for Reston to use to his advantage. Markel ruled supreme for decades, until Arthur Hays Sulzberger's son, after becoming publisher in the 1960s, decided that it was time to retire the septuagenarian Markel. It took the young publisher three days, he said, to screw up his courage to inform Markel of his decision. When he did confront him, Markel raged: "You're ruining my career!"

Prelude, despite its criticism of much of official Washington, did contain some praise for the denizens of the Office of War Information (OWI), including the poet Archibald MacLeish, who was also the librarian of Congress, and Elmer Davis, a former *New York Times* reporter whom Roosevelt had recruited from CBS to run that office. Reston endorsed MacLeish's formulation that the Axis powers were operating a "strategy of terror," while the Allies were following a "strategy of truth." Reston praised both MacLeish and Davis for trying to release all militarily "safe" information.

Reston's praise of Davis was surely uncalculated, but the former *Times*man must have noticed the power of Reston's propagandistic argument before he approached Arthur Hays Sulzberger and asked him to lend Reston to the OWI. Sulzberger agreed, as did Scotty and Sally. They moved back to London, taking up residence at Claridge's Hotel, where many Americans were billeted. In August 1942, Scotty wrote a chatty, four-page letter to Krock explaining what he later called his "minor propaganda chores." It fell to Reston to deal with little upsets like the one caused when an American soldier walked into a London hotel juggling a pair of grapefruits and then proceeded, in Reston's words, "to slice both of them open, shower them with sugar, and gulp them with a flourish." This was understandably annoying to the British, who had seen precious little fresh fruit since the war began. He also told Krock about an incident in which two U.S. soldiers, having been overserved with liquor, started kidding Churchill's daughter Mary about the three stripes she was wearing on her uniform. They gibed that she had gotten them only because of her father's position. Mary said something tart in reply. The soldiers grabbed her and gave her a spanking, with "30 or 40" swats involved. "The story," he told Krock, "has gotten around here despite the fact that [the ambassador] had arranged for it to be suppressed in the British press."

"The colored troops are also quite a problem," Reston wrote, using what was then an acceptable, at least to white people, description of African-Americans. "Whatever Colonel Blimp thinks about them in India," Reston wrote, lumping the citizens of South Asia with "the colored" from America, "they treat them pretty well here. The negroes [sic] are invited wherever the white boys are and a lot of the Southern boys resent it. This has led to several incidents which have created a problem for Eisenhower and his public relations men."

The experience in the embassy taught Reston several important lessons. There is a natural limitation to what a journalist can really know about the people and the policies and the struggles he or she covers, and many reporters never really understand that fact. A reporter who has, for example, spent time inside a presidential campaign will forever after approach writing about such an enterprise with a certain modesty. Reflecting on his service as a minor government bureaucrat, Reston concluded that life inside the government was a good deal more complicated than it looked from outside. The journalist sees only a fraction of any reality, and Reston seems to have learned in London to avoid writing too much more than he actually knew. Reston said he came to admire the embassy staff members with whom he worked in London. He learned to appreciate the intelligence and talent that is often present in the American diplomatic corps below the level of the secretary of state, who was often appointed, Reston opined, only because he looked like a secretary of state. It was not an incidental lesson, since Reston later mined the State Department for many a good story unavailable from the top.

Finally, Reston learned he had little stomach for propaganda work. His task often involved writing factual statements about American policy to counter various Nazi propaganda initiatives, delivering the statements to Foreign Secretary Anthony Eden's parliamentary secretary. A question would be arranged in Parliament and Eden would respond based on Reston's working paper. The intoxication of journalism – the proximity to power – often leads reporters to want more, to actually *be* powerful. Some then skip out of the trade and into government, usually as a press secretary to a candidate or public official. In a small and easy way, Reston solved this outsider-insider dilemma while posted to London. Although he was not unhappy doing his bit for the war effort and noted in his memoirs that he was counseled by the American ambassador that what he was doing was "better than carrying a gun," he realized that "government propaganda . . . was a tricky occupation I could never master or enjoy."

In London he had a pair of chance encounters that profoundly influenced his career. He had the good fortune to work for a man named Wallace Carroll, who was running the OWI operation in London. Carroll, Reston later discovered, had been instrumental in the propaganda effort that duped the Germans into believing that an invasion of Europe would precede the Allied push through

North Africa. Years later, when Reston was in charge of the *Times* Washington bureau, he made Carroll his deputy, bringing in the kind of management skill the bureau chief sorely needed.

But Reston's biggest boost from the London posting again involved Arthur Hays Sulzberger. Reston had not actually seen the *Times* publisher since the Christmas-season dinner he and Sally had attended a couple of years earlier. Sulzberger had been traveling in Scotland and stopped by to pay a call on the American ambassador. He had some questions about how the U.S. delegation was countering Nazi propaganda and Reston was summoned to explain. Sulzberger did not recognize him. Sulzberger made a second call on the embassy and Reston was again summoned. This time Ambassador John Winant mentioned that Reston was on leave from Sulzberger's own newspaper. Sulzberger, Reston recalled, was highly embarrassed and quickly asked Reston to come to his hotel later for a chat. At that meeting Sulzberger observed that if Reston could serve the ambassador so well, why not do the same for the publisher of the *Times*? He suggested that when Reston's tour at the embassy ended, he should come back to New York to work directly for him, helping with speeches and assisting him in thinking about the future of the newspaper after the war. Reston readily agreed and Sulzberger followed up with a formal letter when he returned to New York. "London was obviously my lucky town," Reston wrote in his memoirs. But Reston was often in the right place at the right time, and it wasn't merely luck.

CHAPTER 7

MR. GUS

IT IS NOT exactly a dream of young reporters to become an administrative assistant, a sort of business bureaucrat, even if the person being assisted is the owner of the newspaper. But Reston was not hesitant about moving back to New York to work for Arthur Hays Sulzberger. He understood the opportunity for what it was: a chance to become personally close to AHS, as he was universally known from the initials he signed at the bottom of his office memorandums.

Sulzberger was an attractive and powerful figure, widely admired by those who worked for him even though he had married into the newspaper business. He had been born to an established upper-class Jewish family in New York City and his mother's forebears had even fought in the American Revolutionary War. His social credentials were superior to those of the Ochs family and it gave him a bearing and self-confidence that permitted him to be unintimidated by his father-in-law, who had made it a condition of his daughter's marriage that Arthur Hays join the *Times*. Arthur had done so eagerly, since he was working at his father's cotton-goods trading company, where he was outranked by his older brother. He took full command of the *Times*, with Iphigene's full support. Arthur Hays was adamant that his middle name always appear, having discovered that another Arthur Sulzberger, from a family of meat packers, also lived in New York. He was gracious and urbane, and had traveled extensively as a young man. He loved the theater, was fond of writing funny poems and drawing cartoons. He was a stylish dresser and loved frank conversations and good whiskey. To Reston, Arthur Hays, then in his early fifties, must have been the very essence of what a successful, civilized man should be.

The new assistant took an office on the fourteenth floor of the *Times* building, near Sulzberger, and began writing speeches for the publisher. Despite the brevity of his experience and Arthur Hays's august stature, he also penned memos pointing out the shortcomings of the newspaper. When Sulzberger followed up on those Reston suggestions with which he agreed, the established editors began to regard the new man in the executive suite warily. He was seen, Reston recalled in his memoirs, as "the spy on the 14th floor." He could be charming, but he also had sharp elbows.

Sulzberger was eager to visit the Soviet Union to see for himself how America's new ally in the war effort was doing. FDR wanted to give Sulzberger permission to go but was wary of having to grant the same privilege to other newspaper owners. He insisted that Arthur Hays travel in his capacity as a vice president of the American Red Cross and report back on how American aid was being deployed by the Soviets. Sulzberger decided Reston would go along both as companion and note taker.

At the time, it was impossible to approach Moscow from the north or west because of the German military presence. On June 10, 1943, they began the circuitous journey that was to take them from Washington to Miami, south to Brazil, across the Atlantic to Africa, into the Middle East, north along the Caspian Sea, and finally to Moscow. Before he left, Reston left instructions with Sulzberger's son-in-law, Orvil Dryfoos, to send flowers to Sally every Sunday and left sentimental, handwritten notes to go with each delivery.

Carrying Army Transport Command tickets that gave them number one priority on the military planes, the publisher and his aide took off from Washington in a great Boeing Stratoliner to begin the thirteen-thousand-mile trip, bitten off in roughly thousand-mile chunks. Reston passed the time on the long hops playing gin rummy with Sulzberger, typing notes for an extensive diary of the adventure, and on the very first leg of the trip, getting airsick when the plane hit a storm over the Carolinas.

It was anything but a luxurious trip, at least in the beginning. Breakfast in Puerto Rico was ruined for Reston not just by the greasy ham but also by a giant cockroach that raced across the steam table as he was being served. In the jungle of what was then British Guiana, where the American military had carved out an airbase near a dirt-poor village, he recorded his "shock" – a word he used with indubitable sincerity, since he had never been in the undeveloped world – at the primitive conditions: "The huts . . . had obviously been built by hand with rough pieces of wood of all sizes . . . [and] were full of holes, dirty, obviously verminous and unsanitary. By the side of the road was a sort of rough ditch in which the women were washing and rubbing their clothes on stones, and back of this ditch were the houses, several of which also served as stores. In one of these, amid a filth of flies and squalor, hung sides of beef." It was Scotty's first look at real poverty, way beyond what he had known as a child in Scotland, poverty without any hint of what he thought of as civilization. Nonetheless he reported faithfully that he and Sulzberger were served a "pleasant but violent concoction" of heavy rum and lime juice that made the pair "extremely loquacious."

Reston's diary items about his boss had a relaxed but respectful familiarity that showed his ease at being in Arthur Hays's company. He noted with a gentle sarcasm that before leaving Washington, Sulzberger bought "a number of intellectual publications" such as *The Case of the Dangerous Dowager,* by Erle Stanley Gardner, that were widely shared with the other passengers and crew on the trip. When they got to Natal in Brazil, they went to the mess hall hoping for a nice steak dinner. Instead they ate "burned stew and coffee so black that it left a plimsoll line around your cup." Reston filled up on bread and peanut butter, but Sulzberger, "with a stomach like a cement mixer," downed the military chow.

They flew out over the Atlantic, sleeping overnight in the chilly plane until they set down on Ascension Island. Reston marveled that the navigators had found this lonely island. On they went to Accra, in what was then British-occupied territory. There they found the American soldiers homesick and prone to believe, in a variant of the isolationism Reston had found in Washington, that the folks at home were going hungry while America was sending all its food to England. On the way to Khartoum, they stopped overnight in Maiduguri, in the north of what is now Nigeria. After visiting the mud-and-dung town of 60,000 people, he and Sulzberger discussed the morality of colonial occupation but concluded that at least until the end of the war, the system had to be maintained. They landed outside Khartoum the next day and on the way to the base stopped at a small monument commemorating the 1898 conquest of the Sudan by British general H. H. Kitchener. He had managed to lose only fourteen soldiers as his forces slaughtered 20,000 spear-carrying Africans. There Reston and Sulzberger got a little preview of things to come in Africa when they noticed that a protective fence had been built around the monument. They were informed that "the natives had been throwing stones at it to remind the newly arrived American soldiers that the natives still did not like the British or any other over-lords who might want to settle in their country."

Sitting upright in metal bucket seats, they flew overnight to Cairo, where they finally reached a proper hotel. "AHS takes to this flying like a swallow," Reston rhapsodized. "Six days in the air without normal food or sleep, he took one look at the soft beds, hot and cold running water and endless quantities of fresh food – and decided that the thing to do was to get out of the place as soon as possible." After a busy two days making the rounds of diplomats and other journalists, the pair took off before dawn for Tehran. They went over the Suez Canal at two thousand feet, buzzed the northern part of Jerusalem at three hundred feet, and saw Baghdad from the air. Reston observed that "AHS had always wanted to fly to Baghdad on a magic carpet and here was his wish come true."

Tehran was the key point along the route by which the Soviets received Allied supplies. Truck caravans and trains moved goods and matériel from the Persian Gulf north to the Iranian capital. North of Tehran, the Russians took over, nearly occupying that part of the country. The *Times*men were put aboard a Russian plane at five o'clock in the morning – without breakfast, Reston noted – for the final legs of their journey.

At a fueling stop in Baku, they began to learn how the Soviet Union worked when Reston's diary was examined and partly translated by security personnel. Breakfast was caviar, boiled eggs, bread, tea, sausage, radishes, and pound cake. The pair exchanged dollars for rubles with a Swedish diplomat who was along on the flight. Reston couldn't resist documenting that they had gotten twelve rubles to the dollar instead of five, making the cost of their breakfast four dollars, not ten. "AHS ate the caviar like jam," he noted. After Baku they refueled in Astrakhan, and then again in Kuibyshev, where Sulzberger, tempted by his mastery of three Russian words – *chei* (tea), *nyet,* and *da* – decided to buy some victuals. When the publisher noticed the flies swarming around the teapot, Reston reported that AHS used two-thirds of his Russian vocabulary: *"Nyet chei.*" They landed in Moscow on the evening of June 21, eleven days after leaving Washington.

By coincidence, their first full day in Moscow was the second anniversary of Hitler's catastrophic declaration of war against the Soviet Union. Partly because of the incredible heroism of the Red Army, the course of the war was turning against Germany. Sulzberger and Reston were billeted at the elegant and spacious Spasso House, then the American embassy and now the U.S. ambassador's residence. As they went to bed on their first night, the Russians were lofting their antiaircraft balloons, expecting a commemorative raid against the city. Nothing happened and Reston observed that "the Hun evidently has no bombers for anniversaries now, so we slept quietly and woke to find the morning sun streaming over the city."

Sulzberger was permitted to attend the annual meeting of the Red Cross and its Muslim counterpart the Red Crescent. He attempted to find out whether, as had been rumored at home, the Russians had developed a new and powerful pesticide to combat the body lice that carried typhus. He was told they had, but the secretive Soviets denied him any further information. That was to be typical: polite hospitality along with limited information offered reluctantly and overlaid with a constant suspicion of the Americans. Sulzberger and Reston managed to have a session inside the Kremlin with the Soviet foreign minister, the mustachioed, pince-nezed Vyacheslav Molotov. Inside the great compound, they noticed that huge camouflage nets had been draped over the interior buildings to protect them against air strikes. The occasion was stiff and formal until the Soviets brought out sparkling burgundy, champagne, and chocolates. The drink animated Molotov, who bore down on Sulzberger, wanting to know whether the *New York Times* was the official voice of the Roosevelt administration. When the publisher told him the paper was independent but supported FDR, Molotov demanded to know which American newspaper was the official adjunct of the administration.

The drinking went on so long that Sulzberger and Reston missed the opening curtain at the Bolshoi and had to wait until the beginning of the second act to watch *Swan Lake*. Wrote Reston: "We didn't have much native ballet in Dayton, Ohio, so I'm not much of an expert on the subject; but it should be reported that the female is graceful and beautiful in this part of the world too and, with the aid of Tchaikovsky, she is well worth beholding." He may not have seen much ballet, but he did notice that the Russians had changed the ending, allowing the swan to live as a way of bolstering national morale. After the performance, the men walked out into Red Square and, like countless visitors year after year, were swept away by the grandeur of the towers and domes of the Kremlin and Saint Basil's. They saw couples walking arm in arm and heard the *Pathetique* over the official loudspeakers at every corner. "We felt fine," wrote Reston, "and if it hadn't been for those OGPU [intelligence] agents in the car back of us, we would have been convinced that . . . it really is all 'one world.'"

But they soon began to see just how the great workers' government dispensed its favors. At a street market in Moscow, they watched a person try to sell a dried-up heel of bread to passersby, a man with a handful of hairpins and another with a single comb plead for customers, and a woman with two miniature fish attempt to peddle them for a few rubles. Sulzberger noted in a contribution he made to the diary that he had seen a woman with a child beg for handouts outside a bakery, while another woman crawled on hands and knees along the street, "her head dropped forward like a thirsty horse." "One thing is clear," Reston concluded mildly, "there is a sharper contrast between the amount of food allotted to the privileged political military class and the amount allotted to the poorest sections of the population here than in either Britain or the United States." The official meals, Reston wrote, were "so lavish and ostentatious that no sensitive man in wartime England or the United

States would have dared serve them." A luncheon with the Russian ambassador to the United States, on home leave and showing the Americans around, was held at a mansion in Moscow, with a menu that began with vodka, then mounds of caviar, more vodka, buttered rolls filled with rice, cold fish, spring salad, mushrooms and cream, sturgeon, breast of turkey, breasts of chicken and partridge, fresh green peas and cauliflower, strawberry ice cream, all washed down with more vodka, red wine, white wine, sparkling burgundy, and followed by coffee, chocolates, and a battery of liqueurs. Perhaps wanting to put the best face on the excesses of our wartime allies, Reston concluded that the official extravagance was rooted in a sense of inferiority that led the hosts to try to impress the guests. He also reported, perhaps out of a sense of gratitude for all the Soviet Union had brought to the war effort, that "there is general agreement that the officials are at the same time doing a lot to increase the advantages of all the people and the regime has greatly improved the people's lot since the last war."

Even when they finally left the city limits of Moscow and drove west to where the Nazis had recently been routed, they continued to be well fed in field tents and at an underground hospital. They passed through a town named Vyazma, once home to 60,000 people, that had been totally destroyed by the Nazi invasion and the Soviet counteroffensive, except for church towers saved as landmarks for artillery fire. It was here that they were able to understand the colossal cost of the war to Russia.

Back in Moscow the publisher and his aide were invited to visit a troop train that was to be returning the wounded to the capital the next day. They were asked at what time they would like to visit the train and answered they would be available whenever the train arrived. No, they were told, the time would be at ten in the morning, for their convenience. When they got to the train station, they soon discovered that the train had arrived an hour before and the wounded, both ambulatory and on stretchers, had been forced to wait in the train for the American visitors rather than be taken to the hospital. Sulzberger demanded that the train be unloaded immediately, but he and Reston were made to inspect each car while the wounded and maimed waited. "It was a small incident," Reston recorded in the diary, "and perhaps we drew too many conclusions from it, but I have never seen anything which illustrates so clearly the totalitarian state's contempt for the individual. As we were looking into the cars, I looked at AHS's face and he at mine, and I guess I looked pretty glum, for he came over and remarked: 'Don't let this make a communist out of you!'" The sarcasm was designed to cover up the real horror of the scene. When Sulzberger got home he told Iphigene: "It was a horrible sight. Scotty and I had to hold back our tears."

As they took stock of their trip, the two men concluded they hadn't learned all that much, except that the Soviet Union was a difficult and closed state and would be especially troublesome after the war. "The Russians looked like the kind of people to have on our side and not against us," Reston opined. "I wouldn't want to bring up my boys on their philosophy because I don't think even good ends justify any means and I don't think efficiency and material comfort are very good ends, but I don't want my kids to have to fight them either. In another twenty-five years, I can see a tremendously strong and self-sufficient Russia, perhaps the strongest military power in the world, and I want to make the best honorable deal with them that can be made." It was a simple philosophy about how to deal with the Communist threat, neither belligerent nor accepting of the Soviet system. The trip had left him with no illusions about the Soviet Union, an attitude critical to the balanced and moderate analysis he brought to his writings as the Cold War intensified.

*   *   *

The two men came out of Russia, through Tehran and Cairo again, across North Africa to Tripoli, then to Gibraltar and London. Sulzberger saw Churchill, who told him that "the long agony is slowly coming to an end." The *Times*men flew back to New York by way of Iceland and Labrador, arriving in the late afternoon on July 30. The official record of their running gin rummy contest showed Sulzberger with a comfortable lead. Ever after, in their informal correspondence, Reston addressed AHS as "Mr. Gus," a corruption of the Russian word *gospodin,* meaning "mister." Sulzberger addressed Scotty as Pectoh, the Cyrillic rendition of Reston. The two men were friends for life.

CHAPTER 8

SCOOPS

BACK AT WORK for Arthur Hays on the executive floor, Reston continued to provoke older editors who preferred to run their separate baronies without much interference, especially interference from someone as young and inexperienced as Scotty Reston. Sulzberger was open to Reston's suggestions about improving the paper, but he also recognized he had to support the men who actually ran the newspaper every day. When Reston's criticisms were too pointed and the offended editor complained to Arthur Hays, the publisher would from time to time return a Reston memo with this admonition, in his own hand, at the top of the page: *"Achtung!"* Reston got the message, but he was not about to stop his own attempts to move up the ladder.

Reston had little respect for managing editor Jimmy James, who coincidentally was the uncle of future *Times* columnist Russell Baker, whom Reston would eventually bring to the paper. He described James years later as "a dumpy little Virginian who dressed like a racetrack gambler and carried a walking stick." James was especially sensitive to Reston's critical memos to Arthur Hays because, according to Reston, James's "skin was a lot thinner than his skull." But despite his ability to irritate the top editor, Reston did not have much real traction at the paper, writing memos, not news stories. For his part, he did not enjoy being cooped up in New York. He never did appreciate the city. Meanwhile, Washington's importance as the news capital of America was growing and Reston wanted to be there.

James, eager to be rid of Reston, was delighted to comply with Scotty's request for a transfer. But bureau chief Arthur Krock again saw trouble coming. He had been sent down to Washington ten years earlier and had longed to return to New York to work his way up the ranks of top editors. He harbored some resentments over the paper's refusal to put him into contention for greater responsibilities and believed that to some extent his Jewishness, which he did much to hide, had something to do with this failure. Yet Krock had become a power in Washington, writing his own column and befriending the powerful, including Joe Kennedy and his son Jack. Krock helped arrange publication of Jack's Harvard thesis as the book *Why England Slept*. If Krock wasn't going to make it to the top in New York, he certainly wasn't about to cede any ground in Washington, especially to Reston with all his connections to the publisher.

When Arthur Hays broached the subject of Reston's return with Krock, he objected politely but strenuously. He wrote to Sulzberger: "I should welcome Reston back here, of course, but I don't know what I should have for him to do. . . . He resists any routine assignments, the bulk of which we necessarily have, and I can't think of any roving assignment that wouldn't upset the machinery of the bureau." Sulzberger was not persuaded and assured Krock that Reston would be a good citizen. Reston understood the problems he faced with his editorial superiors, so he extracted an agreement from

Sulzberger that would permit the reporter to operate quite independently from Krock and even from James. Reston was to be in the bureau but not a totally integrated part of it. James, eager to show Scotty the door out of New York, asked him first to sit in as London bureau chief for a few months so the war-weary Raymond Daniell could have a rest. Scotty and Sally dispatched their sons to Dayton to stay with his parents and headed back to England.

Near the end of their temporary stay in London in early 1944, a Washington correspondent for the *Times* named Turner Catledge turned up after an arduous global trip reporting on the wonders of the Red Cross's services to American fighting men. The assignment had, of course, been suggested by Arthur Hays. Catledge was an elegant Mississippian who would later become the top editor of the newspaper, and who would eventually clash disastrously with Reston. Catledge was at that time Arthur Krock's top choice to replace him as bureau chief, should that awful event ever become necessary. But in the winter of 1944, Sally and Scotty extended every courtesy to Catledge as he finished his story.

The Restons had been invited by Lord and Lady Astor for a weekend visit to their stately country home, called Cliveden, on the banks of the Thames River in Buckinghamshire. The couple was the very epitome of English gentry who had been enthusiastic supporters of Chamberlain and his appeasement of Hitler. The featured attraction at Cliveden was always Nancy Astor, an American-born Southerner. She was the first woman to sit in the British Parliament, a crusader against alcohol, and an avid devotee of Mary Baker Eddy's Christian Science church. She was especially glad to see Catledge, whom she greeted by asking, "Where is that Southern white trash?" Shaking his hand, she proclaimed that she, too, was Southern white trash, which was patent nonsense. Catledge remembered that he and Reston began the weekend by secretly downing a couple of whiskeys in their rooms to fortify themselves against the prohibitionist ethic of Nancy. But the teetotaling came to an end when American flying ace Jimmy Doolittle arrived for Sunday dinner and asked for a tall scotch and water. Lord Astor gave his butler the key to the liquor cabinet, and Reston and Catledge eagerly joined in, as did the Astors' two sons.

Doolittle had won fame by leading a bombing raid against Japan a few months after the attack on Pearl Harbor, doing little damage but boosting American morale. He had been awarded the Congressional Medal of Honor and promoted to general. He was in England commanding the Eighth Air Force, then heavily involved in bombing Germany. After the dinner, Nancy Astor sat herself on the floor at Doolittle's feet and read aloud from her Bible and Christian Science tracts. She then cajoled Doolittle into recounting the details of his heroic raid on Tokyo.

Some weeks later the Restons, along with Catledge, sailed back to New York aboard the *Queen Mary*, zigzagging across the Atlantic to avoid German submarines. The great British luxury liner had been turned into a troop ship and had just dropped an army division in Scotland. Going home, it was loaded with four thousand wounded soldiers and a few hundred civilian passengers. The noncombatants were all given jobs to do: the Restons and Catledge put out the ship's newspaper. When he got home, Catledge met with Arthur Hays Sulzberger, who explained that the long assignment writing about Red Cross work abroad had been preparation for the job of foreign editor. AHS then added a strong hint that Catledge would eventually replace Jimmy James as managing editor. But first Catledge covered the 1944 presidential campaign, and when the election was over, Sulzberger enlisted Catledge to accompany him to the Pacific on another of his Red Cross inspection tours. Catledge made the trip, played gin rummy, and was apparently a bit more fun loving and a better drinking companion for the publisher than Reston had been. After James died in 1951, Catledge was named managing editor and remained in that position until the late 1960s, when his clash with Reston effectively ended his career.

"Arthur Krock received me back to the Washington bureau in 1944 with his usual restrained courtesy," Reston recalled in his memoirs, "but we soon ran into trouble." Sulzberger had promised Reston a wide franchise but had never bothered to ask Krock how he felt about the matter. And Krock felt strongly about it; he wanted Reston on a very short leash, within the rigid hierarchical and beat structure in the bureau. He offered Reston the minimal assignment of covering foreign embassies. "He gave me the impression that I would need a visa to venture elsewhere," Reston remembered. "For a while, he revived my old immigrant's dread that somehow I didn't fit in or wasn't wanted." Reston was right to feel this way. Years later, his struggle with Reston long over, Krock told an interviewer that "Mr. Reston is not exactly what you would call a cultivated man." But stirring Reston's insecurity also stirred his ambition, and that was a big mistake on Krock's part.

Krock was an imposing figure at the *Times* and in Washington. Roosevelt disliked him intensely for his conservatism, mockingly referring to him as "that Tory Krock-pot." But he, along with syndicated columnist Walter Lippmann and David Lawrence, owner of the conservative news magazine *U.S. News & World Report* and also a widely syndicated columnist, were the opinion powers in the capital. Krock was not about to cede any of that power to a young go-getter like Reston. But Reston, as he had while working as Sulzberger's assistant, actively campaigned to let reporters take a more analytic approach in their newswriting. He argued, presciently, that with the advent of radio, the role of the newspaper had to change. It could no longer be the first bearer of news; it had to explain the *why* of what happened, not just the *what*.

Years later in his own memoirs, Krock tried to create the impression that it was he who had recruited Reston to the bureau in the first place. Krock laid it on thick:

> I remember Reston on first professional and personal acquaintance as young, good looking, eager, and gifted with personality, intelligence, charm and an instinct for asking the right questions of the right people that induced every news source he dealt with, however highly placed or reticent with the press, to tell him what he wanted to know. I remember him as possessor of an uncanny "nose for news" – the quality that renders a reporter the gestator as well as the chronicler of news before it officially happens. And as endowed with a talent for pithy phrase making that conveys to the readers of the news the essential factor of perspective.

It was a remarkably accurate assessment, but it was not one he shared with his superiors at the time.

Reston, on the other hand, took a poke at Krock in his memoirs, quoting former secretary of state Dean Rusk's recollection that when he first joined the Kennedy administration, Krock had written him saying that if he, the secretary of state, wanted to call on him, he would be most welcome. What Rusk had actually written in his memoirs was that both Krock and Walter Lippmann had sent such messages. Reston had early on begun cultivating the powerful Lippmann, making sure that when *Prelude to Victory* was published, Lippmann got a free copy. The same year, Reston wrote fawningly to congratulate him on a particular column, urging him to "keep it on your desk and rewrite it every week for the next few years." Lippmann was every bit as full of himself as was Krock, but Lippmann was to be a Reston mentor and Krock was an obstacle. Not surprisingly, Lippmann got a pass when Reston commented on the arrogance of the Washington columnists who preceded him.

Krock, Reston wrote, "didn't run the bureau, he presided over it." The older man kept a disciplined schedule, "regular as a metronome." Reston noted that Krock's driver delivered him to the office at ten in the morning, and he lunched precisely at 12:30 P.M., always at the Metropolitan Club, always at the same table. "He was much in demand at the embassy dinner table," Reston wrote disapprovingly. "I was never at ease at such gatherings." In later years, Scotty and Sally did their share of working Washington dinners, which are so much a part of the life of that company town, finding themselves in just as much demand as Krock had been. And like Krock, Reston eventually became an habitué of the men-only Metropolitan Club, which was the very epicenter of the Washington establishment.

Reston had been noticed enough to have been offered twice his salary and much more freedom by the *Times'* archrival, the *New York Herald Tribune*. Over the years, as other offers came his way, he always managed to let his superiors at the *Times* know about them, as would any smart and ambitious person, before turning them down. But Scotty's biggest break came quickly, in the fall of 1944 when the Allied powers, sure that the war was coming to a victorious end, convened a major conference in Washington. The aim was to discuss postwar arrangements for a new international organization that, unlike the failed League of Nations proposed after World War I, would help preserve the peace. Reston's confinement to diplomatic doings suddenly became a wonderful opportunity. The delegates were to meet at an elegant early-nineteenth-century Georgetown mansion called Dumbarton Oaks.

The security around the conference was extraordinary, with guards on all the doors and reporters left to stand outside and wonder what was happening inside. Reston attacked the story with all his charm and guile and with one huge advantage: he already knew one of the Chinese delegates. His name was Chen Yi, and he was son-in-law of a former classmate of Iphigene Ochs's at the Columbia School of Journalism. In her own memoirs Iphigene recalled having flirted with Chen Yi's father-in-law, a Chinese nationalist named Hollington K. Tong. Chen Yi became friendly with Marian Sulzberger and her husband, Orvil Dryfoos, who secured Chen a position as an intern on the *Times* and then introduced him to Scotty. Later at the conference, the reporter worked him like the master of soft-soap he was becoming. How wonderful it was that Chen had risen so fast in the world. How impressive that he already knew the positions the major powers would take at the conference. What a terrible shame it would be not to share those positions with citizens of the world who had suffered through the war and would be affected by the decisions at Dumbarton Oaks. "Without the slightest delay," Reston recounted in his memoirs, "he opened up a big briefcase and handed me the whole prize, neatly translated into English."*

Scotty had the Sulzbergers to thank one more time for this huge bonanza. Still, it was Reston who got the scoop about the negotiations to create the United Nations. That impressed even the wary Arthur Krock, who, when presented with the story, "looked like a guy who had just won the Kentucky Derby," Reston recalled. The *Times*, rather than dump the whole trove on their readers, tortured their competitors and the Allied governments by running the full text of each major nation's position one by one, day after day. Chen Yi helped Reston to follow up as the conference continued, with detailed reports on discussions during the seven weeks of the proceedings.

---

*In his memoirs, Reston misidentified his source as Joseph Ku, who several years after Dumbarton Oaks was posted to the Chinese embassy in Washington. The confusion was straightened out in a letter to Reston by Mr. George Kao, a friend and contemporary of both Mr. Chen and Joseph Ku. In a return letter, Reston acknowledged the mistake and thanked Mr. Kao for setting the record straight.

It wasn't just other newspapers that were upset; the participating governments were outraged. The American secretary of state, Edward Stettinius, accused the British of leaking the documents; he assumed that since Reston had worked in London, the Brits must be his source. (The *Times* itself, in a book published in 1975 by one of its writers about the decade of the 1940s, endorsed the idea that the source was one of Reston's "old London acquaintances.") Stettinius even carried his complaints to New York to Arthur Hays Sulzberger. The secretary warned that continuing publication could undermine the entire conference. Arthur Hays told him, according to Reston, that if Allied unity was so weak that it could not bear the publication of the preliminary position papers, it would be better to face that fact right away rather than after the war.

Trying to soothe the angry diplomats, Reston wrote a letter to Stettinius swearing that the British were not the source for his stories. Reston showed the letter to the British delegate, Lord Halifax, who said that he accepted what Reston claimed but would have no further dealings with a reporter who was involved in such skullduggery. The Soviet Union's delegate, Andrey Gromyko, who later became foreign minister, protested directly to Krock, who handled the complaint with his usual elaborate courtesy but gave Gromyko no satisfaction, save to say that he would pass on the diplomat's disapproval to his bosses in New York. Walter Lippmann called Reston to reassure him that his trouble with the Roosevelt administration over the story wouldn't hurt him. But the American government wouldn't let the matter drop, ordering the FBI to investigate the leaks. They never found the source.

Despite the strictures Krock tried to impose, Reston was becoming a figure in Washington and roamed rather freely around town. For his tremendous scoop on the Dumbarton Oaks conference, Scotty Reston in 1945 won the first of his two Pulitzer Prizes, the highest honor in newspaper journalism, an important public tribute to his reportorial skills, and a huge step on his way up the ladder. His work drew the notice of the ranking minority member of the Senate Foreign Relations Committee, a self-important and very isolationist Michigan Republican named Arthur Vandenberg. Reston had met him on his first posting to Washington and at first thought him a "pompous windbag . . . who could strut sitting down." In a lecture years later, Reston said that, frankly, he "did not admire him." "I had just come back home at the end of the London Blitz to find him still thinking that we could do business with Hitler. I thought him intellectually wrong and personally vain." But Reston's opinion changed, teaching him the lesson that "many limited men achieved good things and many good men did bad things." Reston altered his view of Vandenberg when the senator rather abruptly jettisoned his isolationist views, a change that Reston helped bring about.

Prior to the Japanese attack on Pearl Harbor, Vandenberg had been loudly warning against American involvement in the war in Europe. Even after the fall of France, he opposed Roosevelt's lend-lease program to aid the nations in Hitler's path. He had been a determined opponent of FDR's domestic New Deal program as well. He was, in short, a very conservative mossback from the American heartland. But after Pearl Harbor, he began to rethink his views about America's place in the world, abetted to some extent by his nephew, Hoyt Vandenberg (who eventually became the head of the U.S. Air Force). Hoyt Vandenberg convinced his uncle, if the evidence of the attack in Hawaii was not enough, that modern air war could be conducted across oceans, thus putting an end to American invulnerability. The public turning point came in early 1945, when Vandenberg was preparing a major Senate speech on the increasingly troublesome U.S. relationship with the Soviet Union. The Michigan senator had begun to imagine himself as a possible presidential candidate and was trying to cut a larger national figure by speaking out on major issues.

According to Reston's own account, he ran into Vandenberg in a Senate hallway quite by accident and was invited to the senator's office to look over a draft of the speech. It was becoming abundantly clear by then that Stalin was getting ready to carve out a big role for himself after the war, especially in Eastern Europe. Roosevelt and Churchill were about to meet Stalin at Yalta to discuss the postwar world and Vandenberg wanted to urge the Western allies to resist Soviet expansionism.

Reston read the speech, which had already gone through almost a dozen drafts on the senator's own portable typewriter, and found it, in his words, "well documented, vividly expressed and, in my view entirely fair." But Reston added that he felt it "was only half a speech," which "defined the problem without suggesting why the problem existed and without suggesting what ought to be done about the problem." Reston urged Vandenberg to address the underlying cause of Soviet aggressiveness, which was fear of future threats from Germany. Why not, Reston said, offer the idea of a treaty among the Soviet Union, France, Great Britain, and the United States dedicated to opposing any future German expansion. The idea obviously appealed to the senator, who checked it out with other Republicans such as John Foster Dulles, who later became secretary of state for President Eisenhower. On January 10 Vandenberg delivered the speech, complete with the Reston treaty notion, on the floor of the Senate. It said that the alternative to Soviet (he called it Russian) expansionism was "collective security" against future attack and concluded: "I know of no reason why a hard-and-fast treaty between the major allies should not be signed today to achieve this dependable end."

Vandenberg, once a leading isolationist, was now urging America to help ensure the future peace in Europe and it caused a huge sensation. Vandenburg helped end the long resistance of his party to an activist American stance beyond the oceans. He appeared on the cover of *Time* and was hailed, with good reason, as the godfather of a new bipartisan foreign policy. The oration became known as the speech heard around the world. Vandenberg gave Reston fulsome credit, telling a press conference that the newspaperman had planted the treaty idea in the senator's head. And Reston praised the speech in the *Times,* calling it "wise and statesmanlike," obviously feeling no need to recuse himself from commenting on an event in which he had been a participant. The Soviets openly rejected the idea of such a treaty, but that did not change the fact that Vandenberg had set his party off on a very new and more responsible course in international affairs. Reston's involvement was noticed widely in Washington. Henry Wallace, Roosevelt's vice president in his third term, commented that it was "one of the bright feathers in the cap of the New York *Times* that Reston was able to make a Christian out of Vandenberg when it was needed the most." Reston, asked by other reporters about Wallace's comment, replied coyly, "As a courtesy to the senator and in the interest of truth I feel that I must say that, honestly, I didn't save the Republic; it must have been some other reporter."

Reston had not been the only reporter Vandenberg consulted before his speech. One other was Walter Lippmann, who frequently crossed the line between journalist and participant by writing speeches for politicians he admired. Lippmann, no slouch at trumpeting his own influence, embroidered his role over the years, telling his biographer, the historian Ronald Steel, that he and Reston had actually written the speech for Vandenberg. Steel says he never saw any documentary proof of this assertion and that he had simply accepted Lippmann's version as the truth.

Three years after the speech, in May 1948, Reston published a piece in Henry Luce's *Life* magazine arguing Vandenberg's suitability to be the Republican nominee for president. The article was one of a series the magazine ran making similar arguments for all the Republican possibilities who might unseat Harry Truman: Robert Taft, Harold Stassen, Earl Warren, and Thomas Dewey, the eventual nominee. Reston made no mention of his role in Vandenberg's conversion but cited the speech as major evidence of the senator's suitability for the presidency. "The important thing about that speech, however, was not that Vandenberg made it," Reston wrote, "but that the American people responded with such enthusiasm." The piece was close to an endorsement of Vandenberg, and Reston's superiors at the *Times* properly chastised him for playing the role of advocate. Reston himself later concluded that writing the Vandenberg story for *Life* was a "foolish mistake."

Reston remained close to Vandenberg, a wise decision, since the senator became chairman of the Foreign Relations Committee. He was such a good source that historian Arthur Schlesinger Jr. sent Reston a note on April 5, 1948, warning that "well informed security sources have expressed concern to me over Senator V. on the ground that his mistress, an English lady named Patterson, is believed to be a British agent." When Reston was preparing his memoirs more than forty years later, he wrote to Schlesinger asking about the note: "Does any of this make sense to you?" Reston said it hadn't made any sense to him back then and still didn't. Schlesinger didn't answer Reston and later said he had no recollection of the note or of the source of his information. Reston, of course, did nothing to pursue the dirt contained in the Schlesinger note. That was not the sort of story that interested Reston, partly because of his own distaste for such personal journalism and partly because it would have burned Vandenberg, an important source.

On April 20, 1952, Reston reviewed Arthur Vandenberg's son's collection of the senator's papers in the *Times Book Review*. In describing the speech, Reston wrote:

What is interesting about this is that only a few days before the January, 1945, speech was delivered it did not contain any such proposal at all. The speech originally was a protest against Russia's policies in Eastern Europe, and particularly in Poland. The speech was, as Mr. Vandenberg wrote in his diary six months later, shown to several reporters in Washington. One of them told him it was a good speech but that it offered nothing concrete or positive, that it was merely one more complaint against Soviet policy and would do nothing but aggravate the frustrations of the people about Soviet policy.

Asked for a suggestion about what could be proposed, the reporter then outlined the proposed treaty which would take the debate on the post-war settlement out of the realm of generalities and into the realm of the concrete by offering an American alliance. Sen. Vandenberg decided at the last minute to adopt the proposal, and the response to it was, as he later said, "so sensational it bowled me over."

Reston again failed to mention that said reporter was himself.

Eventually it became a settled truth in Washington that Reston had written the speech. As the times changed and public suspicion of politicians and of the establishment press's closeness to those politicians increased, Reston's rumored collaboration with Vandenberg became a symbol of a kind of relationship that was inherently corrupt. But shortly before his death, I asked Reston again whether he had written the speech. He was frail and his conversation a bit disjointed in the aftermath of a stroke. But he answered clearly and precisely: "I never set finger to typewriter for any politician in this town."

CHAPTER 9

WISE MEN

RESTON MOVED QUICKLY to parlay his new prominence by wiring himself into high-level Washington sources, and not just Republicans like Vandenberg. The senator, still grateful for Reston's help in making him a sudden statesman, continued to provide the newsman with scoops, inviting him to stop by his apartment from time to time. Now that the senator was cooperating with the new Truman administration's foreign policy and was chairman of the key Senate committee dealing with it, Vandenberg had excellent access to secrets. As Reston wrote later, "I thought it only fair to relieve him of his burden."

Reston continued to collect sources in the late 1940s, men – and they were always men then – who had started in subordinate positions in government and politics and along with Reston increased their power and visibility over time. Weeks before its official announcement in 1947, Dean Acheson, deputy secretary of state, leaked to Reston the fact that the administration intended to ask Congress for the breathtaking amount of $16 billion for a bold and imaginative plan to help rebuild postwar Europe. The story naturally ran on the front page of the *Times*. Reston's scoop on the plan, known formally as the European Reconstruction Program and informally as the Marshall Plan, after its principal author, Secretary of State George C. Marshall, earned him an early-Sunday-morning phone call from Vandenberg, who denounced the scheme as "goddamned foolishness" but then later helped push the plan through Congress.

Despite the scoop he gave Reston, Acheson had little regard for the press in general and dealt warily even with Scotty, mostly out of respect for his reporting skill. Once Acheson became secretary of state, he periodically banned his aides from talking to Reston when he felt the reporter had been too critical or "too nosy." But even Acheson could not completely resist Reston's charms. One of Acheson's greatest struggles in office was trying to defend the State Department's Alger Hiss, who had been accused of being a Soviet agent by Whittaker Chambers. Even as evidence mounted that, at the least, Hiss was not telling the truth about his relationship with Chambers, Acheson was loath to condemn his subordinate. Asked by the press about it, Acheson rather obscurely referred reporters to the Bible, specifically the twenty-fifth chapter of Matthew. Reston convinced the *Times* to print thirteen verses of the scripture to help Acheson make the point that he was simply showing Christian charity to the beleaguered Hiss, not arguing one way or the other for his guilt or innocence. Acheson, Reston recalled, thanked him for the favor. The two were close enough that Reston would drop humorous notes to the secretary, with the salutation "Dear Dean." He signed them "Yours, Scotty."

Still, the relationship was not all Reston expected. He wanted to be on the inside, to know what was going on, and to be trusted to be careful in how he used it. On February 10, 1950, Reston, then the *Times'* diplomatic correspondent, delivered the first William Allen

White Lecture at the University of Kansas. Known as the Sage of Emporia, White had been the publisher and editor of the weekly *Emporia Gazette,* where his editorial eloquence and good sense made him the very model of an American small-town editor. It was a high honor for Reston to have been selected to give this first address, and he used the opportunity to settle some scores with Acheson. The secretary's attitude toward the press, Reston said, was like his strategy in dealing with the Russians.

> In both cases he follows an aloof policy of containment. He is determined to block the expansionist tendencies of reporters in the field where he thinks they have no rights. . . . While he does not dislike reporters personally, he apparently thinks they are presumptuous, superficial and often selfish and indifferent to the public interest, irresponsible with secret information, much too distrustful and skeptical of officials and far too interested in being first with any story rather than being right and careful with what he regards as the main story.
>
> Despite these complaints, [Reston continued] I also happen to think that Dean Acheson is incomparably the ablest Secretary of State the United States has had since Henry L. Stimson, but on this question of public information, no contemporary public official has contrived to do so little with so much.

Characteristically, Reston, while making a point about Acheson's inaccessibility, wanted to be fair and to avoid terminally insulting the secretary. Lamenting a time in the past when the secretary of state would meet daily with the department press corps, Reston acknowledged that the flow of events during the Cold War made such intimacy impossible: "Mr. Acheson is lucky if he sees Mrs. Acheson once a day, let alone taking time out for regular private chats with a press corps that is larger than the Senate and House of Representatives combined."

Reston had by then a keen sense that he was now the cream of the journalistic crop and made the case implicitly that he should be trusted more than many of his colleagues. He described the contest with the secretary of state as a game in which "responsible officials and responsible reporters, as distinguished from the old-fashioned scoop artists, gossip mongers and saloon rail journalists, are playing cops and robbers with each other." The newspaper business, he acknowledged, had "at least its share of chumps and scoundrels," and he urged that "we shouldn't take ourselves too seriously." He was, however, seriously dedicated to the notion that the more he could find out, the better for the health of the nation. He thoughtfully recounted the limited public discussion of the decision to develop the hydrogen bomb, arguing that even such a fateful and sensitive problem needed public airing before a final decision was made. "There should of course be some means by which the responsible reporter and the responsible official could discuss, in private and with mutual confidence, the implications of the President's dilemma over the H-bomb." As much as he wanted the trusting access Acheson had denied him, he also understood that, in the end, it was the reporter's job to find out what was happening. The answer was not "adopting softer standards of reporting," he said, meaning that cozying up to the powerful was not going to improve the level of public information and discussion. With sharp prescience, he indicated that "the power of the government is growing all the time and our skepticism will have to grow with it. The power of the executive to decide issues in the secret stage of negotiations with other nations is growing all the time and this, I fear, is going to impose new obligations on reporters and probably bring them even more into conflict with officials than in the past."

Scotty and Sally's friendship with Acheson deepened after he left office and entered private law practice in Washington. Reston would talk to him from time to time, to glean his often ascerbic opinions about what was happening in the government and to get his counsel on foreign policy, a subject on which Acheson was long consulted by succeeding Democratic administrations. He told Reston he hated being a lawyer and missed the action in government, comparing being out of office to "the end of a love affair." The two would lunch together, sometimes with another journalist. In a 1958 letter to Supreme Court justice Felix Frankfurter, Acheson described a midday repast with Reston and columnist Stewart Alsop. During lunch, Acheson had remarked on an eight-hour meeting that Senator Hubert Humphrey had had with Nikita Khrushchev and wondered whether during the ordeal Humphrey had needed "to take a leak." Reston, according to Acheson, said he had already put this important question to Humphrey and then regaled his lunch companions with the story. Humphrey had told Reston that yes, they had taken a break. Humphrey used the stall nearest the door and Khrushchev the one farthest away, with a translator occupying neutral ground in between. Humphrey said that as they were buttoning up, he told Khrushchev the situation reminded him of a story from British foreign secretary Clement Attlee. Attlee was meeting in the war cabinet one day when he and Churchill had to be excused and found themselves at opposite ends of the stalls. "Isn't this unusual modesty for you, Winston?" Attlee asked. "Not at all," said Churchill, "I'm just suspicious of you socialists." "Why?" asked Attlee. "Because," answered Churchill, "whenever you see a means of production in good working order, you want to nationalize it."

The Restons were occasional dinner guests at the Achesons' country home in Maryland, where they marveled at the handmade furniture the old diplomat was turning out. In addition to writing his Pulitzer Prize–winning memoirs, *Present at the Creation,* which Reston said he, among others, had urged the statesman to write, Acheson took a few turns at short fiction. Sally Reston wrote Acheson praising some of the stories. Acheson sent a humorous note back to her claiming the stories were the work of "a close relative of the same name who showed great and early promise, but who unhappily took to drink. . . . Your note delights me into the belief that the poor but gifted chap may finally have found his metier."

By the mid-1960s the Restons and the Achesons were quite close, although not frequent companions. Sally Reston wrote a note to Acheson while Scotty was visiting Vietnam in 1965. She lamented seeing the Achesons only now and then, writing, "I pick you and Alice up like pieces of a rare but broken crystal, never seeing you whole in shape and form and light." In his memoirs Reston proudly noted that when the Achesons installed electrical lighting in their Maryland country home, they gave their old kerosene lamps to the Restons for use in their cabin at Fiery Run, Virginia, with this message: "I have tried, without success, to light your way. Maybe these will help." Reston quoted Acheson's own summation of his official life as having "for the most part left conditions better than we found them." This, Reston concluded, must be "the most understated epitaph of recent history." Acheson, Reston wrote in his memoirs, was the best of the fifteen secretaries of state he had covered, adding that Acheson would not have been impressed by the praise, "for he had a limited regard for those who preceded and followed him."

Washington, especially in the 1940s, was really a small company town. Friends and neighbors were often converted to sources. John J. McCloy, a self-made establishment lawyer and a founder of the Council on Foreign Relations, happened to live across the street from the Restons' first house in Georgetown. On the occasion of a dinner party arranged suddenly by her husband, Ellen McCloy found the need to borrow a roasting pan from Sally. The two families stayed close over the years; Richard Reston became a close school chum of the McCloys' eldest boy. McCloy grew into the consummate Washington insider and "wise man" involved through a series of administrations in the highest level of diplomatic policy making. He was quite discreet in his dealings with the press in general, but while he wouldn't blab secrets, he did provide useful guidance to reporters, and especially to Reston. McCloy dealt with Reston in the interest of increasing public understanding of public policy, not in the pursuit of personal attention and big headlines. McCloy was that Washington rarity, the reluctant, self-effacing source who provides the really useful information.

In his memoirs Reston recounts being tipped off by another source that McCloy was unhappy with Truman's decision to drop the atomic bomb on Japan. He approached McCloy, consistent with his usual tactic of finding the disgruntled and then getting them to talk, but the closemouthed McCloy rebuffed him. But Reston knew a good story when he smelled it, and he persisted for years in trying to get McCloy to tell his story about the White House debate on the bomb. McCloy told him he would deal with the issue in his memoirs, but he died before completing them. Reston still persisted, and managed, through McCloy's children, to obtain their father's written version of the debate, which he appended in its entirety to his own memoirs.

It was a scoop from beyond the grave in which the old statesman recounted how he had advised President Truman that he could avoid dropping the A-bomb if he called for Japan to surrender and followed that, if necessary, with disclosure of the force of the new weapon. If that didn't produce the desired result, McCloy advocated a demonstration blast in an unpopulated place. Reston paid him tribute as a man "who never saw a problem he didn't think he could solve." He was the perfect example of the sort of official Reston admired: smart, reasonable, discreet, not self-aggrandizing, and most important, full of knowledge about what happened behind the scenes. Reston wrote affectionately that whenever over the years he had reason to thank McCloy for his help, McCloy would answer, "Thanks, too, for the roasting pan."

Supreme Court justice Felix Frankfurter was another of the smart insiders to whom Reston attached himself. They were probably introduced by the justice's one-time clerk William Bundy, with whom Reston had worked at the Office of War Information. Frankfurter was close to Acheson and often walked along to work with him. The justice was also a friend of McCloy's, who, like Acheson, had studied under Frankfurter at Harvard Law School. William T. Coleman was a Frankfurter clerk in the late 1940s, along with Elliot Richardson – both men became cabinet members in the Nixon administration. Coleman remembers frequent occasions, sometimes as often as once every other week, when Reston would show up at the Court for lunch and a good gossip with the justice. Frankfurter would bring Reston into the clerks' areas. The men would talk about what was going on in the world and Reston would later write about it. Most frequently the conversation was focused on international affairs, and because of Frankfurter's close friendship with Acheson, the justice became a way for Reston to get around the secretary of state's skittishness in dealing with him.

Frankfurter loved the hurly-burly of politics and was full of opinions about what the elected leadership ought to do. He also loved to lecture Reston about the failures of journalism, and specifically about the failures of the *Times*. Some mornings the justice would have his driver stop in front of Reston's home, summon the journalist to his car, then deliver what Reston called "a torrent of amiable abuse." Sally remembered joining Scotty for some of these encounters, sitting on the curb beside the justice's car. Frankfurter and his wife were childless, and Bill Coleman described the justice's friendship with the Restons as a kind of substitute family arrangement. Reston credits Frankfurter with inspiring him to establish his own system of "clerks" modeled on the high court's practice of taking young lawyers and making them assistants to the justices. For years Reston recruited new college graduates and used them as researchers, personal assistants, and sounding boards for his ideas. Nearly all of them graduated to good jobs on the *Times*.

When Frankfurter was seventy-nine years old, he suffered what was apparently a mild stroke, which the doctors at the time described as "an acute cerebrovascular insufficiency." Reston, recalling the frequent chastisements the justice had doled out at the curbside, wrote affectionately in the next day's *Times* that this diagnosis was clearly wrong:

> It was not an "insufficiency" of blood that did it, but an over sufficiency of ink and nonsense. This city is an intellectual midden of illogical rubbish, and anybody who ever watched the Judge read a newspaper about events in Washington knows that he would get an average of at least one spasm on every page. . . . If he is a little tired, it is because he has paid attention to so many things and inspired so many youngsters here and in Cambridge over so long a time. . . . There is now some talk here of replacing him on the Supreme Court of the United States, but this is as silly as the doctor's bulletin. They may eventually put somebody in his place, but they won't replace him.

Not long afterward, Frankfurter did retire from the Court because of his illness.

The nearly genetic impulse of any reporter is to know what is *really* going on and to be the first to tell the world. Proximity to the powerful, to the people who make the decisions, who debate the policy internally, is the path to that knowledge, so it is wrong to think of these cultivated relationships as merely a kind of social climbing. Building a list of contacts is the basic work of a reporter. The ability to get a timely phone call accepted or returned and a critical question answered is a fundamental task of journalism. Whether it is government or business or even a matter involving individuals, the difference between the official, self-serving version of events and an objective, informed version can be vast. Especially in Washington, the great reporter has accumulated a series of sources who trust the journalist enough to tell him a fuller version of the truth than is normally put before the public. This is what Scotty Reston did with such dexterity and skill and it is why he very quickly became one of the best reporters Washington had ever seen. The "wise men" with whom Reston did business also offered the rather spottily educated and somewhat insecure immigrant a window on the larger world. Their knowledge, which he absorbed as he picked their pockets for scoops, was a part of his ongoing self-education, a project begun in earnest when he first got to Washington. One of the earliest documents from his Washington years, contained in the papers given to the University of Illinois after his death, was an overdue notice from the Library of Congress dated February 5, 1942, asking for the return of two books about Thomas Jefferson borrowed the previous autumn. He kept reading such works all his life, always trying to catch up.

The reporting that came out of these high-level contacts very quickly boosted Reston to national attention, not just because he had won a Pulitzer Prize, but because his access lent great accuracy to his reports. In 1945, in a story about the promotion of Turner Catledge from the Washington bureau to assistant managing editor in New York, *Time* magazine called Reston "fast rising and a kinetic and knowing reporter." In 1947, Reston figured out through a bit of detective work that Secretary of State James Byrnes was about to leave that post. His snooping forced the White House to announce the departure ahead of schedule and earned Reston another mention in *Time,* along with this observation: "On the *Times,* where some newsmen are inclined to sit back on their big, fat prestige . . . Reston remains an unusual reporter . . . a cocky, calculating Clydebank boy."

Reston's enterprise surprised even his own colleagues at the *Times.* In 1945 the newspaper sent a team of correspondents to San Francisco to cover the formal beginnings of the United Nations. Reston, on the strength of his Dumbarton Oaks reporting, was assigned to do the main story. But on a day when a major announcement was expected from British foreign secretary Anthony Eden, no one could find Reston. The editor running the coverage rearranged the writing assignments, fearing that Reston wasn't going to appear. As the time for the announcement grew near, there was still no Reston. Suddenly the doors to the *Times* workroom opened and in walked a clutch of English diplomats carrying portfolios. Behind them came Anthony Eden, chatting with Scotty Reston. Arthur Krock was dumbfounded. "You have to hand it to the little guy," he said grudgingly.

And it was surely grudgingly. Access meant scoops and scoops meant power within the *Times* organization. Reston had been pressing hard against Krock's dominance as the *Times'* voice from Washington. In May 1946 Krock wrote an anguished letter to Arthur Hays Sulzberger complaining about a new typographical device, the so-called Q head, that had been invented to give the more analytic Reston reportage a look distinct from the news columns. To Krock it seemed that Reston had been given a virtual column to compete with his. Krock complained that he should have been consulted about such a momentous move and now felt his standing had been diminished. "I think my service to the *Times,* in general and in particular, should impel you at all times to stand against any dilution of my position here," Krock wrote. The august bureau chief took further umbrage, adding:

The latter observation, of course, is on the theory that the head of your Washington bureau continues to be responsible for what is published from this bureau. If that is no longer true, and Mr. Reston is at the head of an independent Washington bureau, then my point is a very different one. The Q head extension would then be only a part of a larger and more doubtful system. . . . But until you are ready to make him the Washington correspondent [the *Times'* designation for the bureau chief], I think he should not be given an equal status with me here in any particular. The Q head gives him that in a particular way that is important in my sight if not in yours. If I do not seem to you to have deserved the status I describe, or to deserve it no longer, then I still submit that it is not good organizational theory to dilute my position in any way as long as I hold it.

Arthur Hays dismissed Krock's plea summarily, saying he didn't care whether they put Q, R, or S headlines on Reston's work.

That exchange came less than a month after Reston had directly requested of managing editor Jimmy James that he be allowed to do some domestic political coverage in addition to his work on the diplomatic beat. Reston obviously knew that as important as foreign policy news was in those days, American politics was even more important to the paper's news coverage. But the appeal for an expansion of his franchise raised a problem. James sent a memo to Sulzberger saying that the request contradicted a promise he had extracted from Reston that he would clear all his assignments through Krock, even though he was not technically answering to the bureau chief. When everyone finally agreed that Reston could go to Ohio to cover Senator Robert Taft's race for reelection, Reston was urged to depart immediately. Remarkably, Reston refused. Krock told James that Scotty was not prepared to depart Washington for several days, forcing them to make other arrangements to cover Taft's speech. James explained all this to Sulzberger, and with a full understanding of the sensitivity of the Reston matter, concluded his memo hopefully: "I trust you will regard this matter as handled properly."

At about the same time, Krock wrote Turner Catledge that while he still believed that only Catledge was up to the job of one day replacing him, he understood that Catledge was not interested in the Washington job. Therefore, Krock wrote, "[I] shall now devote myself to an effort to develop someone else if, as and when. Reston may be able now, or when the time comes, to handle the executive end, but I feel very unsure of that. Also his eventual ambition seems to be toward another job on the paper." The notion that Reston was aiming somewhere else on the paper was wishful thinking, and Krock followed with a pathetic plea to Catledge saying that he wanted to stay on the *Times* as long as the paper would have him. Besides, he added, "I have nothing to live on except what I can earn."

There were times when Sulzberger himself became a bit uncomfortable with Reston's prominence. He wrote to Reston saying he thought a piece about General Marshall had been too critical. "But what bothered me was not this," AHS wrote, "but the feeling, rather, that you sounded too much like a columnist. I am in hopes you will understand that this is not intended as a compliment. The next time you are up here, let's talk this thing out a little more." Later he sent a memo to Krock noting that Reston had been on the radio quite frequently, something the *Times* generally discouraged.

AHS finally tired of the whole struggle and informed Reston he was to be brought in under Krock's supervision. But he informed him very carefully. "In doing so," Sulzberger wrote to Reston, "we will guarantee that you will not be given any picayune assignments. In fact, I think I am entirely safe in saying that you will be given the same degree of latitude as you now have. By merely making this change in the table of organization I think we will clear up some of the differences, expressed or unexpressed that I know have been present." AHS told Reston that his letter had not been shown to Krock and that he awaited Reston's response. The next day, Reston wrote back that he'd prefer to just cover the major foreign stories and write explanatory background pieces the rest of the time. But he knew when to retreat. He told Sulzberger that whatever he and James and Krock worked out will be "satisfactory."

Krock spoke with Reston and reported in his usual pompous prose back to James:

> I had a talk with Mr. Reston, and he is entirely willing to become a regular member of the Bureau and conform to the light regimentation, which, in his instance, this formality will impose. Between now and the time he leaves on his European trip he and I plan to work out the arrangement on a day-to-day-basis in the hope and belief that by the time he returns we can have devised a modus operandi that will make him happy in his work here. He understands that this will probably mean covering more news stories and writing fewer S-heads [a variant of the Q heads], but he is entirely willing to put this on a trial basis. I have showed Mr. Reston this letter, and he agrees that it states the result of our conversation.

It wasn't just the domestic power structure of the paper that Reston was crowding. The European trip mentioned in Krock's letter set off Cyrus L. Sulzberger, a cousin to Arthur Hays, and the paper's chief European correspondent. C. L. Sulzberger wired that he objected to not being informed that Reston was planning to arrive on his turf, an invasion Scotty repeated over the coming years, further angering the very proud and very territorial Sulzberger.

In April 1948 Reston wrote to Arthur Hays Sulzberger advising him that he had been asked to represent the *Times* at a conference. He also managed to let the publisher know he was in high demand outside the newspaper, informing him that he was serving on Harvard president James Conant's Neiman Fellows Committee, which went on to found the first midcareer academic program for journalists; that he was serving on the board of directors of the Woodrow Wilson Foundation; and that he was to address a group of Harvard students later in the month. The same year, Reston was recruited by Max Ascoli, an academic political philosopher and husband of an heiress to the Sears, Roebuck fortune, to plan a new, liberal magazine. Together with Lippmann, Arthur Schlesinger, and others, he helped Ascoli create the *Reporter,* which until the late 1960s was perhaps the best news magazine in America. Late in the year, Reston wrote to Sulzberger applauding the fact that AHS had publicly denied a rumor that Reston was leaving the *Times* to edit the magazine. "The offer was made and refused long ago," Reston noted. "Since then I have continued to discuss the project with him purely on the basis of friendship. But beyond this personal advice, there is nothing new. A Merry Christmas to you and your family from us." While Reston had turned down the editor's job himself, he suggested to Ascoli that he hire Wallace Carroll, for whom Reston had worked in London during the war. Carroll was installed in Washington as the acting editor before the magazine's formal launch but left the *Reporter* when Ascoli decided to move operations to New York. Reston did, on occasion, write a freelance piece for the magazine.

Finally, in 1948 Scotty won himself a piece of the political coverage, thus inserting himself into the central story of that year. He kept pushing to get his own views of the news into the paper, sometimes going too far or being too cute by half. Covering the whistle-stop campaign of New York governor and Republican presidential nominee Thomas Dewey, whom he didn't much like, Reston wrote that the candidate's train "departed the station with a little jerk." He and the editors who permitted that to appear in the paper were all reprimanded.

CHAPTER 10

THE RESTONS OF WOODLEY ROAD

ON THE FOURTH of July, 1946, the Restons added a third son, Thomas Busey Reston, to the family. The coincidence of date, Scotty joked, took some careful policy planning. Nine years younger than eldest brother Dick, Tom was designated by his father as the family's "fall crop." Scotty was working pretty much nonstop, leaving the care of the boys largely to Sally and a succession of cooks and nannies who came and went over the years; even after the boys left home years later there was always full-time help in the house. As Scotty admitted ruefully in his memoir, he "was off much of the time climbing the ladder at the *Times*, or chasing politicians or diplomats at some important conference, the importance of which now escapes me."

They were still living in Georgetown when seven-year-old Jimmy, who was watching a softball game in a park near the house, was struck squarely in the face by a foul ball. He turned around in tears, staggered away, and walked directly into the path of a bus. He was knocked to the street. The bus then nearly backed up over him before a pedestrian screamed for the driver to stop. Scotty and Sally were away in Illinois visiting Sally's parents, and Jimmy was in the care of his Grandfather Reston, who had come to Washington to look after the boys. Jimmy was taken to Georgetown Hospital with a fractured skull. There he stayed for three months, finally returning home still bandaged around the head. It was an extremely close call.

After Jim's bus accident, Sally and Scotty bought a primitive cabin in an idyllic Virginia pasture near a romantically named little stream called Fiery Run. The idea was to have a weekend place away from Washington that would be both a retreat from Scotty's work and a bucolic playground for the boys. They bought the cabin, ten acres of land, and the remnants of an old water mill and the miller's house. It cost $3,400, much of which they borrowed in a mortgage. The place had no roof or electricity or running water. Jim Reston Jr. still remembers carrying the family's night soil out to a trench, where it was covered with lime for sanitary disposal. As they improved the cabin over the years, it became central to the family's life. For those millions who read Reston regularly, a Fiery Run dateline signaled a column more philosophical and lyrical than his usual Washington reports. And for those young journalists he inspired who did not know just how humble the cabin was, the notion that Reston would repair to his country home on weekends only added to their notion of the man's grandeur.

In 1951 the family moved out of Georgetown to the Cleveland Park section of northwest Washington, a gracious neighborhood of big, informal houses and old shade trees, one of which grew in the backyard of the house at 3124 Woodley Road. The enormous tree had a low, sturdy branch that an adventuresome boy could reach with a jump from the garage roof. The first floor of the house had a large living room and fireplace, a dining room, a pantry, and a kitchen. At the top of one flight of stairs was a hallway that led to a library where Scotty worked. Up three more stairs were three bed-rooms including a master suite occupied by Scotty and Sally. On the top floor was another bedroom sometimes occupied by live-in help.

The house sat close to the imposing National Cathedral and to Saint Albans School, where all three boys finished high school. The price tag for the house was $45,000. It needed, he estimated, about $3,000 or $4,000 worth of repairs and renovation. In the spring of that year, Scotty first called and then wrote to Arthur Hays Sulzberger seeking help with the house purchase. "The reasons for buying are both personal and professional," he assured the pub-lisher. "My total savings are approximately $18,000 [a testament to his frugality, since that was nearly equal to his annual salary at the time]. They are all in bonds and are therefore melting in the infla-tion," he wrote, explaining that they were going to take a $21,000 mortgage and use $15,000 of their savings as a down payment.

"To pay this kind of money for a house and hit you for the loan in the bargain seems a form of wickedness to my Scottish con-science, which is why I called you on it in the first place," he wrote. Two days later, Sulzberger wrote back saying, "We would be glad to let you have $12,000 against the purchase price of your home. . . . There will be no interest on the loan, but it is understood that you will repay it at the rate of $100 a month."

The house would be the Reston home for thirty years, until Scotty retired and he and Sally moved to a spacious townhouse in the center of Washington. In Cleveland Park, the Restons were neighbors to a growing who's who in the capital. Walter Lippmann lived nearby in a house once occupied by the dean of the cathedral. Other well-compensated or well-off newspeople also congregated there. They formed an early elite of the Washington journalism crowd, made up of those who could afford top prices for big homes. On top of the house price, they also had to pay the private school tuitions that were an accepted necessity in a city where the heavily

African-American public school system was kept in poverty by the stingy and Southern-controlled Congress that ran the capital.*

Life on Woodley Road revolved around Scotty's work. He often got home after the boys had been fed, usually by the cook, but they would join their parents to share the news of their day. Jim recalled those moments fondly: "There was a kind of ritual in our household when he would come home from work. We would already have been fed and they would sit down and have a drink. There was always a sense of excitement about what he was doing that he would impart to her over that drink. There was a lot of that sharing in a kind of rit-ualized way. He had this very sentimental thing he used to say fre-quently. He pitied people who went to work every day and hated what they did. He was so blessed to have found himself in a profes-sion where he got up every morning and was excited about what he was going to do." On occasion, a famous person would come to din-ner, and these events could be burdensome for the boys; at least Dick remembers them that way. The youngsters were required to sit attentively and were often quizzed later on what they had learned. Like many families with parents who had experienced the pain of the Great Depression, waste was thought sinful. The boys were re-quired to finish everything on their plates, and Dick remembers his brother Jim, then a somewhat finicky eater, often sitting alone at the table until his food disappeared.

When the family dined together, Scotty ran the table. There was little casual jabbering. Scotty would report on what he had been work-ing on and expected discussion of the events of the day from the boys. The conversation leaned heavily toward public affairs. Even the occasional punishment that was meted out had a political cast. Dick remembers having to memorize part of a speech by Adlai

*After the Restons moved out, the house became a revolving residence for Wash-ington's top television journalists, including Tom Brokaw, Charlie Rose, and NBC's Washington bureau chief Tim Russert.

Stevenson after one transgression. But there was also a good deal of high-minded fun. While his public demeanor was often dour and serious, Scotty possessed a charming, absurdist sense of humor with which he leavened the family's affairs. Tom recalls his father puckishly asking Jim, who was taking Latin in school, to translate the Lord's Prayer. Jim attempted, haltingly, to do so. When he rendered his version of "thy will be done," Scotty interrupted to say that Jim had actually translated the line as "Thou ist washed up." Recalled Tom: "We all loved it, including Jim, for Dad's humor was light enough that it was hardly ever employed as a weapon."

It was Scotty who got the household moving in the morning. He was a heavy sleeper but an early riser. Sally was the opposite. Reston fancied himself something of a short-order cook, having worked in a Dayton diner when he was young, and insisted on making proper breakfasts for the boys, pancakes, eggs, and often a Scottish porridge that the boys hated just as their father had. He was a great user of kitchen gadgets and made all manner of concoctions in his blender, including once, Dick remembers, a slurry of carrots and milk that was less than a success. Scotty would read three or four newspapers over his breakfast and usually insisted that the boys read at least the front pages, in addition to their favored sports sections, before they left for school.

All three boys remember their parents as treating them evenhandedly. The older two were the athletes and remember Scotty showing up for only an occasional game; more often it was Sally who served as family fan. Tom was born with cerebral palsy, which partially crippled his right leg and arm and kept him out of sports. The ailment was described as "a spastic leg" by his parents. Tom for years was forced to wear a leg brace in the evenings to stretch his muscles. The brace was attached to a heavy shoe; his brothers remember his clomping around the house in the device. That disability, Tom's brothers believe, made him the closest of the three to their mother.

While Scotty is not remembered as either cold or distant by the boys, they don't have many recollections of notable warmth. He was conditioned by his own upbringing. Scotty avoided the emotional turmoil of his parents' home by maintaining a kind of studied calm in his own household. Sally remembers Scotty simply retreating into his den when he was angered. Tom recalls his father tousling his hair affectionately from time to time, but not hugging and kissing in the way now favored by psychologically aware parents. Dick does remember a snowy night when they still lived in Georgetown when his father awakened him in what seemed like the middle of the night and swept him off to go sledding in Montrose Park. The fun seemed to go on for hours, with Dick clinging to his father's back as they hurtled down the hills, then trudging back to the top for another go. Dick also remembers being forced to wear what he called "those Scottish tweed knickers, until I begged him to stop making me wear them." The knickers were what Scotty had desperately wanted to wear when he first went to school in America, the replacement for the short pants and long stockings that were the object of such derision from his Dayton schoolmates.

Dick was a rambunctious kid, always pressing against the limits his parents tried to set. In an entry he typed for his sporadic diary, Scotty noted that Dick's theme song, derived from the old spiritual, should have been "nobody knows the trouble I've been." He described Dick at about age ten as "a Huckleberry Finn character, big for his age, a little heavy and, as his Uncle Bill once remarked, 'a one man blitzkrieg.'" While enrolled in public schools, he was an indifferent student who, Scotty noted, "contributed more to the physical and mental decline of his teachers than anything else." Finally Scotty and Sally decided that the rigors of Saint Albans would be better for Dick than the public schools in the District of Columbia, so Scotty took Dick to take the entrance examination at the exclusive school. When he picked him up after the test, he asked his son how it had gone. "It was a cinch," Scotty said Dick replied. A few days later, the school reported that Dick had performed below standard in each element of the test and, worse, had played around in the room during the exam. Asked by the monitor whether he enjoyed doing the work, the cheeky Dick had responded, "Sometimes I do and sometimes I don't."

This exasperated Scotty to the breaking point and he applied what he described as Dick's "first solid whipping" – more painful, of course, to the spanker than the spankee, Scotty averred. The punishment induced a miraculous change in attitude on the part of the young Reston. A new test was arranged and Dick made his way into Saint Albans, where he became a star athlete and a decent student.

Scotty could muster a dreamy sentimentality about the glories and importance of family. But at least one of the boys, looking back at his childhood, thinks that the sentiment was false, that his father was preoccupied and not really involved in the childrearing enterprise. Sally was more available emotionally. But she too ceded top priority to her husband and to his career. Jim Reston remembers being in awe when his father would retire to his study on the second floor of the Woodley Road house and close the door to write. "It was almost a kind of religious experience in our household." Jim said. "Partly it was the sound of the old typewriter. He had incredibly strong hands and short stubby fingers and he would just beat the shit out of that typewriter. And the smoke of that pipe would come out from under the door. The feeling was 'this is really impressive and don't get anywhere near that.'"

Although Scotty and his work were the main themes of life in the house, the subtext was his devotion to Sally and his never-ending efforts to please and impress her. He relied on her judgment and her opinions, often phoning her from work to try out a line from his columns to see if she thought it worked. On the mornings his column appeared, he would wait with apprehension for her to read it, hoping for her approval and being disappointed if her praise was lukewarm.

"It was the obvious thing," said Jim Reston, "the kid from nowhere, from a hardscrabble early existence, who suddenly finds himself in the presence of this beautiful and extremely popular girl. And for the rest of his life he is trying to say he is worthy, trying to prove himself to her. Certainly, when he was older, his total reliance on her was evident then, for virtually everything. She was not a secondary figure at all. She adored him and was extremely respectful of what he did and honored what he did. I think she tremendously admired his discipline, his ability to concentrate with chaos all around him."

In another time Sally Reston would have demanded a career, and judging by the quality of the writing she did do, she would have been a success. In that era Scotty's success was her success, and he worked hard to give that to her. Looking back on their life together, Sally could manage only one criticism of her beloved husband: "He worked too hard." Implicit in that simple statement was her observation that he was not as involved with his sons as she would have liked. Others, like the young journalists Scotty brought into the Washington bureau to work as his clerks, thought that he was pretty hard on his sons, especially as they got older. Said one of those assistants, who was devoted to Scotty and thought he treated his clerks with an almost paternal concern, "It was a lot easier to be his clerk than to be his son."

He grew more demanding with the boys as they began to think about colleges and careers. There was never any doubt from any of his three sons that, loving newspapering, loving the *Times*, and loving Washington and politics and world affairs, he wanted them to follow the same path. The message was unmistakable. Even when the boys were young, they were named "editors" of what Scotty later called "my first newspaper." It was known as *Reston's Weekly* and was printed on an old hand-cranked mimeograph machine in the basement of the house. It carried a jolly chronicle of the family's doings, always written by Scotty, announcing events like anniversaries and basement cleanings. On the Restons' fourteenth anniversary, Christmas Eve, 1949, the mimeographed sheet headlined, truthfully: "Fulton-Reston Romance Going Great after 14 Years." The story said that "Mr. Reston, interviewed by the editor of this paper, said he thought Mrs. Reston looked prettier tonight than he had ever seen her before. And brother, that's something." The family paper chronicled comings and goings, as when a "cook that couldn't cook" had departed. Tom's dog Spunk, a black cocker spaniel, was reported housebroken on Tom's authority, but a dissent from that opinion by Scotty was recorded as well.

Turning out his little family paper was a way Scotty tied himself to his sons and to the family's life, doing what he did best, writing and reporting. The house paper was sent to forty or fifty of the family's friends, with the expectation that they would subscribe for a few cents a copy. The paper had a "board of directors" including some of Washington's most prominent journalists, like Eric Severeid and Edward P. Morgan, the ABC radio commentator. An item in the *Weekly* once noted that Morgan had just returned from traveling with the president and was expected at dinner that week. Scotty used the "board" as an excuse to get his friends together now and then for meetings held around a Ping-Pong table in the basement.

In a diary entry written on New Year's Day, 1947, Reston seemed a happy man. "Snow fell all last evening," he began. "By the turn of the year it had covered the town, which made it hard on the revelers. At the same time, appropriately enough, it beautified this perplexed world and gave it a new start." The Severeids had been there for dinner the night before, along with Arthur Schlesinger Jr. and his wife. "They went about one o'clock and Sally and I went to bed sober and happy."

Sally, he noted, was in good health "and looks remarkably and wonderfully like the girl I met 15 years ago last month. I have been rewarded in my life with many loyal friends, but here is the dearest and truest of them all." Vowing to "give back to life, to the very best of my ability, something that approaches the service and satisfaction that life has given to me," he noted with a bit of Calvinist self-flagellation, "I cannot truly say that I am satisfied with my contributions as they are at present. Like my generation, I have been restless and often ineffective; in my job, I have made progress in this past year, and yet I cannot truthfully say I have written what I might of the confusion and lack of philosophy of my time. . . . I hope to do more in the coming year." That evening before bed, he and Sally read aloud from the early chapters of Walter Lippmann's *Preface to Morals,* which surely gave both of them a sense of wanting to try harder in the new year.

The turn of the year seemed to inspire Scotty to produce his sporadic diary notes. On January 1, 1950, when he was forty years old, he wrote that "the Restons ought to start the fifties with a little gratitude. . . . We have our health; we still have all four of our parents; the children are growing up, it seems, with a sense of decency and responsibility . . . and it seems to me that we have more respect and love for one another now than ten years ago, if that is possible." He and Sally and the boys did indeed have much to be grateful for. They had provided a childhood and a home for their boys that far surpassed what Scotty had experienced, both in comfort and in security. That was not a bad way to measure one man's progress, but there was much more to come.

CHAPTER 11

HIGH POLITICS

HE MAY NOT have been the best father in the world, but by the 1950s, Scotty Reston was the best reporter in Washington. His command of the capital's news sources was impressively productive. In October 1950, for example, as America waged war in Korea, Reston learned that the Indian ambassador to China had warned President Truman that the Chinese would enter the war if the American forces crossed the thirty-eighth parallel and began to approach Chinese territory at the Yalu River. His reporting went unheeded. General Douglas MacArthur had repeatedly advised the president that neither the Chinese nor the Russians would intercede in the conflict. He was surprised when a force of 400,000 Chinese troops crossed into North Korea, hid themselves in the mountains, and then attacked the advancing American troops. MacArthur retreated south and his army suffered major losses.

Although Reston was still covering the diplomatic beat, he never missed a chance to find and develop new sources he calculated would one day benefit him. In late 1951, when Sally's parents were both near their death – her father would die only a few months after her mother's passing – Scotty and Sally were visiting them in Sycamore. Reston used the opportunity to phone Adlai Stevenson, then governor of Illinois. Reston doubtless met Stevenson at the San Francisco conference when the UN was founded and had known him in Washington when Stevenson served in the national government before becoming governor. The Truman years were coming to a close and Stevenson was a possible candidate for the Democratic nomination.

As Reston told the story in his memoirs, Stevenson could not see him on that trip but did promise to get in touch when he was next in Washington. He kept the promise in January, calling Reston at home at eleven o'clock one night from his hotel. He told Reston he had just seen the president and that he wanted to talk about the meeting. Reston put on his pants over his pajamas and hurried downtown to the second-rate hotel in which Stevenson (who, Reston said, was "as tight as a Pullman window") was staying. Reston throughout his career would catch important people at critical and often anguished moments. These people had a habit of telling the truth to Reston, seeking his advice and his confidence and trusting him to be judicious in what he made public of these conversations. They saw Reston as someone outside the political process to whom they could talk candidly, but at the same time a knowledgeable player in the political game who would understand their trials and dilemmas.

Truman had just promised Stevenson his personal support if he would stand for the Democratic presidential nomination. Stevenson had resisted the idea, but Truman famously argued that "if a knuckle-head like me can be president and not do too badly, think what a really educated smart guy like you could do in the job." Stevenson poured out his doubts about running for president to Scotty. He worried that perhaps the right thing for the country was for the Republicans to take power after two decades of Democratic rule. He thought that Lord Acton was only half right and that the absence of power also corrupted. Perhaps, he thought, it would be healthy for the Republicans to govern again, partly to educate the Grand Old Party in the modern realities of international politics. Besides, he said, if Eisenhower were the nominee, no one, himself certainly included, could beat him. "I like being governor of Illinois," Reston quoted him as saying. "Nobody needs to save the Republic from Ike Eisenhower, and couldn't if they tried." As Stevenson sat on the edge of his hotel bed, Reston argued that "when your number comes up in a democracy you have to go, especially if the president asks you." Even months later, as he was about to be nominated by his party, Stevenson still brooded privately to Reston, who recorded the conversation in a news analysis piece, about looking for a way to get out of the race. Writing in the *Times* after the two political conventions of that summer, Reston noted authoritatively that candidate Stevenson never felt "he was particularly fitted for the job."

Nonetheless, Reston admired Stevenson's mind and his speaking ability as well as his unusual candor. The candidate, who was divorced from his first wife, told Reston that a woman had approached him at a campaign stop and asked how he thought he could hold the country together if he couldn't even keep his family under one roof. Stevenson said it was one of the toughest questions he was ever asked and really didn't have a good answer. Both Sally and Scotty knew Stevenson's former wife and visited her during the 1952 Democratic convention in Chicago. The woman told the Restons that she felt that her former husband's new fame was a threat to her own life. She pulled a small pistol out of her handbag, declaring, "Adlai should never be president. Never." Reston never wrote a word about this encounter until he recorded it in his memoirs four decades later. Today a reporter in that situation would call the Secret Service.

In retrospect, one would expect that his close familiarity with Stevenson and his respect for the Illinois governor's mind and mind-set would have made Reston a strong Stevenson supporter. He was not. His friend Eric Severeid eloquently stated the case for Stevenson, crediting him with bringing

> a luminosity of intelligence unmatched on the American scene today; he has caught the imagination of intellectuals, of all those who are really informed; he has excited the passions of the *mind;* he has not excited the emotions of the great bulk of half-informed voters, nor among these has he created a feeling of Trust, of Authority, of Certainty that he knows where he is going and what must be done. Eisenhower does not create that feeling, or that illusion, because, God knows, he is empty of ideas or certitude himself.

But Stevenson's lack of single-mindedness in the pursuit of the presidency turned Scotty Reston off and he reported later that he voted for Ike in 1952. Perhaps not coincidentally, Arthur Hays Sulzberger and his editoral page editors also supported Eisenhower. Shortly after Ike took office, Stevenson made a speech harshly criticizing Secretary of State Dulles's policies as amounting to "dollar diplomacy." Reston weighed in immediately, criticizing Stevenson for being too quick to differ with the new administration. But when a collection of Governor Stevenson's speeches was published the same year, Reston described them as "something quite extraordinary in the political literature of the Republic . . . undoubtedly the finest collection of speeches made by any Presidential candidate since Wilson and maybe in this century . . . , surely among the finest ever crowded into a single presidential election by a single individual."

*   *   *

In 1956 Reston judged Eisenhower's first term as fairly passive. He worried as well about the incumbent's health. This time Reston voted for Stevenson, even though Scotty deplored the fact that Stevenson had abandoned much of the idealism that marked his first presidential campaign, in favor of a heavy – and futile – reliance on Democratic machine politicians. In his memoirs Scotty concluded that Stevenson ran for the presidency as "a spectator, as if somebody else were doing it." The candidate, Reston wrote, "seemed to see his public life as something outside himself, often referring to himself in the third person." Years later, in a conversation with *Washington Post* publisher Kay Graham, Reston concluded rather bluntly that Adlai Stevenson was "a loser."

Scotty's youngest son didn't feel that way at the time. In 1956, when Tom was only ten, he got caught up in the Stevenson cause, stuffing envelopes and decorating his room on Woodley Road with campaign posters and banners. As his father went off to New York to work on the election-night story, knowing that Stevenson was again doomed, he told Tom it was time to clean up his room and move the Stevenson memorabilia to the attic. Tom obeyed the order but was so disappointed by Stevenson's landslide loss that he moved up to the attic to be close to the posters. There Scotty found him writing an imagined acceptance speech of his own – "Fellow Americans, fellow Democrats, I accept your nomination."

Scotty told the story of Tom's disappointment to a friend of Stevenson's, who in turn told the candidate. Stevenson dashed off a note to Scotty and Sally: "There's one Democrat who will be READY. Tell Tom I love him; that I apologize; that in 1952 I didn't want to be ready; in 1956 I didn't have time to get ready, and in 1980 I'll be cheering for him – here or there." Tom, unlike his athletic brothers, was much more attracted to politics and public affairs, perhaps as a way of sharing part of his father's life. Stevenson was obviously touched by the boy's disappointment and also respectful of Scotty's stature in Washington. Yet Scotty's lack of enthusiasm for the Stevenson candidacy stands as a fine example of his ability to befriend the powerful without forfeiting his own judgment about their strengths and weaknesses.

Reston genuinely liked Ike — it was difficult not to — and especially liked his decisiveness as compared with the Hamlet-like Stevenson. The hero of the Allied victory in Europe had, as Reston once put it, "a smile that lit up like a Broadway sign." Scotty first met him in London when Eisenhower took over command of the Allied forces. "I learned early in Washington that it was a bum idea to have heroes or even intimate friends in government," Reston wrote in his memoirs, "but Ike put a strain on that ideal. . . . We all took a shine to him." In the 1952 campaign, Reston traveled extensively with Eisenhower. Despite his national popularity, Ike faced a tough fight for the nomination with Robert Taft, who was favored by the conservative wing of the GOP. At the nominating convention in Chicago, Reston was actually in Ike's suite at the Blackstone Hotel watching some of the convention proceedings on television with the candidate himself. The reporter remembered watching the famous Eisenhower temper erupt when the conservatives tried to suggest he would go the way of Dewey if nominated by the party.

While Reston found Eisenhower personally attractive, he had a clear-eyed view of his weaknesses. Partway through the general's first term as president, Reston decided, as he wrote in one of his columns, that Ike had become "a symbol of the atmosphere of the time: optimistic, prosperous, escapist, pragmatic, friendly, attentive at moments of crisis and comparatively inattentive the rest of the time." He thought that Eisenhower was often too distant from his own administration's policy discussions, especially the option of a preemptive strike against the growing power of the Soviet Union, a notion that Reston often discussed privately with Secretary of State Dulles. In fact, it was Reston himself who finally forced Eisenhower to engage on that issue. At a press conference in 1954, Reston asked Ike directly what he thought of the concept of "preventive atomic war." With the authority only a war hero could bring to the question, and with a clarity that often eluded the syntactically challenged president, Ike dismissed the notion entirely. "A preventive war, to my mind, is an impossibility today," Eisenhower said. "How could you have one if one of its features would be several cities lying in ruins, several cities where many, many thousands of people would be dead and injured and mangled. . . . That isn't preventive war; that is war. I don't believe there is such a thing, and frankly I wouldn't even listen to anyone seriously that came in and talked about such a thing." It was an important question and a direct and sensible answer, ending a dangerous policy debate. By 1956, after the president had suffered a serious heart attack, the conventional wisdom held that he would not and should not seek a second term. Ike had apparently been undecided about the idea, even before his heart attack. But after a well-publicized séance with his heart specialist, Paul Dudley White, the president announced he would indeed run again. Reston managed to ride with Dr. White as he was driven to the airport the day after he issued an optimistic report on the president's health prospects. Reston wrote that White seemed to be putting the president's happiness ahead of the needs of the country.

It was through Foster Dulles that Reston did his most important work covering the Eisenhower administration. Dulles liked and trusted Reston and spent a good deal of time with him in off-the-record sessions, giving him an informed, even intimate, picture of the workings of the Eisenhower foreign policy team. "I spent more time with him," Reston recalled, "than with any other secretary of state from the forties to the nineties." Reston delighted in his private meetings with Dulles, noting later the secretary's odd habits of stirring his whiskey with his finger and twirling his key chain as the two men talked policy and politics. Reston appreciated Dulles's efforts to keep the Republican Party from lapsing into the isolationist stance that Arthur Vandenberg had helped to end, but his own more nuanced understanding of the Soviet Union, born in part from his own wartime trip there with Arthur Sulzberger, led him to think Dulles was too reflexively anti-Soviet for the nation's own good. Still, Reston appreciated the private Dulles as "generous, thoughtful and even amusing."

Eisenhower's greatest accomplishment in foreign policy was, of course, the engineering of a truce in the bloody war in Korea. With the involvement of troops from China, what had started in the Truman years as an attempt to roll back Communist incursions into South Korea was threatening to become a much larger war in Asia. In his first year in office, Eisenhower decided to bring covert pressure on the Chinese to get some sort of peace. The administration sent word to Beijing privately through Indian diplomats that it was considering the use of atomic weapons in an expanded war. Almost simultaneously, Dulles told Reston the same thing, including the fact that large bombers and atomic weapons had been moved to bases closer to the Chinese mainland. The secretary regarded Reston and the *Times* as an important tool of diplomacy.

Dulles, like Reston, was a Presbyterian, although the diplomat took his religion much more seriously than did the newspaperman. But the common affiliation gave Reston an opening to poke and jab at Dulles's policy of massive nuclear retaliation as the means by which America would try to contain Soviet expansionism. Reston remembered asking Dulles how he could square his religious belief in the sanctity of every human life with his nuclear doctrine. "He was visibly uncomfortable with this question," Reston wrote in *Deadline*, ". . . [but] he liked these philosophical wanderings."

Not all of his dealings with Dulles were as pleasant. Reston reported in his memoirs that during Ike's second term, Dulles confronted Reston with the accusation that the *Times* had been consistently unfair in its coverage of the administration's foreign policy. The secretary said he had considered going to Arthur Sulzberger about the problem but instead decided to deal directly with Reston, who was by then the paper's chief in Washington. The two apparently had a stiff exchange of views, with Reston defending in particular his analytic Q head pieces as fair comment on the daily arguments within the administration. Dulles replied lamely that the paper was getting too much information from foreign-embassy sources. Reston argued back that he and his colleagues used embassy sources because the State Department was not as forthcoming as it should be. Reston said it was the only serious confrontation he ever had with Dulles but that it did not poison their subsequent dealings.

There was, however, another source of constant irritation between Dulles and Reston and between Reston and Eisenhower. It was the issue of how the Republican president and his top advisors should have been dealing with the ominous rise of Senator Joseph McCarthy of Wisconsin. With increasing malevolence, McCarthy was using American distrust and fear of the Soviet Union to attract attention to his unsavory self. Dulles was often irritated when Reston bearded him on the question of whether Dulles was using his own brand of anti-Communist rhetoric as a way of currying favor with the demagogic McCarthy. "Be fair, hang it," Reston quoted Dulles as saying in exasperation when Reston raised the issue. "The State Department is not a school of moral philosophy." Reston recalled Dulles explaining: "I probably dislike the obstructionists even more than you do, but we need their votes or at least their neutrality or we won't have any foreign policy at all."

Reston himself had felt the sting of the fervent anti-Communists in the later years of the Truman administration when, almost on a whim, he cabled a series of questions to the Soviet dictator Stalin. It was not an original ploy; others had tried the gambit before. But amazingly enough, doubtless because of the coming change of administrations and the stature of the *Times*, Stalin cabled back some answers, which the *Times* then printed verbatim. Both questions and answers were anodyne. Reston asked whether Stalin thought the United States and the USSR "can live peacefully in the years to come?" Answer: "Our countries can continue to live in peace." He asked whether the Soviet leader would welcome negotiations with the incoming Eisenhower administration for the purpose of arranging a meeting with the president. Answer: "I would react favorably to such a proposal." But the story drew shrill criticism of the newspaper for giving Stalin a forum.

The affair angered Arthur Sulzberger, partly because he had not been told beforehand by any of his editors that the questions had been asked and answered and were to be printed. Sulzberger distanced the paper from the whole matter and rebuked Krock, who wrote back two days after the letters were printed to apologize for the lack of consultation and make sure the publisher knew it was Reston's scheme, not his. "I am so instinctive and experienced a team-player that I wonder myself why I never thought of discussing with you and Catledge Reston's idea of sending those questions to Stalin."

Reston took a starchier tone with Sulzberger in a letter he sent the publisher a few weeks later. He objected to editorials the paper ran criticizing its own publication of Stalin's views and public statements by the New York editors disassociating themselves from the incident. Feeling abandoned by his boss and mentor, Reston wrote with passion and eloquence about the need to be able to report freely.

He argued persuasively that the goal of American policy should be to reach some accommodation with the Soviets and spoke out against the growing popular notion that negotiation with the Soviets was useless. "If we are in the business of watching and inquiring about the course of events in the camp of the enemy, why should we not question there as we question in every other capital in the world?" he asked Sulzberger pointedly. "It is my hope," he wrote, "that whatever we do about reporters, whatever we say about the wiles and propaganda lies of Stalin, we contribute nothing more to the idea that negotiation is useless." It was a letter remarkable for its cogency, for its willingness to disagree directly with Sulzberger, and for its very reasonableness in the face of harsh criticism. "If we don't say to each other what is in our hearts," Reston concluded, "the whole basis of our professional relationship, and what is more important, of our friendship, will be gone."

The incident illuminated two things about Reston. He was willing to be quite direct with his mentor Sulzberger. And more important, his basic take on the Cold War was that it was not a confrontation that could be won by force of arms. He had seen the Soviet Union in wartime; he understood its concerns about invasion and its need for security. He had little patience with those who were feeding popular fear of the Soviet Union.

He had an equal impatience with those who would not stand up to the fear mongers like Joe McCarthy. Reston reported in his memoirs that while Dulles refused to criticize McCarthy directly, he was happy to whisper to Reston on background about McCarthy's lies and public drunkenness. "He [Dulles] had a cunning way of telling me all about them without asking me to do anything about it or putting it off the record," Reston recalled. He was troubled enough by this arrangement, he wrote, to seek the guidance of his editors about whether he should continue the close relationship with Dulles. But

Reston also understood that Dulles had a motive for his intimacy with the newsman, and it helped Reston weigh the information Dulles provided.

After all, Reston knew how to work the angles in the news business, where he could get an advantage, where public disclosure would help one side or another. And soon Reston would use that understanding to garner one of his greatest scoops, at the same time delivering a serious blow to Joe McCarthy.

CHAPTER 12

THE GREAT FEAR

BY 1953 THE large American obsession about Communist infiltration of government – and the press and schools and just about any organization one could imagine – was reaching nearly hysterical proportions. The anxiety was not completely irrational; there had been a passel of Soviet agents uncovered. Alger Hiss, though never convicted of espionage, had been found guilty of perjury for denying he had ever dealt with former Communist spy Whittaker Chambers. The Korean War was bloody evidence of Communist expansionism, and the triumph of Mao Zedong's forces on the Chinese mainland had led to shrill political charges that the United States had failed to save China from the Reds – as if that were within America's power. The Rosenbergs had been tried and executed for giving Moscow nuclear secrets that helped the Soviet Union break the short-lived American atomic monopoly. Still, the witch-hunting was exactly that: a perfervid, irrational search for demons to blame. Purges of admitted former Communist Party members and of suspected former members were common across the country. Hollywood was busy blacklisting writers, actors, and directors with ties to the party or other groups once sympathetic to the party. Even the children of one-time Communist Party members were being fired from their jobs. "Did you ever closely associate with your father," one suspect was asked at a congressional hearing.

The poisonous atmosphere presented a classic opportunity for Scotty Reston, one in which he used his contacts, his prestige, and his sense of how the press and the government can work together for the common good. President Eisenhower, although contemptuous of Joe McCarthy, never summoned the political courage to denounce the senator's crude, destructive Red-baiting, which had helped the Republican Party win the presidency. But then McCarthy began using selective leaks of the Yalta conference records to make the case that the American government had rolled over for Joe Stalin. Even the hawkish Eisenhower State Department found his assault destructive to their efforts to deal realistically with the Soviet Union. The solution to the McCarthy-Yalta problem was quite obvious: release the full record of the proceedings. But the British government opposed full release, partly because publication would break the rules of confidentiality required to reach high-level diplomatic agreements and partly because Churchill had been recorded at Yalta making disparaging remarks about the French.

The State Department under Secretary Dulles decided on a classic bureaucratic solution. It announced that it was sending copies of the original documents to twenty-four high-ranking members of Congress for their personal use, knowing full well someone would leak them. The papers would become public, but the administration would avoid direct responsibility for their release.

When Reston heard of the plan at a State Department press briefing, he went directly to Capitol Hill to see the chairman of the Senate Foreign Relations Committee. The chairman agreed with Reston that such a tactic would only make things worse because the leaks of the documents would still look selective and politically motivated. The next day Reston called Dulles's office for an appointment, telling an assistant that he had had a conversation with the committee chairman and that he wanted to share the gist of that conversation with Dulles.

After a morning press conference by Dulles the next day, which Reston attended, the secretary's chief press officer, Carl McCardle, beckoned Reston to join him in the private elevator to his boss's office. Reston told Dulles, who was standing behind his desk, that sending the documents to the Hill was a bad idea that would only make selective leaking worse. He had been told, he said, by the powerful chairman of the Foreign Relations Committee that he agreed and would refuse to accept the document.

By Reston's account, he then reminded Dulles that the two had often talked about the idea of the "calculated leak" and that it would be a good time to use the tactic. Dulles understood immediately and was intrigued by Reston's offer, though he was totally unauthorized at that point to let the *Times* publish the entire body of papers. Dulles then told Reston that McCardle, not the secretary, was in charge of the calculated-leak department. "In accordance with the old rule that when you've made a sale, stop talking, I got up and left," Reston recorded. He and McCardle talked the matter over and Reston left for his office to call New York. The editors there estimated it would take about fifty pages of the newspaper to publish the whole document but told Reston to go ahead. He pressed McCardle for an answer; by evening there was no response.

Scotty and Sally were at home, preparing to go to a glee club performance at their boys' school, when McCardle called from his home in Virginia and asked Reston to drive over. The spokesman exacted a promise from Reston: since the discussions with the British about the release of the papers had not yet been completed, the *Times* would not publish if the two countries could not agree. It was clear to Reston that while McCardle was following Dulles's unspoken instructions, he was apparently doing so secretly. The documents he gave Reston were his own numbered set. If, McCardle insisted, the department security people demanded his copy, Reston would have to agree to return it within fifteen minutes.

Reston drove directly downtown to his office and began to try to figure out how to send two 400-plus-page books of documents to New York. They could not be taken there physically, since they might have to be rushed back to McCardle in the event of a security check. They could not be taken apart and handed in sections to teletypists for the same reason. By five in the morning, they had jury-rigged a photocopying arrangement so that a gang of telegraphers could each type sections of the text for transmission. By two o'clock the next morning, they had managed to finish only one volume. Reston called in one of the paper's photographers and asked him to take pictures of the pages, two at a time. By daybreak they had a big package of film, which they sent by train to New York.

At this point McCardle's assistant called and told Reston the press secretary had to have lunch with him that day. They met at the F Street Club, where McCardle reported that Arthur Krock, totally unaware of what Reston was up to, had called one of McCardle's assistant press secretaries to ask for the Yalta papers. The assistant refused and told McCardle he thought it was wrong of the *Times* even to ask for the documents. But a while later, Krock had figured out what all the rushing around in the bureau was about and called back to rescind his request. That tipped off the assistant that the *Times* already had the papers. At a subsequent staff meeting, the assistant announced the *Times'* scoop. A heated discussion broke out over how the *Times* obtained the documents. An embarrassed

McCardle said nothing. But he asked Reston for a one-day delay in publication so it would occur while he was out of town with Dulles.

Reston conveyed the request to Turner Catledge, the managing editor, but the two decided that since the transmission of such a massive amount of material would soon be known, no delay was possible. Reston called McCardle with the bad news. And soon the secrecy was broken. The *Chicago Tribune*'s office in New York was, oddly enough, located in the communications room of the *Times*. The *Tribune* staff figured out what was up and told the home office. Turner Catledge turned down a plea from his Chicago counterpart to share the documents and the cost of transmission, so the *Tribune* reached out to Illinois senator Everett Dirksen, who called the Republican leader of the Senate, who in turn persuaded Dulles to release the papers publicly. The *Tribune* also photographed the pages and rushed out a special section to some of its readers the next morning. The *Times* made all its editions; the paper, and Reston, got all the credit. It was, Reston thought, "a pretty good job of reporting."

It was journalism at its best. The publication of the documents was a genuine public service. The *Times* readers and the nation as a whole benefited from the disclosure of the Yalta agreements because they could make informed judgments about the ongoing accusations from the McCarthyites that a pro-Communist conspiracy contaminated the top ranks of the government. The Yalta episode was also an example of Reston at his best. The combination of his access to the top players and the trust they placed in him made his reporting work. His sharp understanding of how the news would affect the policy debate was what led him to propose the "controlled leak" to Dulles. His position at the best newspaper in the country was the final asset he brought to the game. Apparently within minutes of the request from Reston and without regard to the fact that printing fifty pages of text without advertising would be costly, the leadership of the *Times* recognized its journalistic duty and did it, without hesitation.

But the scoops also benefited Reston. The more he exercised his journalistic power, the more power flowed to him. Later that year, on October 18, 1953, his regular column on the editorial page of the paper began to appear. In the spring he had won his third award from the Overseas Press Club in New York for best interpretive writing about foreign affairs. In the winter he was inducted into the Gridiron Club in Washington, an elite organization of the city's top journalists, whose sole function was to hold an annual dinner to make enormous fun of their politician guests. The politicians invited to join them were expected to pitch in with their own self-deprecating humor.

The only losers in the Yalta incident were the Red-baiters, exactly whom Reston wanted to be disadvantaged. He had never liked McCarthy and had used his reporting and analytic writing to try to dull the impact of the Wisconsin Republican's increasingly hysterical and unsubstantiated charges that the U.S. government was riddled with Communists. Reston's was not the most powerful journalistic voice criticizing McCarthy. Columnists like Marquis Childs and the Alsop brothers – Joseph and Stewart – were more direct and forceful. So was Drew Pearson, whom McCarthy, in a drunken rage, punched senseless in a Washington men's room one night. None other than Richard Nixon was the only witness. "This one's for you, Dick," McCarthy said as he assaulted the columnist. These writers, however, had the advantage of being able to produce opinion pieces. Reston was, in the early period of McCarthy's ascendancy, still writing news and analysis.

Reston, reflecting years later on the way the press dealt with McCarthy, found little to praise. He called the period "painful" and found his own performance inadequate, despite his role in the release of the Yalta papers. "At the beginning of McCarthy's campaign," he wrote in his memoirs, "I treated it as political theater, then reported his gradual decline, and tried to get out the facts he was suppressing. But it wasn't until 1954, when I had the greater freedom of writing a column, that I was able, along with many other colleagues in the press, to take a stiffer line."

His "stiffer line" wasn't all that stiff and never had the impact of Edward R. Murrow's television exposé of McCarthy. But Reston did take on Eisenhower's timidity toward the Wisconsin senator. After one particularly egregious charge by McCarthy, Eisenhower inched away from the senator by urging Congress to establish standards of fairness. Reston dismissed the notion, writing in a column in 1954 that "there is little evidence that the Congressmen are being faithful to their own consciences, let alone to the conscience of the nation. Not only the young ones, dazzled by his [McCarthy's] success, but the old-timers to avoid his wrath." He lectured the president by quoting Woodrow Wilson's observation that it was only the president who represented the entire nation. But it was a mild rebuke. "We were, I'm sorry to say, intimidated much of the time by the popularity of McCarthy's lies and his charges that his opponents were 'soft on communism,'" Reston wrote in his memoirs.

In part, the poor performance of the press in bringing McCarthy to account was, Reston explained later, rooted in the "cult of objectivity" that was the dominant journalistic ethic of the time. Most newspapers felt they were doing their duty to their readers if they simply reported accurately the lies McCarthy was telling. Worse, a significant portion of the American press supported McCarthy's position, if not his methods, quietly enjoying the circulation-building sensation the senator caused.

Often, however, the intimidation of the press was quite direct. In 1953, Arthur Hays Sulzberger received an anonymous tip that Reston himself would become a target of McCarthy's witch-hunt. Nothing ever came of that. When Reston became bureau chief, he assigned a man he called in his memoirs "the best congressional reporter we had" to cover McCarthy. The job was to report anything new the senator had to say but "to avoid repeating his undocumented charges." Since so little of what McCarthy said was ever documented, it's hard to imagine how the reporter was to proceed. But McCarthy didn't like the way he was being covered by the *Times* and rolled out his usual weapon to settle the score. On the floor of the Senate, McCarthy charged that the correspondent had once been a member of the Young Communist League. Reston and his bosses in New York were stunned and embarrassed. After the reporter admitted his earlier affiliation, Reston wrestled with what to do. He and the paper could have simply stood by the reporter, pointing out that the association was long ago and in a different time, that his reporting had been fair, and that they were taking no action. Yet the fact that the reporter had not divulged his vulnerability upon being assigned to cover the world-champion Commie hunter was a serious ethical mistake.

Reston wrote to managing editor Catledge:

> I don't think our reporter was fair to the paper or to me or to his other colleagues in the bureau. If I had a responsibility for other sections of the *Times*, where no political material was handled, I would not feel that this record had destroyed his usefulness to the paper. To fire him outright would seem to me too drastic, and an unnecessary cruelty not only to him but to his wife and three children. But I am clear that he has forfeited the confidence of this bureau and cannot continue to do the kind of work expected of him here.

The man was transferred back to the New York office, where, Reston said, he did "excellent work" until he retired. Still, the reporter's career was ruined, and he served out his days in relative obscurity. Reston was, however, right about the fact that his correspondent had been compromised, and his solution was relatively humane.

Much more so than the way Arthur Hays Sulzberger dealt with a similar problem that arose in 1955. Mississippi senator James O. Eastland, angered at the *Times'* criticism of his segregationist views, launched an assault against the paper by subpoenaing thirty of the paper's staffers to be questioned about past Communist associations. Sulzberger took the view that staff members who took shelter under the Fifth Amendment's right against self-incrimination, as many of those subjected to McCarthyite inquisitions did in the period, would be fired from the paper. Several were. Even their union, the Newspaper Guild of New York, fearfully refused to protest their dismissal. Others openly confessed their past associations with the party but refused to name other party members. For that refusal they were indicted for contempt of Congress. Eventually they won reversal of their convictions on appeal, including one case that went to the Supreme Court.

It was not journalism's finest hour. Sulzberger had given a public speech before the Eastland investigation in which he had said he would never employ a known Communist on the paper but criticized those who refused to stand up to the anti-Communist zealots. "It is the lack of plain, old-fashioned guts on the part of those who capitulate to them" that bothered him the most, he said. When the Eastland committee went to war against the *Times,* Sulzberger approved a tough and eloquent editorial defending a free press and attacking McCarthyism. But such resistance was rare. Across America editors who knew better published McCarthy's charges. The Great Fear, as author David Caute called it, cowed them into the most muted criticism, if they permitted themselves any criticism at all. They printed guilt-by-association charges, some of which came from the FBI, in their fervor to expose Communist infiltrators. Together the politicians and the press nearly drove the country mad.

*   *   *

By 1954 the anti-Red purges began to devour some of the nation's most eminent scientists, especially those who had been involved in developing the first atomic bomb. Most prominent was J. Robert Oppenheimer, the man who ran the Los Alamos labs and directed the invention of the A-bomb. Oppenheimer had once associated closely with Communists; his wife and brother had been party members, which was not unusual at the time, particularly among Jewish intellectuals who were aware of the Nazi genocide in Europe. Several other scientists had also been party members, but Oppenheimer had never made any secret of his associations. The new element in the Oppenheimer case was a letter sent from a congressional staff member to the FBI alleging that the scientist had actually leaked atomic secrets to the Soviets.

Reston happened upon this story before any other reporter and it occurred in a characteristic way. He boarded an airplane from Washington to New York one morning. Seeing an empty seat next to Oppenheimer, he quickly planted himself next to the scientist. As any good reporter would, Reston saw a chance to talk to someone in power, maybe pick up a story in the process. He recalled that Oppenheimer "was not visibly overjoyed" when the journalist introduced himself. "I never mentioned anything about Oppenheimer's work, and yet he seemed unaccountably nervous in my presence and obviously under some strain," Reston wrote in his memoirs. By this time Oppenheimer already knew of the accusations against him and had been prohibited, on the order of President Eisenhower, from seeing any secret materials of the Atomic Energy Commission. But nothing had yet been made public about the case.

When he returned to Washington, Reston, following his superb instincts, began asking, "What's wrong with Oppenheimer these days?" Gradually he heard bits and pieces of the story. He tried to see the scientist, but Oppenheimer was out of the country. He was referred to Oppenheimer's lawyer, Lloyd Garrison, in New York.

Reston recounted to Garrison the tidbits he had dug up in Washington. The lawyer filled in the details, but on condition that Reston refrain from publishing the material before Oppenheimer had a chance to prepare answers to the charges against him. Reston struck a deal. He would hold off on the story of America's most prominent atomic scientist's being investigated for espionage. In return, Garrison would give Reston and the *Times* the exclusive story, once Oppenheimer was ready to respond to the charges. Reston's editors in New York agreed to hold off. "In fifty years on *The New York Times*," Reston wrote in his memoirs, "I was involved in quite a few cases in which the immediate competitive interests of the paper conflicted with the honor of an individual, and on not a single occasion in my personal experience did the *Times* put its competitive interests first."

Reston held to the agreement, despite his worries that J. Edgar Hoover was sure to leak the Oppenheimer charges to Joe McCarthy. Soon McCarthy began hinting he was about to charge the government with harboring "atomic energy spies." On the day Oppenheimer's supposedly secret hearings began before a government board of inquiry and Oppenheimer was able to argue his own defense, Reston broke the full story. The board was furious that the matter was now public. President Eisenhower, Reston reported in his memoirs, told press secretary James Hagerty he thought Oppenheimer "was sure acting like a Communist . . . using all the rules they use to try to get public sentiment in their corner." Eventually Oppenheimer lost his security clearance and was driven from the high councils of the American defense establishment. When the details of his eccentric life and contacts became known, public opinion turned against him, though he was never convicted of espionage. The settled wisdom became that Oppenheimer had become one of the most prominent victims of the Great Fear and that he was guilty of nothing more than being, in Reston's words, "an oddball."

The case, Reston wrote, "troubled me for years." He worried that his scoop had inflamed the board of inquiry against Oppenheimer and had thus led to his banishment. As he began writing his memoirs, he called Oppenheimer's lawyer, Garrison, in New York, who assured him that "the cards were stacked against Oppenheimer" before the *Times'* story was ever published and that had McCarthy been the first to air the story, things would have been even worse for the scientist. "I had no personal feelings about Oppenheimer," Reston recalled. "I had used him to get an important story and he had used me for his defense." There is no more pungent expression of the relationship between reporter and public figure. He and Oppenheimer were playing an old game and they both played it honorably. Reston could have set off a sensation by printing only the charges against Oppenheimer weeks ahead of the scheduled hearings, attracting much attention to himself and his paper. He still got the attention when he wrote the first big story about the case, but he had avoided a one-sided smear that likely would have made Oppenheimer's situation even worse.

Still, Reston always believed that Oppenheimer had been railroaded on insufficient evidence and somehow he should have been more on Oppenheimer's side. There is no doubt that McCarthyism was a factor in Oppenheimer's disgrace. So was a bitter political feud between Oppenheimer and Dr. Edward Teller, the father of the H-bomb, the production of which Oppenheimer firmly opposed. But Reston's part in the Oppenheimer case is above reproach. He did his job. He was fair to Oppenheimer. His restraint produced a more balanced story. The public and the democratic process were well served.

"Wee Jimmy" Reston, Scotty's father. In his retirement he copied his son's columns in longhand. (Courtesy of the Reston family)

Johanna Reston, Scotty's mother. She had a sharp tongue and preached hard work and ambition. (Courtesy of the Reston family)

James B. Reston at the University of Illinois. Lack of money and preparation made him insecure, despite his athletic ability. (The Reston Collection, University of Illinois Archives)

Sally Reston during her college years. She won Scotty's heart and changed his life. (Courtesy of the Reston family)

Reston as an Illini letterman. This picture was sent to relatives in Scotland as
proof of the lad's progress. (Courtesy
of I. A. Reston)

Reston was captain of the golf team.
They won the Big Ten championship
his junior year. (The Reston Collection,
University of Illinois Archives)

Reston (second from right) with his new colleagues from the London bureau of the
New York Times. (The Reston Collection, University of Illinois Archives)

Scotty and Sally in London during World War II. He was loaned to the Office of War Information by the *Times*. (*The New York Times*)

Arthur Hays Sulzberger in 1951. "Mr. Gus" was Reston's mentor and friend. (*New York Times* Photo Archive)

Iphigene Ochs Sulzberger and managing editor Turner Catledge in 1965. She was a huge Reston supporter; Catledge was replaced by Reston in 1968. (Charles D. Hogan, *The New York Times*)

Orvil Dryfoos in 1961. The publisher and Reston spoke nearly every day. (*The New York Times*)

The Restons of Woodley Road. Scotty and Sally with Richard (on couch), James B., Jr. (holding dog), and Thomas in 1960. (Noel Clark, Black Star)

Reston (left) wasn't enthusiastic about Allen Drury (center), who left the *Times* after writing *Advise and Consent*. Scotty forced White House correspondent William White (right) to quit the paper. (The Reston Collection, University of Illinois Archives)

Abe Rosenthal (left) picked his friend Jimmy Greenfield (right) as the new Washington bureau chief. Reston blocked the maneuver. (*The New York Times*)

Reston took over the top editor's job, but clashed repeatedly with and was ultimately replaced by Rosenthal. (*The New York Times*)

Reston (far left) presided over the editorial board meetings, here with Senator George McGovern (back to camera) in 1968. (Charles D. Hogan, *The New York Times*)

Reston speaking to a press association meeting about his acquisition, the *Vineyard Gazette*. (Mark Lovewell)

Eldest son Richard Reston and his wife, Jody, were the saviors of the *Gazette*. (Alison Shaw)

Arthur Ochs "Punch" Sulzberger (center), Abe Rosenthal (left), and *Times* lawyer James Goodale at a press conference explaining the publication of the Pentagon Papers. (J. Manning, *The New York Times*)

Attorney General John Mitchell (left), who brought suit to stop publication of the Pentagon Papers, speaking to Reston in Washington. (The Reston Collection, University of Illinois Archives)

Reston interviewed Zhou En-lai during his 1972 trip to China. (*The New York Times*)

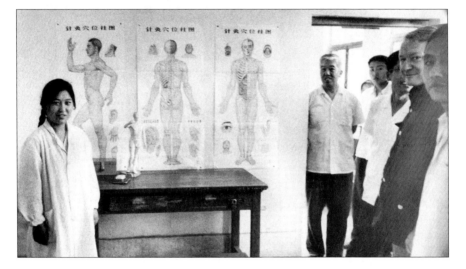

Reston visiting a hospital in China before he was rushed to one himself for an emergency appendectomy. (Sally Reston, *The New York Times*)

Reston with Henry Kissinger (The Reston Collection, University of Illinois Archives)

CHAPTER 13

THE OTHER NEWSPAPER FAMILY

JUST A FEW blocks down the street from the house on Woodley Road was Walter Lippmann's home. Reston had his eye on Lippmann for years, recognizing him as the preeminent American columnist and opinion leader of the center-left, flattering him with an occasional piece of fan mail and making sure he got an early copy of *Prelude to Victory* when it was published in 1943. As Reston became more and more well known, not just as a fine and diligent reporter, but as an interpretive journalist, he drew closer to Lippmann. Their letters now began with the salutations "Dear Walter" and "Dear Scotty." The Restons were frequently at the Lippmanns' for dinner and the Lippmanns occasionally dined at the Restons'. The two men enlisted each other to support their friends for membership at the Metropolitan Club, the most exclusive social grouping in the capital, and the Century Association in New York, a club of writers and artists, musicians, and patrons of the arts, both of which at the time excluded women. These affiliations were testimony to the fact that James B. Reston had *arrived*.

Lippmann was much the older of the two. He had helped found the *New Republic* magazine in 1914 while Reston was still a boy in Scotland. Through his writings, and then his direct service in the government, he had influenced President Woodrow Wilson's attempt to form the League of Nations and was present as a negotiator at the Treaty of Versailles. Before Scotty had even graduated from college, Lippmann had started writing his column "Today and Tomorrow," which eventually appeared in more than 250 newspapers around the country. Reston admired him deeply and felt free to tell him so. Lippmann was an often remote and sometimes cruel man, but when he admitted Reston into his circle, it was evidence of Reston's talent, accomplishment, and growing place among the powerful in Washington.

Lippmann was a much deeper thinker than Scotty Reston, a man who could write thoughtful books on the large philosophical issues facing the nation while turning out newspaper opinion columns closely rooted in current politics and international affairs. He had been tutored by William James and George Santayana at Harvard. Reston used Lippmann in a similar way, as a teacher to expand his mind and broaden his perspective. Lippmann in turn used Reston, as he did other young reporters, as his legman, since the columnist did not choose to report the news as such. His columns were based on the news but were more commentary than factual investigation. The little news nuggets he came upon and decided not to use, he often passed on to Reston.

Reston often sent Lippmann copies of his own private memorandums to Arthur Hays Sulzberger, recounting background sessions with policy makers. These reports were thorough accounts of the substance of the conversations, but typically Scotty threw in some colorful tidbits for the delectation of his highly limited readership.

As an addendum to his report of a session with a second-tier State Department official, Reston noted the official was privately critical of the secretary of state. In a six-page memo about a dinner conversation with that same secretary of state, John Foster Dulles, Reston noted that the secretary had two stiff bourbons before dinner and was privately worried whether President Eisenhower would be too freewheeling in private conversations with other heads of state at an upcoming summit meeting. It was not just his own background reports that he sent on to Lippmann; he also sent along confidential reports that came to him from his *Times* colleagues.

These dispatches were invaluable to Lippmann. When read today, they are amazingly frank and serious conversations between the government and the press, usually done for the background information of the correspondents but loaded with enough incendiary material to spark huge headlines had there been any breach of confidentiality. In Reston's memo about the dinner with Dulles, the secretary of state is reported musing about the possibilities of a preemptive atomic war against the Soviet Union. "As you know," Reston quoted Dulles as saying, "there are men high in this government who believe that we cannot avoid a major war with the Soviet Union and, therefore, that we should take advantage of what lead we have in the atomic field now." "On the other hand," Reston wrote, "the Secretary realizes that the power of the new weapons has forced a reevaluation of the whole idea that principle can be served and society defended by modern war." Dulles ended this discussion by commenting: "Of course, we cannot just allow them [the Soviets] to go on taking one place after another." Here was the second-most-powerful figure in the American government musing about the pros and cons of a preemptive nuclear assault on the Soviet Union! That debate, of course, was not confined to the government, and had Reston and the *Times* chosen to violate the ground rules of the Dulles conversations, it would have been front-page news and would have fed an already emotional debate about how to the deal with the Communist menace.

It was not just the discussions of high policy that were illuminating. In the same session, Reston commented to Dulles that "the President seemed very remote from both the internal crisis of McCarthy and the foreign policy crisis of Southeast Asia." Reported Reston: "He [Dulles] nodded agreement to this, but did not comment. I added that this sense of remoteness was increased by what seemed to me to be a major public relations blunder; that is to say, the President, while not taking the lead on the major issues of the front pages, was permitting himself to be photographed almost every day with some unimportant ceremonial aspect of his job. Mr. Dulles agreed that this was unfortunate." Imagine what could have been done with that exchange in the next day's newspapers. But Reston, as he did throughout his career, felt being trusted with Dulles's private feelings about the president and understanding the shape of the debate on foreign policy were ultimately more important than reaching for a headline. After this screamer, DULLES DOUBTS IKE'S COMPETENCE, would there have ever been another private dinner with Reston in attendance?

With no television, no Internet, not even a national newspaper, Lippmann's was for a time the most important single editorial voice in the country.* Despite that, Lippmann was not recognized by the Pulitzer committee until 1958, more than a decade after Reston had won his first prize. When Lippmann finally did win the Pulitzer, Reston sent him a handwritten "Dear Walter" note saying: "Sally and I send you our warm congratulations. This is so obviously overdue that I have often felt a twinge of shame that I should have such

*As thoughtful as most of Lippmann's columns were, they were not always prescient. His first column in the *Post*, printed on July 5, 1938, carried a Paris dateline. Lippmann wrote that "barring incidents that cannot be foreseen . . . there would seem to be no great probability of war in the near future. . . . Neither Germany, nor her uneasy partner, Italy, has the resources to conduct a great war."

an award when the man I admired more than anyone else in our profession was passed by. Anyway, the wrong has been corrected at last and I am sincerely happy."

When Lippmann reached his seventieth birthday, Reston organized some of his colleagues to write tributes to their mentor's fifty-year career for a book called *Walter Lippmann and His Times*, which included appreciations by Reston, columnist Marquis Childs, historian and mutual friend Arthur Schlesinger Jr., diplomat and scholar George Kennan, and others. Reston's own contribution to the book concluded by saying, "I know that he has given my generation of newspapermen a wider vision of our duty. He has shown us how to put the events of the day into its [*sic*] proper relationship to the history of yesterday and the dream of tomorrow." That passage described exactly the effect of Lippmann's tutelage on Reston.

Lippmann was quite the social lion in Washington, and in addition to the Restons, his circle included Justice Frankfurter and a former Frankfurter clerk, Philip Graham. Graham was married to Katharine Meyer whose father, Eugene Meyer, was the owner of the *Washington Post*. Phil Graham had begun his career at the paper after he returned from World War II, and in 1948 Meyer turned over control of the *Post* to his son-in-law and daughter, giving Phil Graham 3,500 of the 5,000 voting shares and his daughter the remainder. Lippmann was one of the first national columnists Eugene Meyer added to the paper to give it prestige and heft, and the columnist became a friend and advisor to Meyer and then to the Grahams.

Lippmann and his wife often played tennis with the Grahams on the Meyers' private court, and he and his wife entertained the Grahams and the Restons. And they all repaid his hospitality. Scotty took to calling the great man Walt as he came to know him better. Soon the Restons and the Grahams were fast friends too. Kay Graham, whom Scotty affectionately called Kate, and Sally were busy with their children and would attend ladies' functions, like the Congressional

Wives luncheons. The two of them recalled one such affair at which each lady present was asked to rise and speak about how she had spent her summer. Both were mortified because the congressmen's wives all spoke about campaigning for their husbands, while Katharine and Sally had been merely tending to their families' lives.

Phil Graham and Scotty had a bantering, masculine relationship that included a good deal of mutual taunting and kidding. On the golf course, Phil would keep up his chatter right through Scotty's backswing, his exuberance unchecked by the etiquette of the game. Phil had taken up golf in middle age; Scotty had the game from his youth, but it had become quite rusty. On a vacation they took in Nassau, the two couples were playing the ninth hole at the exclusive Lyford Key Club. Reston uncorked a huge hook off the tee, over the road, and right through a plate glass window in the Bank of Canada office. "We were just broken up to the point where we were weeping, we were laughing so hard," Kay Graham remembered. Scotty and Phil, like two juvenile delinquents, went sheepishly into the bank and volunteered to pay for the window. "I believe they were not allowed to do so," she said.

"We had such fun with Scotty. We'd spend the evenings together and he would say, now this is going to be the topic of conversation," Mrs. Graham recalled. "The one I remember most was he said, 'Graham' – he used to call him Graham – 'what is going to take the place of poverty in your family and mine with our children?'" Phil Graham had come from a relatively poor family, although not quite as strapped as the immigrant Restons. By the 1950s, the Restons were financially comfortable but had nothing approaching the wealth of the Grahams. Despite the huge income gap, the topic was not at all frivolous to Reston, who understood that his children would never face the economic challenges that had shaped him. In a meeting years later in which Kay Graham and Scotty and Sally were reminiscing about their lives to help Kay prepare her own superb autobiography, Reston elaborated on the subject: "It was a very interesting question. I noticed, for example, our own children today are a bit envious of those of us who grew up in the Depression, in the sense that there is confusion about what are they going to do. You were going to get a job; we were not sitting around talking about will I go to law school, will I go into journalism, will I go into business, where will I go to college, all this stuff, you know, that this generation goes through. Poverty made things simple."

Sally and Kay usually did the cooking when the couples vacationed together. But one night the men undertook to prepare dinner, and the event was rare enough that the women remembered it decades later. The men served hamburgers and salad, but with great fanfare prepared a written menu with laughable, faux French names describing the humble fare. The men managed to use every pot in the kitchen and left a complete mess. "We laughed so much and had such a good time," Kay Graham remembered happily. They were young, comfortable, secure, and important. Those sunny days would not last.

The couples became so close that the Grahams decided to make Scotty and Sally the legal guardians of their children. The Grahams had begun to worry about the risks of flying on airplanes together, and rather than go separately, they chose to make careful provision for their children in the event of a disaster. "We loved them [the Restons] in the real sense that we felt the values and the integrity were there," Kay Graham said. "So what we did was ask them if they would take our children if we ever went down in a plane. We willed them the house and a certain amount of money if they had to bring up the children. That only shows how we felt about them."

Phil Graham, rich and powerful by marriage, had high energy and self-confidence that made him at some times a magnetically attractive figure and at others a repellantly, aggressively negative human being. Reston held his own with Graham, but he recalled years later that he was actually intimidated by his friend. "I was in constant awe of Phil," Reston told Kay Graham as she was preparing her memoirs. "I admired him immensely. He seemed to have none of the doubt and tortures I had as a young reporter. I'd never had anything like his confidence." The pleasing Phil Graham was actually a bipolar personality who would charm his friends when he was not shocking them with his rude and aggressive behavior. Graham's dark side often showed itself in his mocking denigration of his wife, often done in public, which made the Restons uncomfortable. "He was brutal, you know," Scotty recalled. "His humor was wounding." When he drank too much, which was not infrequently, he could also be quite profane. "Our problem with him was his vulgarity, his use of vulgar language in front of my wife," Scotty said. "I found it very repulsive and I told him so."

Still the Grahams and the Restons remained great friends. In 1953 the longtime editor of the *Post*'s editorial page resigned because of poor health. Phil immediately offered the job to his friend Scotty. Reston was not really tempted; his loyalty to the *Times* and the Sulzbergers was total and he wisely worried about working for his complicated friend Graham. Reston was also troubled by Graham's open use of his position to back political candidates: he was a major booster of Adlai Stevenson both in the pages of the newspaper and among his powerful friends. But Reston did seek outside advice, most prominently from Lippmann, who urged him to join the *Post* because the *Times* was already a superior paper and the *Post* was very much a work in progress. Moreover, Lippmann did not seem to share Reston's affection for the Sulzbergers.

It was no surprise in small-town Washington that the offer from Graham got back to Arthur Krock. Krock had continued to complain to the publisher about Reston's independence from the normal constraints of the bureau. But he had learned from Sulzberger's rather pointed refusal to do anything about his protests that Reston was destined to succeed him. For Krock it had become a matter of hanging on as long as possible. Krock once encountered Scotty's eldest son, Richard, in a supermarket in Georgetown. Krock was still the bureau chief, but when he said hello to Dick, the young man replied, "Oh, you're the man who works for my father." Krock himself spread the story around Washington as a way of ridiculing Scotty's ambition. But when the Graham offer was laid on the table, Krock knew it was time to get out of the way before he was pushed from New York.

In his memoirs Krock characterized his eclipse as a selfless move in the greater interest of the *Times:*

> By 1953, he [Reston] had made himself, in my opinion, so essential a member of the Times staff that when he was tempted by the prospect of much more money and greater personal publicity by the *Washington Post,* I offered to recommend him for the position I had occupied for twenty-one years – The Washington Correspondent. My proposal was agreeable to the management. It was agreeable to me, since it would enable me to concentrate on my daily and weekly editorial column and dispense with the cares of administration. And, of course, it was agreeable to Reston, fulfilling as it did an ambition of his of which I had long been aware.

Some years later, in an interview for the *Time* magazine cover story on Reston, Krock explained the transfer of power more succinctly, borrowing the famous military circumlocution for defeat: "I didn't retreat. I merely withdrew to a previously prepared position."

Graham took Reston's refusal graciously, but he didn't give up the notion of bringing his friend to the *Post.* In late 1958, in negotiations that continued well into the next year, Graham tried again. This time he offered Reston the title of associate editor, with a vague promise of participating in what "I suppose is called policy making."

He proposed to roughly double Reston's pay to $100,000, including a profit sharing bonus, and give him a regular column and syndicate the column around the country, with any annual proceeds over $40,000 going to Reston. He tossed in the option to buy 1,000 shares of nonvoting Post Company stock. Later he offered a $250,000 life insurance policy, to be paid for by Reston with an interest-free loan from the company, and raised the stock option shares to 3,000. He told Reston that while he delayed a decision he had "blown" $50,000 because the company stock had increased handsomely in the interim. He said he would make Reston an executor of his will, giving him a say in who would control the paper after Graham's death. "If that isn't enough," Graham wrote jokingly in his long-hand proposal to Scotty, "I'll give you Kay, Lally, Donnie, Billy, Steve and Glen Welby," naming his wife, his children, and his country estate. Knowing of Reston's loyalty to the Sulzbergers, Graham even offered some advice on how to cut the cord to the *Times*. He suggested that Reston say "that no one has ever been more fortunately treated and been more appreciative, but that your love of residence in Washington and the unusual chance for participation in ownership offer advantages to your family which the Times could not and should not grant and which you, for the sake of your family, should not decline."

Once again Reston turned him down. In a few more years, there would be one more Graham family effort to lure Scotty Reston away from the *Times,* but by then the move was born of tragedy and desperation.

CHAPTER 14

BUREAU CHIEF

SCOTTY RESTON WAS surely ambitious for himself. Beyond that, however, he was ambitious for his newspaper. He had pressed hard and successfully to permit more interpretive writing in the *Times;* in the process he made it a much better newspaper. Now he wanted to bring in more writers in his own mold. Not satisfied to be the paper's top man in Washington, he wanted his bureau to dominate the coverage of the capital. So when he took over Arthur Krock's chair as the Washington correspondent, Scotty Reston began to change the bureau in a dramatic way. For Krock, being bureau chief meant an orderly and untaxing existence, with much of his energy saved for the evening's social whirl. For Reston, becoming part of the management of the *Times* meant trying to turn his part of the paper's operation into an alert, aggressive organization. The Washington bureau had often served as a dumping ground for reporters who were not making their mark in New York. Reston refused to take the castoffs from the home office and started to recruit the best talent he could, most often outside the existing staff of the *Times*. Just as he had done as a reporter, he set out to shake up the existing order in the bureau and, by example, the entire sleepy world of Washington journalism.

The most important person Reston brought in to help him as bureau chief was Wallace Carroll, whom he had once recommended to Max Ascoli as the start-up editor of the *Reporter* magazine. Carroll, Reston wrote in his memoirs, "could have edited the Gettysburg Address and made it better." Carroll came to Washington from the *Winston-Salem Journal* and he, almost as much as Reston, helped build what was to become the best collection of newspaper journalists under one roof in the capital. It was Carroll, more than Reston, who ran the bureau day-to-day, warred with New York, and handled the personnel problems. As an editor, Carroll was not only good but tough. When David Halberstam joined the *Times* years later, Carroll made him rewrite his first story for the paper five times. Carroll was forceful in describing the state of the newspaper as he found it in 1955. "The *Times* was only a mediocre newspaper then," he said in an interview. "They spent so much money that they were well-thought-of. Old man Sulzberger thought he had a good newspaper because he spent enough money to have a good paper. But they did very little by way of recruiting. News clerks were taken in from New York schools and they made their way to the desk. Their idea was to make things read like the Associated Press. These were the people who set the tone of the *Times*."

The bureau was no prize either. It was staffed, Carroll recalled, "with very mediocre people." They would play pinochle all day over at the Pentagon press room or on Capitol Hill, then come back and pick up the Associated Press stories and write their own versions," Carroll said. "The guy covering the Pentagon was a very charming man, but he'd write the same story every six weeks and New York would put it on the front page every six weeks." Reston remembered that the man covering the Supreme Court would return to the office with the printed opinions of the justices, write a one-paragraph lead, then scissor some selections from the majority opinion, paste them on his copy paper, write a paragraph of transition, then scissor and paste some fragments of the minority opinion. End of story. Reston was so contemptuous of this practice that he uncharitably named the man in his memoirs, calling the technique "the Lew Wood treatment." Carroll blamed Krock for the laxness, saying he thought Krock hadn't really cared about the quality of the bureau. Reston noted that Krock had bothered to hold only two bureau meetings during his tenure, one the day he took over the job as Washington correspondent and one when he relinquished the post to Reston.

The bureau was housed on an entire floor of an undistinguished office building on Farragut Square, just three blocks north of the White House. The reporters sat together in a large newsroom, their desks facing in one direction and so close to each other that they could hear their neighbors' phone conversations if they cared to. The clacking of typewriters as deadline approached produced a kind of white noise that afforded a few hours of relative privacy. Reston installed himself in Krock's old office, a glassed-in space in one corner of the bureau, with his secretary outside. Except when he retreated to write his column late in the day — almost always very late in the day and very close to deadline — the door was open. He was accessible to the staff and enjoyed walking out into the newsroom, seating himself on the corner of a desk, and picking the brains of his reporters. He would make suggestions from his own contacts around town, offer the mildest criticism of the stories already in the paper, all the while puffing on his pipe and acting like an affectionate uncle. "I never saw him get angry with anyone," says Max Frankel, whom Reston recruited to the bureau and who eventually became bureau chief, then executive editor of the *Times*. "I remember once lying to him about some small thing, and then ten minutes later sheepishly going into his office to confess. Even then, he wasn't angry." Reston would ask his reporters where a story came from and then follow up with his own ideas about how it might be advanced. He believed every good scoop would beget another one, and he drove his reporters to keep digging. When he felt something was missing from a story the paper had run, he would engage in a kind of Socratic dialogue with the reporter until, miraculously, the reporter himself would realize what more needed to be dug up.

One of Reston's first new hires was Anthony Lewis, then a reporter on the tabloid *Washington Daily News,* a generally undistinguished product of the Scripps-Howard chain that eventually failed. Lewis was on the verge of winning his first Pulitzer Prize for his coverage of the McCarthy hearings, which Reston probably knew in advance of hiring him. Bringing in Lewis was a bold move. He had already served four years at the *Times* in New York, where, as he put it, he was "hopelessly miscast" working for Lester Markel's Sunday department. Reston assigned him to cover the Supreme Court and the Department of Justice, but not in the Lew Wood way. Reston sent him off for a year's training at Harvard Law School, increasing Lewis's acumen. Reston was especially proud of Lewis and of his own smart choice when Justice Frankfurter called Reston to praise a piece Lewis had written summarizing a set of the high court's rulings. "I can't believe what that young man achieved," Reston remembered Frankfurter's saying. "There are not two justices of the Court who have such a grasp of these cases." Lewis eventually became a contender to be Washington bureau chief, was London bureau chief, and then became a regular columnist for the op-ed page. Years later he was a pawn in a power play inside the paper that resulted in his mentor Reston's first defeat in a long career of masterful inside maneuvering.

To young reporters in Washington, just being noticed by Reston was an unforgettable experience. Tom Wicker, who later succeeded

Reston as bureau chief, remembered the moment he met Reston as if it had happened the day before yesterday. Wicker was involved in a boating accident on the Potomac and his picture appeared in the evening newspaper. He was working for the *Winston-Salem Journal* as their Washington reporter. The following day, Wicker went for lunch in the Senate dining room. As he sat down he realized that Reston, whom he recognized as the most famous newspaperman in the capital at the time, was eating across the table. Wicker thought it impertinent to sit so close to power and edged away. Reston, without preamble, growled: "Wicker, what the hell were you doing in that river?" The perfect ending of the story, Wicker concluded, would have been for the great Reston to offer him a job on the spot. But that came a bit later.

Russell Baker was a young reporter based in London for the *Baltimore Sun* when his lyrical writing style caught Reston's attention. Baker was due to be transferred to the paper's Washington bureau when a letter arrived from Reston. Recalled Baker: "[Reston's] name was typed on the envelope under fancy lettering that said 'The *New York Times* Washington Bureau.' It was a thrilling envelope to look at, and I spent a lot of time enjoying the pleasure of looking at it before slitting it open. Getting a letter from James Reston was even more exciting than getting a letter from James Cagney would have been. I didn't want to spoil it by opening it too soon and discovering it was only a form letter asking for ten dollars to help support the Old Reporters' Home."

"Scotty Reston was the most exciting man in American journalism . . . ," Baker wrote in his memoirs.

He was journalism's new shining star, the man of the future at the *New York Times,* and, so, a celebrity whose career had been reported as fully as an up-and-coming politician's. Even in faraway London, heavily absorbed in myself, I'd been excited to learn the *Times* had given Reston its top Washington job. Maybe a new age had dawned at the *Times,* a paper where dull, plodding earnestness had become such a tradition that *Time* magazine referred to it with a reverential sneer as "the good gray Times."

Baker either saved Scotty's letter for decades or remembered it verbatim, because he reproduced it in full in his memoirs: "This is just a note to tell you how much I have admired some of the dispatches you have sent from London. I was told that you were coming home soon, and I should like very much to have a talk with you. I don't know whether you are wedded to the Sun, but, in any event, I should like to meet you when you get back." Baker remembered being both pained because he felt a strong loyalty to the *Sun,* where he had begun his career, and delighted at the idea that he might one day work for Reston. "I wrote back right away," Baker remembered, saying he was happy at the *Sun* but certainly not "wedded" to it.

After Baker began covering the White House for the *Sun,* he ran into Reston in the pressroom. Baker is an often sardonic man with such a powerful sense of the absurd that covering the predictable rituals of Washington eventually became unbearable for him. He once told me that he knew he had to get out of daily journalism and on to his humorous column when he started thinking that presidential elections really were only "quadrennial exercises," the hackneyed newspaper phrase so overused every four years. Baker vividly remembered first meeting Scotty Reston:

There was an old-fashioned, boyish look about him. With black hair, slightly curly, and a wide mouth that smiled readily, and a brow so serene that it seemed never to have scowled. At first glance he looked as if he might have stepped down from an old photograph over the velveteen settee in a 1912 parlor. The eyes told a rather different story. He had the shrewdest, wisest, most disconcerting gaze I had ever seen on an honest man. Old-fashioned or not, he was the most self-confident person I had ever met, and I liked him instantly. . . . It was love at first sight. Only forty-four years old, he was just a shade too young to be my father. A big-brother perhaps. During the talk that followed I was so dazzled that later I could remember nothing that passed between us.

Reston continued throughout his career to hire the best he could find, with a special eye to finding expertise in specific fields. He understood before many of his contemporaries that the world was getting too complicated for the generalist journalist, and he understood that because he recognized his own limitations. Economics was a dark hole of ignorance for him and so, over a lunch at the Metropolitan Club, he hired Edwin Dale from the *New York Herald Tribune.* "Scotty was above all things a good human being," Dale remembered. "He was also a superb reporter, with all the subtle qualities that requires, thinking ahead on events, creating the correct distance in relationships with important people, neither too close nor too hostile, and it was in the days when it wasn't quite so fashionable to be too hostile toward the government. He was a good recognizer of talent. He was not a profound man. He was not an intellectual. He was very thoughtful, but he was not the kind of man, like George Will now or Charles Krauthammer, who can quote by the yard from old Kierkegaard. He was not that deeply read, although he read plenty. His reporting, even as bureau chief, remained top, 100 percent quality forever."

Dale believed himself to be more conservative politically than the *Times* and most of his colleagues. "Reston was a scrupulously fair man," Dale recalls. "I don't know if he had any political passions at all. If forced under penalty of death, I certainly would not put him down as a conservative, but I would say it only that way. I never felt any pressure to alter a story."

To help Dale on the economics beat, Reston hired Richard Mooney, who had first met Reston in 1955 when Mooney was a Neiman Fellow at Harvard and Scotty was a guest speaker. "Everyone in the room was hoping to catch his eye and be swept away to Washington," Mooney remembered. "Well, it didn't happen." But two years later, the dream came true and Mooney went to work for Reston in Washington. What was it like to work under Scotty? "Wonderful. Scotty had hired quite a few people of my age, most over six feet tall, and one noticed that. Russ Baker, Allen Drury, Tom Wicker, and I. But when you think about it, it's what short people do." Mooney found Reston loyal and protective of his men in the endless battles over turf and style the bureau fought with New York, often wading in the next morning to avenge some slight inflicted by editors on his reporters' copy. "It was just wonderful the way that this great man, this imposing, important journalist, was looking after his flock," Mooney said. The two men felt a mutual loyalty and respect, but like many of the people who worked for Reston, they were not close personal friends. "While I fancied I was close to him, there were parts of Scotty that I just didn't know about," Mooney said. "He was a cagey fellow and kept some things to himself." Yet, years later, when Reston desperately needed a friend and a loyal sidekick, he sought out Dick Mooney.

Reston's desire for more and more expertise in the bureau led him to hire John Finney to cover science and atomic energy. Reston had quizzed Jerome Weisner, then president of MIT, and James Bryant Conant, a former president of Harvard, in an attempt to find a scientist who could write for the lay reader. Reston was advised that all the good scientists either could not write well enough or were getting paid too much for their services to make the transition to newspapering. So he hired Finney, a good, smart writer Reston figured could learn the necessary science. Like the others, Finney remembers the protection Reston offered from the inevitable assaults on his handpicked high-profile reporters. Finney had done a series of stories about how scientists were playing both sides of the street, advising the government on policy, then accepting high-paying jobs with companies seeking government contracts. The pieces annoyed the president's science advisor, who complained to Reston. Scotty convened a sort of trial over lunch at the Metropolitan Club, with the advisor and his reporter. At the end of the lunch, Reston delivered the verdict to the advisor: "I think John has a good case."

Reston tried to mold his reporters to his own, highly successful, techniques. Shortly after joining the bureau, Finney made an appearance on the weekly news show *Meet the Press*. "In my nervousness I got rather prosecutorial," he remembered. "There were calls from New York asking who was the new district attorney you hired? Scotty called me aside and said, 'Now John, there are several ways to ask questions. In most cases it's best to be genial and talk in a cooperative kind of way. That gets the most information out of people. Sometimes they will stonewall you and then you have to get tough.'"

Reston was not in any sense a self-indulgent man, but there were limits to his Presbyterian austerity. Finney remembers Scotty asking him to take him to see Hyman Rickover, the ascetic navy admiral known as the father of the nuclear submarine. They had lunch with Rickover in his office; the fare was a boiled egg, saltines, and an apple. On the way back to the office, Reston took Finney to the Metropolitan Club. "Let's get something to eat," he said.

Reston did enjoy his company perquisites. Finney recalls the story of a top editor from New York calling to ask that the bureau car be sent to pick him up. Sorry, there is no bureau car, the editor was told. Every bureau has a car, the editor barked. An investigation was launched and it was discovered that there was indeed a bureau car. It was the Mercedes parked in Reston's garage.

Not everyone loved Reston, and Reston did not love everyone who worked for him. Although he had hired Allen Drury from the

Washington Evening Star, Reston found the congressional coverage he provided rather ordinary. The reason was that Drury had larger ambitions. He was busy writing a novel and didn't let his day job impinge on that effort. When Drury published *Advise and Consent,* winning the Pulitzer Prize and becoming wealthy in the process, Reston was a bit stingy with his compliments. He left it to Finney and others in the bureau to host a celebratory party. Scotty Reston read very little fiction himself; the notion that one of his reporters favored that sort of literary endeavor left him cold.

Drury's eventual departure was, however, instructive. He departed not because of his literary success but because of his frustration at the newspaper. Reston was winning the battle to write his own stories and analysis in a style that was not pedestrian, but he had not yet fully secured that privilege for others. When Drury died in 1998, Russell Baker wrote this account of their unhappiness:

> Both of us came to the *Times* in 1954 with over-inflated expectations. These had been raised by James B. (Scotty) Reston, who ran the Washington bureau and had hired us. Afterward we laughed a bit sourly about Scotty's power, when the hiring was going on, to "take you to the top of the mountain" and show you an improbably glorious future on the *Times.* It did not take long for Allen to realize what a long climb it might be up that mountain. He had a reputation as an elegant writer when he came to the paper. Scotty Reston was then trying to persuade the *Times* to write plain English, and it was assumed that Allen was brought in to promote this campaign. He tried. The results depressed him. In those days plain English was under suspicion at the *Times.* Many stories read as if written by a Henry James imitator with a bad hangover. Incomprehensible English was accepted as evidence of the honest, if inarticulate, reporter; plain English bothered people. Allen was soon finding his pieces being melted down into gray lead or being asked to rewrite them in murkier English.

There were others with whom Reston did not see eye to eye and who suffered for that. The most serious criticism of his reign as bureau chief came from the women – the very few women – who worked there as reporters. The old college athlete, Scotty saw the office as a virtual locker room where men could be men. He rarely used profanity in conversation outside the paper, but in the news-room he could be quite bawdy in his language. When a politician got in trouble, he was heard to say: "Well, he really got his cock caught in the wringer." Once, when Vice President Hubert Humphrey stopped by the office for a drink and a chat, Reston summoned his clerk James Sterba and instructed him to escort Humphrey to the men's room. "The vice president has to take a piss," he said.

"Sally was the only strong woman Scotty could tolerate," John Finney said. There was only one woman working in the bureau when Reston took it over, and she was assigned to cover the First Lady. Another was hired later by Wally Carroll. The most famous story of Reston's Edwardian sexism involved a job offer he made to Mary McGrory, now a distinguished columnist for the *Washington Post* and one of the capital's most thoughtful and incisive journal-ists. In the summer of 1954, McGrory had been writing brilliantly about the Army-McCarthy hearings for the now defunct *Washington Evening Star,* which in its best years had not only McGrory but also David Broder, Haynes Johnson, and Walter Pincus as part of a small but superb staff. "Scotty approached me," McGrory recalled. "He said he didn't really have a slot, but he thought he could fit me in if I were willing to handle the switchboard in the morning. The idea seemed to be that anything would be worth it if you were on the *Times.* You know how Scotty felt about the *Times,* the holy of holies, and kind of a temple of journalism, it was just such a priv-ilege to be there. I thought he must be serious, and anyway I declined. It was such a gross insult there was nowhere to begin, because it showed a mind-set that there was no getting around. I was so embarrassed for him that I really didn't tell anyone at the time."

But the story got around, and after McGrory won a Pulitzer Prize, it became an emblem of Reston's antiquated view of women. He so adored Sally, so valued her full-time support of him, that the notion of a woman working at a real career was almost beyond his imagination. When Ed Dale went off to the Paris bureau, Mooney lobbied Scotty persistently to hire Eileen Shanahan, a former reporter for United Press International and the *Journal of Commerce,* and an official in the Treasury Department. Reston resisted. "We had to lean on Scotty to convince him that a woman could do anything other than cover matters of interest to women," Dale said. It took twelve weeks for him to decide to take on Shanahan, who became one of the most distinguished economics correspondents in Washington.

When she finally joined the bureau, Shanahan immediately felt excluded by the men, who had collectively acquired the nickname Reston's Rangers. One night, about six months after joining the *Times,* Shanahan drew night duty. Scotty was in the office late, saw her working, and said, according to Shanahan, "Ah, honey, they shouldn't make you work nights like this." She turned on Reston and rather forcefully said, "Get out of here with that misplaced chivalry." As she remembers the incident, "He sort of turned and fled. He was a man who was protective of women and didn't understand how condescending that sort of gesture could be. And I think he died not knowing. I always thought Scotty Reston would have been a different man if he would have had just one daughter. He would have had great aspirations for her, not just to marry some swell guy, but in her own right."

Perhaps the most egregious example of Reston's insensitivity to the women who worked for him came in the early 1960s, when a new publisher was named and came to Washington to meet Reston's troops. A dinner was held at the Metropolitan Club for the top men and possible future bureau chief candidates. A lunch was held the next day for the other men in the bureau, also at the Metropolitan Club. The women gathered together to share their anger, and others – not Shanahan – passed it on to the man who was then Reston's deputy, who passed it on to Reston. "If I didn't have the nerve to tell Scotty, I wasn't going to tell someone else," Shanahan remembered. "A few days later, I saw Scotty in his office. He said he was glad to see that I wasn't upset like the others about this silly little business. I said, 'I may have been the most upset.' He uttered this long 'ahhh' and that was the end of it."

About a year after Shanahan joined the bureau, Nan Robertson, a reporter in the New York office, sought a transfer to Washington because her husband was taking a job in the capital. "I had heard that I had three strikes against me," she recounted. "I was a professional woman. Scotty had very old-fashioned notions about women and their lives and about keeping the family together. He did not want women in the bureau. But I thought I would go down and charm the bejesus out of Scotty and tell him I would bring a fresh eye to politics. He looked deeply into my eyes. He had a wonderful, open face and deep hazel eyes. It was the kind of face you want to tell things to. He didn't say no. He was much more oblique when he wanted to be."

After her interview, Reston and Robertson walked out into the newsroom, where they encountered Russell Baker. Knowing what Robertson was looking for, Baker asked Reston whether to encourage or discourage her. "Discourage her," Scotty said. Baker, over what Robertson remembers as a "gloomy lunch," told her that the bureau was no place for a descriptive writer, substituting an account of his frustration for the real reason she was being turned away. "I was heartbroken by it," Robertson remembered. "I loved the *New York Times*." She met her husband in Lafayette Park, told him the bad news, and broke into tears. But when she told editors in New York that she would have to resign and find a job on another paper in Washington, the top brass overruled Reston, marking one of the few instances where his independence in Washington was successfully challenged.

Robertson found the bureau ungenial. "I was not made to feel welcome," she said. "What I found to my astonishment was that Scotty ran the bureau like a men's club. The men didn't even eat lunch with the women, unlike the way it was in New York. The women went out to lunch together and the men went out to lunch together." Robertson observed one of her female colleagues walking through the newsroom saying, "Anyone for lunch?" while the men lowered their heads to avoid the invitation. But Robertson was bolder than the others and soon broke down the lunch barrier.

When Reston died, Shanahan read the obits written by people like David Halberstam and R. W. "Johnny" Apple and Russell Baker, men for whom Scotty had been a mentor. "I can't tell you how full of pain I was reading that and recognizing, for the first time, that he never mentored me," she recalled tearfully. "I called Nan Robertson and we went to the service together. After the eulogies, the young priest asked each of us to think for a moment why we had come. I thought about it. I knew I'd see a lot of people I wanted to see. But that wasn't why I wanted to go. Why did I want to go? In the time available, I figured it out: that despite his great reluctance about women, his total misunderstanding of our aspirations to grow to our full potential – I'm quite sure he must have died without understanding that – despite that, he was so intent upon hiring the best, and hiring the people his people told him were the best, that he managed to overcome that and hire me, with enormous consequences for my life. I don't think I could have become the person I am if I hadn't had those years in Scotty Reston's bureau. I was so personally enriched by being able to be a part of that, and when I thought of that, the pain went away."

CHAPTER 15

WHAT'S GOOD FOR RESTON IS GOOD FOR THE *TIMES*

ARTHUR HAYS SULZBERGER remained Scotty Reston's biggest fan among the managers of the paper. On November 7, 1955, the publisher wrote Reston a note saying: "I find I write you almost every Monday to applaud your column of the day before. Today is no exception." And, as usual, Scotty replied: "Thanks for your note. I assure you that the more repetitious these encouraging notes become, the better I'll feel at the beginning of each week."

But there were limits to the family's approbation. As Ike's second term wore on, Reston was getting more and more critical, and this began to irritate his fans the Sulzbergers. Iphigene Sulzberger once wrote to admonish him for being too tough and Scotty wrote back:

I agree that last paragraph is pretty rough; the point could have been made with more grace. But the point is deadly serious: the fact is that anti-intellectualism is a great danger to our society, as you know better than I, and the further melancholy fact is that the President has done very little from the very beginning to combat it. It is not alone his temporizing with McCarthy for so long, his acquiescence in the vilification of the foreign service, his indifference to the sacking of George Kennan, or his failure to keep his promise to seek out and bring to Washington the best brains in the country regardless of party, but his insistence on spending his pleasure hours with locker-room cronies.

Reston went on to complain about the guest list for a state dinner held in honor of Queen Elizabeth: "Not a writer, not a scientist, not a university president except his brother. The point is not that he should not have the distillers and the businessmen, but that the others should be so generally ignored."

As Ike's second-to-last year in office began, Arthur Hays sent a handwritten letter saying he too thought Reston had been too tough on Ike. Scotty typed this reply:

> I accept your kind reflections. There is a drop of vinegar in the Scotch blood. It runs to irony and occasionally to sarcasm and sometimes it hurts. Iphigene once chided me obliquely ... and, since I love and respect you both, I welcome these gentle admonitions.
>
> Yet, I demur: not in defense of "snide remarks" – on that I agree – but in defense of the principle that we must report the facts, even when they hurt. . . . I have to tell . . . the plain unhappy truth: the nation faltered in 1956–57 because it lacked energy at the political core. This has been the topic of private conversations here throughout the last year. It has to be reported; otherwise, those who know the truth and who know we know the truth will properly say we are not doing our job. . . . I don't want some dusty professor in the future writing that, out of personal kindness or consideration for the President, the New York *Times* ignored what almost everybody knew to be the truth.

Arthur Hays was by this time in failing health and Reston realized that some of the gentle criticism was prompted by Sulzberger's sympathy for the president's medical problems. When Sulzberger mentioned his own frailties in a note, Scotty tried to rally his old friend and patron: "You see the present misery of your life; I see the glory. Who in our profession has been more faithful in redeeming the obligations of a lifetime? Who has carried the baton over rougher ground? Who has taken from one generation a nobler tradition and sustained and enriched it over so many years? Not the Reids, alas; nor the Hearsts; or the Pulitzers; or anybody else I can think of." This was more than mere flattery. It was also the truth: the *Times* was without doubt the best paper in America and it was steadily growing even better.

Sulzberger understood Reston's part in the progress the paper was making and steadily rewarded him. In 1952, for example, Sulzberger granted Reston a $2,500 "expense allowance" that was to be paid quarterly, apparently without too much fuss about accounting for its uses. Explained Sulzberger: "I believe this to be a thoroughly legitimate allowance considering the entertaining you and Sally have to do, the cost of which can not always be covered by an expense report." By early 1953 Reston was the tenth-highest-paid member of the *Times* staff, behind a group of editors and a few correspondents like Cyrus L. Sulzberger and Arthur Krock. Reston had also begun to get stock in the still family-owned company, and by the middle of the 1950s he owned fifty shares of the closely held voting stock, for which he had to pay out of withheld salary. Later, nonvoting stock was given to him as part of a deferred compensation program. The elusive bureau car that was controlled by Scotty was authorized in 1958, along with a driver and with instructions from Sulzberger that the car and driver were to be left for the bureau when Scotty and Sally went on vacation. The Restons continued to visit the

Sulzbergers, both in the city and at their huge country place. Often the visits were followed by notes from Sulzberger's office announcing the return of a pipe or a raincoat or a pair of cufflinks left behind.

There were little tokens as well. When the publisher developed a problem with his feet, he gave his old shoes to Reston, prompting Scotty to joke that he had literally stepped into the publisher's shoes. AHS dispatched a pair of bedroom slippers he had bought in London that he could not wear comfortably, noting that he hoped "neither your feet nor your head have grown in the last few years." Later, a pair of boots came Reston's way, prompting him to remark in his thank-you note that wearing them made him feel like "the central character in High Noon."

In September 1957 Sulzberger was traveling with Iphigene in Asia. While staying in the Strand Hotel in Burma, he suffered a stroke. He recovered, returned to New York, and attempted to continue running the Times Company. But a second stroke the next year while he and his wife were vacationing in Italy further weakened him. Wisely, he had already elevated his son-in-law Orvil Dryfoos to the presidency of the company and thus day-to-day management of the paper fell increasingly to Marian Sulzberger's husband, although not without a good deal of carping and sniping from her frustrated father. Scotty and Sally were about the same age as Marian and had been socializing with her and Orvil for years. The Restons would take the train from Washington, timing their trip to meet Orvil in New York and travel together to the Dryfoos country home in Stamford, Connecticut. The two couples had children of about the same ages, which made for pleasant family weekends. Marian remembered one such outing when Jimmy Reston interrupted the adults' breakfast to complain he had a mouse in his slipper. The grown-ups shooed him away, doubting that a foot and a mouse could occupy the same slipper. Jimmy returned later, still going on about the mouse. When Sally finally checked, there was, sure enough, a small mouse in the toe of the slipper. "They had bought the slippers so big there was room for both," Marian recalled.

The Restons and the Dryfooses were very close. Scotty's years on the paper made him a kind of mentor for Orvil, and hardly a day went by that they didn't talk. Said Marian, "I think he cared about the family. I think he felt like he was part of the family." Scotty called her "Manny," a family nickname Marian did not particularly like. In 1959 Orv, as he was always called, took Marian and the Restons to the Dorado Beach Hotel in Puerto Rico. In a memo to Frank Cox, the company's chief financial officer, Dryfoos explained that he had been ordered by AHS to take a vacation in order to recover from the stress of settling a strike by the newspaper's deliverymen. He had invited the Restons to join him, he explained, and during the trip had secured Scotty's agreement to stay at the *Times* instead of taking over "complete charge" of another newspaper. The dual-purpose vacation was doubtlessly approved as an expense account excursion. If it was during that trip that Reston decided to stay at the *Times* rather than accept a competing offer from Ogden Reid, owner of the *New York Herald Tribune,* it was well worth the price of the holiday. Most likely he had already decided to stay where he was, turning down this, the second offer from the *Trib.*

Reston had used the entreaties from the *Tribune* for another purpose, as he had done with Phil Graham's offer some years before. Scotty wrote a long letter to Orv arguing that his column should be extended into weekday editions, though he denied that the offer from the *Trib* had anything to do with the discussion: "The only connection between the two is that Reid's suggestions stirred up old ideas and ambitions," Reston wrote to Dryfoos reporting on a discussion the day before between himself and Sulzberger.

He placed the two alternatives before me and left no doubt about his preference: First, in due course, accept the editorship of the Times, or, failing that, stay where I am and add – again in due course – Arthur Krock's column to my present duties.

I tried, rather feebly, I'm afraid, to express my appreciation of his confidence, and I indicated, as always, my preference for the latter course, just as he expressed his preference for the former. . . . If we have to remove doubt now, I think you know my decision would be remain here, but if alternate plans are carefully thought through, we need not anticipate the future or be confronted by troublesome doubts at a moment when calm is essential.

Reston wanted to make sure Dryfoos understood just what his father-in-law's intentions were regarding Reston's future. Even as Scotty expressed his desire to continue on in Washington, he wanted to leave on the table for future consideration the possibility of his one day running the entire paper.

Later in the year, Marian Dryfoos, worried that Reston was getting restive, dictated a letter to Scotty: "Are you unhappy? I have so often said that of all the people I know, you are my choice of what I'd like to be associated with and with whom I'd like to put my trust. . . . Might I add as a true Ochs Sulzberger product, please stop before you leap! s/ Love, Manny." She never sent the letter.

In an undated memo obviously written late in 1958, AHS noted that he planned to tell Krock that as of January 1, 1959, he was to give up one of his three columns to Reston, and after another year, he was to relinquish the other columns to Reston. Krock was to be told that he could continue to write a Sunday "News of the Week in Review" column and whatever analytic Q heads he wanted to. Sulzberger planned to lay out the terms of Krock's eventual departure from the paper, giving him three years' salary spread over five years; but if Krock were to die during that period, the payments would by replaced by a pension for his widow.

In November AHS again wrote to Reston about Krock, saying that if he had to give this document a title, it would be "What's Good For Reston Is Good For The *Times*." At the same time, however, he refused Reston's request to be listed by name in the paper's index so readers could find his pieces more easily. The next month, AHS informed company presidents Amory Bradford and Orv that he had given Scotty a $2,000 raise to $50,000 and had approved the purchase of a car complete with a driver. When word of the car deal reached financial officer Frank Cox, he wrote to Orv saying that the normal way the paper helped correspondents buy cars was to pay half the cost up front, then let the reporter expense the balance over four years in lieu of cabs. But he noted diplomatically that he had no objection to the company's buying and insuring a car for Scotty Reston.

CHAPTER 16

JFK

WHILE SCOTTY AND Sally were almost a part of the Sulzberger-Dryfoos family in New York, their adoptive family in Washington was Phil and Kay Graham. The Restons frequently visited Glen Welby, the Graham estate in northern Virginia, and both families fondly remembered the easy times they had together. They both recalled a sign posted by the long entrance to the estate that warned: "Slow Children." Scotty delighted in asking Phil whether or not there were any fast Graham children. Kay recalled how Phil and Scotty would go off alone for long talks about the *Post* and about Washington politics. Phil regularly badgered Scotty about joining the *Post* and Reston kept turning him down. Scotty still objected to the way Phil Graham used his ownership of the paper to insert himself into the political scene. He urged Phil to follow the Sulzberger-Dryfoos example of a studied independence from public partisan activity, to no effect. In 1960 Phil Graham initially supported Lyndon Johnson for the Democratic nomination, then turned into a full-bore enthusiast for Jack Kennedy. He tried to enlist Reston as well, but Scotty was much more skeptical.

The Grahams got to know Jack Kennedy in the late 1950s when he moved into a Georgetown house and became part of the social circle the columnist Joseph Alsop constructed as his way of gathering news. Kay Graham recounts a rather embarrassing evening at Alsop's salon when Phil drank too much and, "visibly and audibly out of control," lectured Jack Kennedy on why he was too young to run for president in 1960. Kennedy displayed the coolness and control for which he was already known, treating Phil Graham as if he were stone sober. He patiently explained that if he didn't run in 1960, he'd wind up serving another term in the Senate, thus becoming "a mediocre senator and a lousy candidate." Kay later recalled: "I was thoroughly impressed by this and each time I saw Senator Kennedy I grew more impressed."

When it became obvious that Kennedy was going to win the nomination, Phil Graham became an important go-between, trying to get Lyndon Johnson on the ticket as the vice presidential nominee. When the effort succeeded, he became a hearty supporter of the Kennedy-Johnson ticket, as did Kay. She remembered trying to convince Marian Dryfoos of Kennedy's worth, while the two were having a swim at their hotel in Los Angeles during the convention. Shortly after, she and Phil hosted a dinner at Kay's mother's house in Washington for Kennedy, Marian and Orvil, and the Restons. The Grahams felt the *Times* families were insufficiently enthusiastic about Jack Kennedy and "wanted to let Kennedy sell himself to the *Times*." Kennedy arrived alone, driving up to the house in a convertible with the top down. But the Restons remembered most a question Sally popped to Kennedy that was, in retrospect, alarmingly prescient. "What will you do about Cuba?" she asked. Kennedy looked at her with complete surprise, as if he already knew there would be trouble ahead. No one remembers his answer, if he ever gave one.

Unlike the Grahams, and a coterie of reporters who became Kennedy acolytes, Scotty was quite skeptical about Jack Kennedy. During his days in London before the war, Reston had heard Jack's father pushing his isolationist line as American ambassador and had disliked him for it. "My first instinct," Scotty recalled, "was to compare President Kennedy to his father. He had all the old man's charm and many of his wayward habits, but unlike his father, he knew the world was round, and was loyal to his party and to his allies. He was a little too clever and fancy for my taste, but he was intelligent, half Irish and half Harvard, irresistibly witty, and like all the Kennedys, recklessly handsome." Reston also disapproved of the very close relationship between Arthur Krock and the Kennedy family. He wanted to avoid, as he put it later, "playing footsie" with the Kennedys the way Krock had.

Two years before Kennedy was nominated, during the midterm elections of 1958, Reston covered Jack's appearance in West Virginia, one of many stops the senator made across the country in support of other candidates whom he hoped would one day return the favor. "He [Kennedy] looked a little self-conscious today riding down the main street of Parkersburg in a scarlet Cadillac convertible with his attractive, young wife," Reston wrote. "Somehow he seemed out of place in a parade with the Democratic donkey and the Parkersburg High School band, especially since few people on Main Street seemed to know who he was or what the noise was all about."

Still, Reston deemed Kennedy a much-improved platform speaker, with "an assurance he did not have two years ago and with a clarity and brevity not usual in political oratory." Reston noted how the Kennedy personality was having its effect, even in Parkersburg: "His clothes and hair-do are a masterpiece of contrived casualness . . . and even with Mrs. Kennedy on the platform, his influence on lady politicians is almost naughty." Reston saw what made Kennedy attractive but was not overawed in the least.

After Kennedy won the nomination in Los Angeles, Reston, just more than a decade older than Kennedy, wrote of the nominee as if he were much, much younger. "He is a remarkably gifted young man," Reston opined, "experienced well beyond the normal expectations of his years, at home in both the intellectual and political institutions of the nation, articulate particularly in the give and take of modern television discussion and debate." He did admire the way Kennedy had taken on the question of his religion, the way he had gracefully passed off ex-president Truman's sharp criticism of his candidacy, and his bold acceptance of a convention-debate challenge by Lyndon Johnson. By October of that election year, Reston had come around to Kennedy, in no small measure because of his own continuing disdain for Richard Nixon.*

In November 1960 Scotty Reston faced his first presidential election night as the Washington correspondent. It was the custom and burden of the capital bureau chief to appear in the New York newsroom and write the main election story every four years. Reston remembered being a bit anxious about the chore. "I was neither calm nor confident," he wrote. "The managing editor, Turner Catledge, an old hand at these parties, was in charge. The newsroom, stretching a full city block from Forty-third Street to Forty-fourth Street, wasn't quite as crowded as Times Square, but almost.... In addition I was surrounded by charts of the states with their electoral votes and batteries of telephones open to our correspondents."

*In a letter to his friend the British philosopher Isaiah Berlin, Phil Graham described his own support of Kennedy as having passed "beyond enthusiasm into passion." He told Berlin of two people who were "closest to our state of mind, in order of non-detachment, Walter Lippmann and Scotty Reston." This is an overstatement of Reston's enthusiasm, given Graham's own unabashed support for Kennedy.

The election was incredibly close: Kennedy won by about one hundred thousand votes, probably thanks to a bit of ballot hanky-panky in Chicago. By midnight, as the second-edition deadline approached, Reston and his editors were far from sure of the result. They, like political reporters since 1948, could not erase the memory of a happy Harry Truman holding up a copy of the *Chicago Tribune* proclaiming "Dewey Beats Truman." After hearing from their correspondents in Chicago and in San Francisco, Reston and Catledge decided to call the election. "Kennedy Elected," blared the headline on the late city final edition, which closed at 3:18 in the morning. They held their breaths and waited for Nixon to concede. No word came from Nixon, and then the two correspondents reported back that neither Illinois nor California was safely in the Kennedy column. Catledge ordered an extra edition, hedging Reston's lead story under the headline "Kennedy Is Apparent Victor." Scotty remembered that he staggered back to Sally and confessed that the whole experience had reminded him of his Grand National steeplechase miscue when he was writing sports for the AP. "All the old immigrant doubts and fears I had long forgotten returned for a few days," he wrote years afterward. Back in Washington, he later shared the night's anxiety with Jack Kennedy, who quipped, "If you think you were scared at the *Times,* you should have seen me."

Scotty Reston was never given to great bursts of praise, especially not of the people he covered, but his column following John Kennedy's stirring inaugural speech was about as glowing as the reserved Scotsman got in print. Reston called the speech "remarkable" for its rhetoric and for the reception it won from quarters as diverse as Republican conservatives and Democratic liberals. He noted with happiness the "revival of the beauty of the English language." But more than that, the speech mirrored the essential Reston: optimistic, moralistic, a paean to the American ideal that the immigrant son of poor and uneducated parents had embraced and had in fact lived. The call to sacrifice for the national good rang true to his Calvinist upbringing. Wrote Reston: "The evangelical and transcendental spirit of America has not been better expressed since Woodrow Wilson, and maybe not even since Ralph Waldo Emerson." He loved the youthful energy Kennedy brought to national leadership, after worrying about the geriatric later years of Eisenhower. Still, he was too smart, too attuned to the ways of Washington, to be entirely swept away. "All those who praised it [the speech]," he wrote, "cannot possibly be so enthusiastic as they sound, unless they are merely reacting to its style and music." And, he noted at the end of his column, the real cost of what Kennedy called for had not been discussed: "Later on he will present the bill to carry this out, and then we will find out who was for this speech and who was against it."

The commentary was vintage Reston: careful praise, admiration with an eye to reality. As much as he liked the speech, and the tone and energy of the new administration, he still had business to conduct with the newcomers. Reston immediately moved to ensure that his interests and those of the paper were protected. He had just been the subject of a *Time* magazine cover story anointing him the most powerful journalist in Washington. He did not need the newsmagazine to bolster his sense of power, but he quickly let the Kennedy staff know who was boss.

The day after the inauguration, Scotty called Kennedy's press secretary, Pierre Salinger, to protest the announcement that the president's movements outside the White House would not necessarily be divulged to reporters. "He said you can't do that, you have to tell the press every time he goes out of the White House, no matter where he goes, because if something happens when he's out of the White House we wouldn't be in a position to cover it," Salinger recalled. "I said, 'Well I don't think anybody is going to attack the president.' We talked for about an hour. He finally convinced me I should tell the press when the president goes out of the White

House. I did discuss it with Kennedy and he wasn't very much in favor of it, but he decided I should go ahead and do it."

Hugh Sidey, then White House correspondent for *Life* magazine, was one of the reporters who had grown especially close to Kennedy and the new president's inner circle. He remembers Reston trying to instruct Salinger on how important it was for the White House to place its calculated leaks in the *Times*. The newspaper's White House man, Bill Lawrence, was, like Sidey and *Newsweek*'s Ben Bradlee, part of the press corps closest to the Kennedy machine. But one of the men Reston had brought to the paper, Tom Wicker, was also covering the White House and was being shut out in favor of the insiders. Reston took steps to make sure his man also got access. He lectured speechwriter Ted Sorensen on the importance of being fair to Wicker, pointing out, "We were here before you came and will be here after you leave."

When Kennedy began holding regular press conferences and opening them to television cameras, Reston immediately saw the threat that direct access to the nation would pose to columnists like himself. He famously denounced the television news conference as "the goofiest idea since the hula-hoop." Ted Sorensen thought Reston objected because, having covered the verbally challenged Eisenhower, he feared this new president would make some huge mistake, live on television, and the wise men from the print press would be unable to correct the error. But Kennedy was brilliantly deft on camera. Performing live on television was the cleverest political move he could have made. With television he could reach past the newspapers, displaying his good looks, his charm, his humor, and his intelligence directly to the electorate. It was the beginning of the end – but only the beginning of the end – of the enormous power columnists like Reston wielded in America.

The televised news conference attracted a clamoring press eager for exposure on the tube. In March 1961 Reston denounced the new horde who were destroying the intimacy he had enjoyed with presidents past. "There are more reporters here than lobbyists," Reston wrote, "and they no longer cover the President; they smother him." Presidential press conferences, once held informally around the president's desk, had to be moved to the huge new State Department auditorium, which Reston decided was "a dandy place for a heavyweight boxing championship, but asking questions in it is like making love in Grand Central Terminal." Reston recognized his own role in swelling the crowd, since he brought his little bureau army, all carefully prepared with an agreed-upon list of questions Reston most wanted answered, in the order of their importance. The theory was that no matter who from the *Times* was called upon by Kennedy, the key inquiries would get made. One way to solve the problem of the mass conference, Reston joked in his column, was to "ban all reporters from the New York *Times*. . . . This would solve the crush in a single stroke." What he most missed, though, was the chance to talk with the president without the whole world watching, let alone all the other reporters in Washington. Reston worked best in private.

While the bureau chief was trying to get Wicker included in the inner circle of White House correspondents, he was having the opposite problem with Bill Lawrence, who was increasingly seen as too close to the Kennedy group. Scotty Reston valued access, but he understood the damage a loss of the appearance of fairness could cause the paper. During the campaign, Lawrence had not been allowed to write about the Kennedy-Nixon debates because managing editor Turner Catledge worried about Lawrence's adoring JFK coverage.

After the campaign, Reston stewed about the Lawrence problem. Lawrence had tripped up before, during the 1956 presidential campaign, when he brought one of his girlfriends, actress June Lockhart, on a campaign trip carrying *Times* credentials. (When Reston found out about it, he denounced Lawrence as having entered a "second childhood.") During the Kennedy campaign, Lawrence had apparently taken up with a woman not unfamiliar to the Kennedy family, and this, too, deeply offended Reston. Now, with the credibility of the paper's coverage of the president at stake, Reston devised a strategy. Kennedy was scheduled to travel to Vienna for his first summit with Nikita Khrushchev. Lawrence, as senior man on the White House beat, would be expected to cover the meeting. Instead, Reston announced that he would substitute for Lawrence as one of the *Times*men going to Vienna. The veteran Lawrence's reaction to such a loss of face was totally predictable: he resigned from the *Times*. David Halberstam described the ploy as giving Lawrence a "revolver with a bullet in it knowing Bill would pull the trigger." Lawrence promptly found a new job as a correspondent for ABC News, which was then under the direction of his old pal James Hagerty, President Eisenhower's former press secretary.

Reston aimed for a difficult balance: he was quick to complain about access to the president and his staff, but he had strong reservations about invading the president's privacy. Tom Wicker recounts the story of how the bureau handled the rumor, which surfaced in right-wing hate sheets, that Jack Kennedy had been married to another woman before he married Jacqueline Bouvier. As whispering about the former marriage spread, deputy bureau chief Wally Carroll dutifully assigned a *Times* reporter to look into it. He was getting nowhere when the effort came to Reston's attention. Reston, in Wicker's words, "erupted." Scotty was outraged, not by the reporter's failure to turn up anything, but by the paper's wasting its time pursuing nebulous, and in Reston's view, irrelevant, scandal. "I will not have the *New York Times* muckraking the president of the United States," Wicker quotes Reston as declaring. And Reston was not alone in his reaction. The prevailing ethic at the time was to avoid discussion of the private lives of public figures, unless there was some evidence that their private behavior affected the performance of their public duties.

The constant challenge was to maintain access for himself and his correspondents but still be fair and thorough in their reporting of the Kennedy presidency. It was not an easy task. One of the toughest balancing acts came early in the Kennedy years. In early April 1961, a supposedly secret CIA plan to send Cuban exiles back into Cuba to overthrow Fidel Castro had become a common topic of conversation among the Cuban émigré community in Miami. The plan was even widely discussed on the streets of Havana. Several enterprising newsmen nibbled at the story, including Karl Meyer, an editorial writer at the *Washington Post,* who had submitted a piece on the planned invasion to the *New Republic.* When White House advisor Arthur Schlesinger Jr. showed an advance copy of the piece to Kennedy, the president ordered him to stop it. Schlesinger contacted Gilbert Harrison, publisher of the magazine, who agreed "like a gentleman and a patriot," in Schlesinger's words, to drop the article.

According to Richard Reeves's account in his history of the Kennedy presidency, the next shoe dropped on April 6. Someone – Reeves says it was a *Times* employee – called the president and read a story slated to run in the paper the next day. It described the invasion plan and characterized the timing as "imminent." The president, according to Reeves, "blew up, banging down the phone and throwing around words like 'treason.'" When he calmed down, he phoned Orvil Dryfoos and asked him to kill the story.*

The editors in New York were already concerned about the piece. The author of the report was Tad Szulc, who had been covering the rumored action from Florida. He had pegged the invasion date at

---

*In his memoirs, Reston himself never mentioned the presidential phone call to Dryfoos. Harrison Salisbury, relying on interviews with Reston and Turner Catledge, concluded that the call was never made.

April 18 and said categorically that it was a CIA-sponsored operation. The story was to run on the top part of page one, "above the
fold" in newspaper parlance, with a four-column headline. When
the bullpen editors who read all page-one stories reviewed Szulc's
story, they had immediately toned it down, striking the April 18 prediction and characterizing the invasion instead as "imminent." Managing editor Catledge quickly decided to show the story to Dryfoos.
The *Times* was already being tagged as pro-Castro because of sympathetic reporting on his revolution by correspondent Herbert Matthews.
Catledge reasoned that if the *Times* was now seen as tipping off Fidel
about the exile force, the paper would be excoriated for helping the
dictator stay in power.

Catledge and Dryfoos called Reston on the speakerphone to find
out what he thought. Reston said he would make some inquiries. He
went to see CIA director Allen Dulles, who had been retained from
the Eisenhower administration, at his home. Dulles told Reston that
the *Times* should not publish the story, for national security reasons,
but that if it did, it should leave the CIA out of it. Reston reported
back to Catledge, who remembered Reston's advice as being to kill
the entire piece. Reston's version was that he had advised getting rid
of the word *imminent* but not killing the piece entirely. On April 7
the story appeared on the front page, under a one-column headline
that described the training of anti-Castro guerrillas in Florida. Oddly,
after all the anguish, the ending of the story, on an inside page, was
followed by a short wire service piece quoting a CBS news report
that preparation for the invasion was in its "final stages."

Kennedy was furious even with the toned-down version of the
story. Dulles complained that Washington needed a British-style
Official Secrets Act. Kennedy urged newspapers to determine the
worth of stories not just by asking "Is it news?" but by weighing
the "interest of national security." Thinking about the story years
later, Reston wrote that he still thought he was right to advise against

predicting the timing of the invasion. But his role even in toning down the story became embroiled in internal *Times* politics and myth making. The bullpen editors had objected strongly to being overruled by Dryfoos and Catledge, mostly because they operated in a kind of bizarre world where, despite their rank well below the publisher and the managing editor, they usually ran the front page the way they wanted to. Moreover, the story was almost exactly right; the invasion took place on April 16. Later, even Kennedy himself fed the notion that Reston and the *Times* had been derelict in not printing all that they knew about the invasion. In a session with Catledge after the invasion fiasco, JFK said – perhaps wishfully, perhaps sarcastically – that if the *Times* had printed the full story, the invasion plan would have collapsed and he would thus have been saved from the worst embarrassment of his presidency. But of course it had been Kennedy himself who tried to kill the story.

"National security" considerations put tough demands on the press. No editor wants to be responsible for the loss of American soldiers. In the era of the Cold War, they were keenly aware of the need not to compromise an administration's ability to maintain the nation's defense. Reston was involved in another incident before the Bay of Pigs in which those concerns led the paper to ignore a good story for the sake of the national interest. For some years during the Eisenhower presidency, the United States had been flying high-altitude spy missions over the Soviet Union in an ominous-looking supersonic jet called the U-2. The Soviets knew about the overflights and had quietly protested them to Washington. The most informed members of the press corps, including Reston, knew about the spy flights. One *Times* correspondent had actually spotted one of the sleek, black aircraft at a military base in Europe, but when he made inquiries about its purpose, the director of the CIA asked Arthur Sulzberger to call off the reporter. AHS checked with Reston and Reston agreed.

Then, in May 1960, the Soviets shot down a U-2 flown by Francis Gary Powers. The Eisenhower government decided to deny that the plane had been spying, explaining lamely, given the extent of knowledge about the flights, that Powers had been on a weather reconnaissance mission and had lost his way, drifting into the Soviet Union's airspace. One rationale for lying was that the airplane had been designed and the pilots trained to self-destruct rather than risk capture if shot down. The United States thought there would be no evidence to rebut the weather-plane canard. But Powers was captured alive, complete with his government-issue suicide pills, and was brought to Moscow, along with the wreckage of his plane, as props in a little Cold War theater. A major summit meeting had been scheduled in Europe for that month; when Khrushchev went to Paris he had plenty with which to embarrass the Americans. Reston was witness to that debacle and reflected in his memoirs about whether he and the newspaper had been right to disclose nothing about the spy flights. "Now, I am not so sure," he concluded decades later. His later doubts, however, were expressed in a time quite different from those in which the decision to withhold news of the spy plane had been made.

When Eisenhower lied about the U-2, it was hardly the first time the government had tried to deceive the people. It was certainly not the first time the press knew that the government was lying and, with a perhaps misplaced sense of patriotism, went along for a time. But the ridicule heaped on Ike and the United States did constitute a turning point, if not the decisive turning point, in the relationship between the press and the government in Washington. Max Frankel, who patterned his own tenure as Washington bureau chief on the style and manner of Reston, even wearing bow ties and smoking a pipe like Scotty, was based in Moscow when the U-2 incident happened. "That was the beginning of the end," said Frankel, "although the era of good feeling had begun to end with those of us who watched the press carrying water for Joe McCarthy. That planted the seeds of adversarial journalism in us."

Reston remained largely sympathetic to those in power and used that sympathy to get them to tell their stories to him. But watching the president of the United States lie, rather stupidly and, worse, ineffectually, made the Washington press corps a bit more skeptical, a bit more leery of collaborating with the government. The practice certainly didn't end, as we shall see, especially on national-security matters. But after the Bay of Pigs, the bureau under Reston produced a tough series on the CIA's shenanigans around the world, a project that would have been unthinkable some years before.

CHAPTER 17

AT THE SUMMIT

THE SUMMIT MEETING in Vienna began with an invitation from Khrushchev to Kennedy in February 1961, only a month after the new president took office. The invitation had been renewed, somewhat to the surprise of the Americans, just after the Bay of Pigs debacle. The Soviet leader had been haranguing the United States about the need for a new arrangement in Berlin that would effectively have given the Soviets control of the divided city. With a bellicose Khrushchev and the Bay of Pigs darkening the background, the stakes at the summit were high. Kennedy felt he needed to impress upon Khrushchev, face-to-face, American resolve to resist Soviet expansion, especially regarding Berlin. More than that, he felt he needed to show the Soviet leader that despite the blunder in Cuba, he was a president in command of himself and his country.

Before he left Washington for Vienna, Reston had extracted a promise that the president would see him privately after the summit meeting. The exclusive arrangement was designed to throw Reston a bone and to smooth his relationship with the administration. Reston traveled to Europe alone, separate from the presidential party, stopping in several capitals to catch up with his old sources. He arrived in Vienna just as the summit began.

Over two long days, beginning on Saturday, June 3, Kennedy and Khrushchev sparred. The wily Marxist was unyielding, tying Kennedy in rhetorical knots. The president's weak performance shocked the senior American diplomats present. "He's a little bit out of his depth," said one. "He's dancing. All he's doing is dancing," said another. Every effort Kennedy made to warn the Soviet leader of the dire consequences if Moscow made a move to oust the Western powers from West Berlin was met with bluster, even anger. "The USSR will sign a peace treaty [with East Germany] at the end of this year," Khrushchev said flatly. "Would this treaty block access to Berlin?" Kennedy asked. "Yes," said Khrushchev. Kennedy replied that signing a treaty was "not a belligerent act" but denying access to Berlin was, and the United States would not stand for it.

At a ceremonial closing lunch at the Soviet embassy, Kennedy presented Khrushchev with a model of the Revolutionary War battleship *Constitution*. Kennedy added a little soliloquy about how after the wars of the past, nations could recover rather quickly, but nuclear wars would destroy countries for generations. The luncheon was planned to be the end of the summit. But Kennedy was unhappy and dissatisfied. He asked for ten minutes alone with the Soviet leader. "This is the nut-cutter," Kennedy told Secretary of State Dean Rusk.

Ten minutes after warning Khrushchev of the possibility of war, Kennedy was in the American embassy. On instructions from press secretary Salinger, Reston had slipped into the embassy early to await the president. He had spent the preceding hours ducking his fellow correspondents so they would not know what he was up to.

Scotty waited in the embassy more than an hour. Suddenly Jack Kennedy arrived. "He was wearing a hat – unusual for him – and he pushed it down over his forehead, sat down on a couch beside me, and sighed," Reston remembered. The room was dark, the curtains pulled to hide Reston from his colleagues waiting outside for a promised official statement.

"How was it?" Reston asked. The answer from John Kennedy was likely the most alarmingly candid conversation any reporter has ever had with any American president.

Reston, describing the encounter in Vienna in his memoirs, makes no mention of the ground rules under which he met Kennedy in the embassy. Most likely they were what today would be described as "deep background." This understanding means the journalist is free to write what he knows of what the principal has said, without ever quoting or in any way acknowledging that the information had come from the source himself. Certainly Kennedy wanted the world to know what had happened. But to describe the disastrous meeting himself would have been to send a cold shiver of fear around the world. His brutal frankness about how badly he felt he had done was perhaps indiscreet, but he also knew he had in Reston a journalist capable of dealing with sensitive information in a careful way.

And that is what Reston did. In a *Times* story that appeared two days after the summit, Reston wrote with nuance and care, never mentioning his direct conversation with Kennedy, never advertising his extraordinary access or telegraphing the president's amazing candor. He did just what Kennedy had expected him to do and just what he should have done. He let his readers know the seriousness of the summit encounter without being sensational or alarmist.

"Mr. Kennedy's reaction [to Khrushchev] was not unlike that of many Western officials who have negotiated with the Russians for the first time," Reston wrote knowingly, but with great understatement.

He approached the conversations thinking he knew what to expect. But nevertheless he was astonished by the rigidity and toughness of the Soviet leader.

... The President left the Austrian capital in a somewhat pessimistic mood about the possibility of agreement with the Soviet Union on Germany and Berlin, nuclear testing and disarmament, and a wide range of differences over the uncommitted and under-developed nations.

Reston characterized the discussions as "acrimonious" and went on to say, without citing his source, that

the President definitely got the impression that the German question was going to be a very near thing, a very delicate and perhaps even a dangerous thing. . . . He also has the impression that there will be very little chance of reaching agreement with Mr. Khrushchev on any of the other major questions now dividing the East and the West. . . . In short, the President's reaction was to confirm rather than minimize his opposition to the present trend of Soviet policy and to increase his determination to look to the defenses of the United States.

And if the careful reader had still not understood that the summit had been ominous, Reston made it clear: "The Vienna talks left the President with the uneasy feeling not only that there was a great gulf between Soviet and United States policy on many fundamental questions, but also that it was extremely difficult even to discuss the matter sensibly because the two sides were giving different values to the words and the terms used."

Reston's account was by far the most informed of those published after the summit. Kennedy later conveyed his pessimism to other columnists — such as Joe Alsop, whom he saw in London on his way home; his friend Charlie Bartlett, the Washington correspondent for the *Chattanooga Times;* and James Wechsler of the *New*

York Post — and to several senators, congressmen, and members of his staff. But it was Reston who was sitting there when the summit was over and it was to Reston that John Kennedy gave his most candid reaction to the Khrushchev encounter. In retrospect, the substance of the conversation between Reston and Kennedy does not seem calculated. It was, as Reston sensed immediately, "no bullshit." And Reston was not there because he was one of Kennedy's intimates; Reston had already had a few shoving matches with the administration. He was in the embassy in the first place because Kennedy cared that Reston have a positive attitude toward him and his administration, that Reston not feel cut out. Reston wasn't a friend, but what he thought and wrote about the government mattered greatly. Kennedy's almost shocking candor was a measure, not of his indiscretion, but of his understanding that Reston knew how to use what he learned, without compromising the president. At some level, John Kennedy knew that the American public needed to understand just how things stood with the Soviet Union. And he knew he could trust Scotty Reston to paint that picture accurately.

Critics have suggested in hindsight that Reston was wrong not to write more directly and more extensively about what Kennedy said in Vienna about his intentions in Vietnam because it was at this moment that the seeds of the disastrous U.S. war in Southeast Asia were sown. Reston came to believe this as well, connecting the Vienna conversation to Kennedy's later moves to send more American advisors to assist the South Vietnamese army in its fight against the Vietcong. In his memoirs he concluded Kennedy "had started the slide." But recent histories, particularly David Kaiser's *American Tragedy: Kennedy, Johnson, and the Origins of the Vietnam War*, dismiss the notion that the confrontation with Khrushchev led inevitably to the disaster in Vietnam. There were numerous subsequent occasions when Kennedy resisted the urgings of various advisors to escalate American involvement. Vienna was not a magic moment that triggered the coming debacle. Kennedy would have his share of responsibility for the war in Vietnam, but in this case Reston's critics are wrong. Reston behaved with consummate professionalism in his handling of this extraordinary piece of access to history in the making. He understood its importance, he conveyed it to his readers, and he protected his future access to the most powerful man on the planet.

The Berlin crisis continued to stew through the summer. Khrushchev alternated between threats to destroy Germany and promises not to block Western access to Berlin. Meanwhile, the economic and political oppression in the East Bloc sent a flood of refugees into West Germany that profoundly embarrassed the Soviets. In early August, Kennedy went on television with a stunning statement: "An attack on [Berlin] will be regarded as an attack upon us all." It was an alarming speech, warning that if force were required "American families will bear the burden of these requests. Studies or careers will be interrupted; husbands and sons will be called away; income in some cases will be reduced. But these are burdens which must be borne if freedom is to be defended." He was desperately trying to signal Khrushchev of his resolve to maintain access to West Berlin. To do so he was willing to speak openly to Americans about the possibility of war, even nuclear war. In mid-August, Khrushchev took the opening Kennedy had left for him. He did not interrupt Western access to Berlin; instead he sealed up East Berlin behind a wall. At the end of the month, the Soviets tested a hydrogen bomb in Siberia, ending a long test moratorium both nations had observed. The Soviet move abrogated a promise not to test first that Khrushchev had made to Kennedy in Vienna. ("Fucked again," said Kennedy to his brother Robert, when they got the news of the test.) The next weekend Kennedy invited Scotty Reston to his family compound on Cape Cod.

Kennedy was still trying to prove his resolve to Khrushchev. The president believed that after Vienna, the Soviet leader did not take his vow to fight for Berlin seriously. At the Kennedy home in Hyannis Port, the president told Reston that he was determined not to be forced out of Berlin but didn't want to say so again, perhaps escalating the ongoing crisis. It would be "helpful," Reston recalled Kennedy saying, for Reston to write on his own authority that this was still Kennedy's firm position. In a column on September 6, ostentatiously datelined Hyannis Port, Reston did just that.

It is now just three months since [President Kennedy] met Nikita Khrushchev in Vienna. Since then the jovial evaporationist has been threatening, every hour on the hour, to obliterate the human race, but Kennedy remains calm and even confident.

He seems perplexed about Khrushchev rather than angry. What puzzles him is why he cannot get down to rational discussion with the Soviet leader about the factual situation in Berlin. . . .

The striking thing about him [Kennedy] is that, after seven months of disappointing negotiations with the Russians, the allies and the Congress, he is taking his frustrations with such equanimity. . . . He is not personal or vindictive in any of his comments about these things. . . .

The main danger is that this calm Kennedy appraisal of his responsibilities may be misjudged in Moscow. . . . Any action which closes U.S. access to Berlin will certainly lead to counter reaction by the West, first in the UN, then in the field of economic countermeasures, then, if necessary, with an airlift or conventional military action on the ground to force the passage of supplies.

Any assumption, however, that the U.S. would acquiesce in the defeat of its compound on the ground without resorting to the ultimate weapons of nuclear power would be highly reckless. For nuclear war in such circumstances is not "unthinkable." It is in cold fact being thought about and planned, and Mr. Khrushchev, unless he wishes to preside over a Soviet wasteland, next door to 800 million Chinese, would be well advised to take this into account. . . .

The ironic thing about all this is that it is Kennedy, rather than Khrushchev, who is ready for peaceful and competitive co-existence. It is Khrushchev who is trying to direct the course of history and Kennedy who is ready to accommodate himself to history on the basis of "co-existence." The question is whether Khrushchev will allow an honorable accommodation to take place.

After the interview, Kennedy and Reston took a stroll on the beach along Nantucket Sound. Reston used the moment to ask the kind of broad question he loved to pose, just to see what sort of mind was at work. "What did the president want to achieve before he rode down Pennsylvania Avenue with his successor?" Scotty remembered asking Kennedy. "He was embarrassed by the question," Reston recalled, "and finally said he had never thought about that." Kennedy was too preoccupied trying to avert nuclear disaster to consider his long-term agenda. And he was a pragmatic politician who spoke eloquently but acted cautiously.

The column that came out of this weekend in Hyannis Port is quite remarkable. The president of the United States had used Reston to send the most apocalyptic message imaginable: the United States was willing to go nuclear over Berlin. It certainly wasn't the first or last time a president had employed a newspaperman to play a card in a tough game of tacit bargaining. But the stakes in this game were the highest possible, and it was Reston who was the natural messenger. The column he produced is a masterpiece of balance: Reston's rather chatty tone, juxtaposed to the hard warning imbedded in the column, all nicely woven. There was no mistaking from whom the message was coming; the dateline, the tone of authority, the description of the president's state of mind and demeanor, made the source of the piece quite clear.

Both Kennedy and Reston appreciated the need to put the message absolutely correctly. To ensure that, Reston submitted the column, or at least the critical warning paragraphs, to the White House for approval. He told his editors in New York he was doing so, and they agreed. As far as can be determined, this was the only time Reston ever did such a thing. Normally, submitting a written piece for approval by sources is among the most forbidden of all journalistic practices. Reston said later he was "not happy with this selective cooperation between officials and reporters," although he was proud enough of the finished piece to include it in the first collection of his columns, *Sketches in the Sand,* published in 1967. In this case Reston and the *Times* understood the incredible sensitivity of what they were about to publish. It is hard to argue with what he did, given what was at stake.

The subtler question regards what effect this sort of collaboration had on Reston's approach to writing about Kennedy afterward. He certainly produced columns praising Kennedy thereafter, but he had also been supportive beforehand. In April 1962 he wrote a column praising the "informality, dignity and wit" of the administration. He was taken by Kennedy's ability to laugh at himself. "If this were merely a change of style it could be welcomed as an agreeable new aspect of political manners and forgotten," Reston wrote, "but it is more than that. It is a reflection of a serious effort by Kennedy to dispel some of the illusion of political life and deal with things as they are."

Reston's admiration for Jack Kennedy was hardly a rarity at that time; it was hard not to be impressed. But the personal access to the president he had achieved was to prove, in the perilous months ahead, invaluable.

CHAPTER 18

MISSILE CRISIS

IN THE SPRING of 1962, Jack Kennedy was traveling the country, gearing up for the midterm elections that fall. He drew a crowd of more than 200,000 in New Orleans and had an audience of 85,000 in California. Reston noted the rising tide of approval for Kennedy and the role of the mass media in feeding that sentiment. "The increasing power of nationwide mass communications is obviously working to the political advantage of the Kennedys," he wrote in his column on May 9. "Not only is the President dominating the political news on national television, but his only competition in the national magazines seems to be his wife, Jacqueline."

While he admired Kennedy's ability to command attention, he also worried that the president's hold on the mass media was creating a lopsided advantage for the chief executive. "As this trend continues," he wrote, "the dangers are obvious. The opposition can continue to express its feelings on the floor of the Congress, probably in the presence of a handful of members and spectators, but the President has an audience of millions at his command any day he likes. It is not a situation that promises to maintain a political balance of power in the United States."

Reston's concern was reasonable, but the imbalance was more a function of Kennedy's personal appeal than of a structural flaw. The very media attention then overshadowing the opposition would eventually prove as potentially destructive for the executive as it was sustaining in Kennedy's day. And even before that year was out, the ability of the Republicans to attract attention would become an important factor in the most dangerous confrontation of the Cold War.

In the summer of Kennedy's second year in office, intelligence reports coming in to the CIA cited an unusual amount of secretive Soviet activity in Cuba. Thousands of soldiers, hundreds of trucks, scores of military freighters were spotted on the island. CIA director John McCone and his analysts soon determined, with the help of high-altitude photographs taken from a U-2 spy plane, that the Soviet Union was busy installing surface-to-air missiles in Castro's country. McCone was alarmed. Soviet assurances that their military assistance to Cuba was purely defensive didn't ring true to him; the missiles being installed were useless against low-flying planes. He reasoned that the SAMs were to be used to knock out U.S. aerial surveillance over the island so that intermediate-range missiles aimed at the United States could be secretly installed. McCone personally warned John Kennedy of this possibility.

The Soviet ambassador and a secret emissary from Khrushchev who spoke directly to the president's brother Robert assured the administration repeatedly that there was no aggressive intention. Kennedy worried about the missiles. But the advice from the Pentagon and the State Department agreed that Khrushchev might be crazy, but not crazy enough to try to upset the strategic nuclear balance by sticking missiles capable of hitting the southern United States, as far north as Washington, only ninety miles from American shores.

McCone and his agents disagreed with State and Defense and were unhappy about the slowness of the White House to see the real threat in Cuba. Either the director, or those lower down in the agency acting with his knowledge, shared their concerns with members of Congress. Soon two Republican senators, Homer Capehart of Indiana and Kenneth Keating of New York, were publicly chastising the Kennedy administration for its passivity in the face of increased Soviet activity in Cuba. In fact, the administration had been anything but passive. Ever since the Bay of Pigs debacle, an insistent Robert Kennedy had led planning for a variety of operations aimed, ultimately, at unseating Castro. The options ran from subversion to invasion to assassination. Naturally, these plans were very tightly held.

In mid-October, as the Republicans spread the alarm about Cuba, Reston saw the president briefly. "Keating's a nut," John Kennedy told Reston, off the record. Scotty's meeting with JFK was followed by a more detailed briefing from McGeorge Bundy, the president's national security advisor and a friend and frequent source of Reston's. For background use, Bundy described the outlines of what had been dubbed "Operation Mongoose," a plan to end the Castro regime.

In an October 12 column, Reston suggested that the argument between those who wanted to invade Cuba and those who advocated doing nothing was too simple: "There is a missing element in the debate — subversion, which is going on all the time on that island." He concluded by stating the administration's policy more clearly than had the administration: "In present circumstances, there will be no invasion, and no blockade, and no acquiescence in Soviet control of Cuba. But there will be total surveillance of Cuba and there will be more turmoil in Cuba than Castro has yet experienced or imagined." Bundy had used Reston to buy time for the administration, by making the case that they were not sitting quietly by as the Soviets militarized Cuba.

Four days later, Kennedy saw the latest photographs from the U-2, which clearly showed offensive nuclear missiles being installed in Cuba. It didn't take the *Times* bureau long to smell that something unusual was happening. The Pentagon correspondent noticed that members of the Joint Chiefs were canceling speaking and travel plans. Another correspondent noted that several foreign service officers had been excusing themselves early from Washington parties. Bobby Kennedy refused to return a call from the *Times'* Anthony Lewis, although in normal times he was easily available to Lewis. Reston tried Mac Bundy, but Bundy said he had nothing to say about the problem, whatever it was. Then he hinted that Berlin was again the issue. Max Frankel, who had joined the bureau at Reston's request the year before, was tracking State Department and diplomatic sources. When he found the German ambassador at home in bed early one night, the bureau figured Berlin was not the problem. Soon the bureau's persistent inquiries caught the notice of the White House. Press secretary Salinger called Reston with a message from Kennedy: the president knew the *Times* would eventually figure out what was up and when it did, Kennedy wanted to be called before anything was printed. It was an amazing acknowledgment of the skills and power of Reston and his staff. It was also a sign that Kennedy knew the country was approaching the most frightening and dangerous moment of the nuclear age.

Reston urged his troops on and by the weekend they picked up intense activity among Latin American experts at the State Department. The president returned early from a political trip to the Midwest, lamely claiming that he had caught a cold. That only heightened

the sense that whatever the problem, it was serious enough to require Kennedy's personal attention. Reston and others in the bureau
concluded that the only explanation for the secrecy and the odd
behavior of the government must be that the so-called defensive
missiles in Cuba had been discovered to be something else. Scotty
told Frankel to start writing for Monday's paper. In the middle of
that work, Reston interrupted Frankel and asked him to listen in on
an extension while Reston made the promised call to John Kennedy.
As Frankel reconstructed it from memory for his memoirs, the
exchange went this way:

KENNEDY: *So you know what it is?*
  RESTON: *Yes, sir. We struck out on Berlin and by a process of elimination
       figured it had to be Cuba, offensive missiles in Cuba.*
KENNEDY: *And do you know what I'm going to do about it?*
  RESTON: *No, sir, we don't, except we know you promised to act and we
       hear you've asked for television time tomorrow night.*
KENNEDY: *That is right. I'm going to order a blockade — a blockade of all
       Soviet shipping to Cuba.*

Frankel and Reston were nearly jumping out of their skins in
excitement over the huge scoop they were about to land. But the
president had other ideas.

KENNEDY: *If you reveal my plan, or print that we have discovered their
       missiles in Cuba, Khrushchev could beat us to the draw. He
       could make some preemptive move or counter with an ultima-
       tum that would force us to take more violent action.*
  RESTON: *You're asking us to suppress the news?*
KENNEDY: *I'm asking you not to disclose what we've discovered in Cuba
       until I have a chance to address the country and the Russians
       tomorrow night.*

RESTON: *Well, that sounds like a reasonable request, but we down here only report the news. This is a decision the publisher will have to make. I'll pass on your request immediately.*

KENNEDY: *Give Orvil my regards and tell him to call me if he disagrees.*

Reston convened all the reporters working on the story and told them of the president's request. Frankel recalled that he urged Reston to delay calling Dryfoos until the bureau could discuss the matter further. Frankel suggested that without betraying Kennedy's disclosure of the planned blockade, they could write about the missiles, which they had found out about on their own. Others recalled the paper's restraint on the Bay of Pigs invasion and later second-guessing about whether a fuller story might not have aborted that operation. And what, some wondered, if other papers had figured out the same thing as had the *Times:* would they look foolish? In fact, the *Washington Post* was getting close to the truth, but a call from Kennedy to Phil Graham led him to soften their story to the point where it disclosed little about the real dimensions of the crisis.

Reston responded to the doubts from his staff by calling back the White House and asking for Kennedy. He was, according to Frankel, who was again listening on an extension, put through to the president almost immediately. Frankel later reconstructed the conversation:

RESTON: *Mr. President, one more question if you will. We all remember the Bay of Pigs and our belief that more advance publicity might have spared our country that humiliation and spared our Cuban friends many casualties. If we hold out on our readers now, are we going to be in a war with the Russians before we print another edition? Some of us wonder whether you are asking for secrecy until after the shooting has begun.*

KENNEDY: *We have taken a whole week to plan our response. I'm going to order a blockade; it's the least that I can do. But we will not*

immediately attack. You have my word of honor. There will be
no bloodshed before I explain this very serious situation to the
American people.

Remembered Frankel: "Though his words were often devious, the
president's 'word of honor' struck us as a genuine and generous gesture. We were impressed not just by the fervency of his response but
by his willingness to submit to our presumptuous cross-examination."
Reston advised Dryfoos to accede to the president's request. The
publisher agreed. Reston never second-guessed his recommendation
to Dryfoos, nor would most historians. The missile crisis was extremely dangerous and early disclosure of the calibrated United
States response could have proved disastrous.

The peaceful resolution of the missile crisis thirteen days later led
Reston to a higher respect for Kennedy. As he wrote in his memoirs,
"Camelot was never my favorite legend, but the more I saw
Kennedy after that, the more I trusted him. He seemed increasingly
steady in adversity." Reston's assessment of Jack Kennedy was further colored by a conversation he had with British prime minister
Harold Macmillan after the missile crisis. Macmillan made the point
to Reston that before both world wars, failure to thwart Germany
led to enormous tragedy. "Kennedy did not make the same mistake," the prime minister told Reston. "If he never did another
thing, he assured his place in history by warning Khrushchev that
this time the United States would not stand aside."

After the Cuban crisis ended, Robert Kennedy was one of the
administration officials chosen to give background briefings to the
press as they attempted to reconstruct the tense days of crisis management. In notes he typed after his background session with Bobby,
Reston reported that Bobby came away from the showdown bitter
and angry about the duplicity of the Russians. "You have to figure —
and I think the President does — that you're dealing with gangsters, and

you have to wear your jock strap at all times," Kennedy told Reston. Bobby attempted unsuccessfully to persuade Reston that domestic politics were never a consideration during the crisis, when Republican hounding of the administration made it plain from the beginning that it would have been politically devastating if Kennedy had taken no action in response to the Soviet threat.

In early 1963 much of Kennedy's domestic program was stalled in Congress and his foreign policy initiatives had yielded nothing. Reston noted "a strange kind of malaise" pervading Washington. He criticized Kennedy for his tendency to avoid political confrontation, which Reston implied was leading to stalemate. Apparently having had another conversation with Kennedy, Reston wrote in his column that JFK "is depressed, for he thought, even at the beginning of the year, that he was gaining on history, and now after only a few tumultuous weeks, history seems to be gaining on him." Little did anyone know.

CHAPTER 19

A BLEAK YEAR

AT THE END of 1962, all the newspapers in New York City were silenced. The printers union, after months of failed contract negotiations, called a strike against four papers, including the *Times*. All the other daily papers closed their doors to present a united front against the printers and other craft unions that had joined in the work stoppage.

It was only the second time in the history of the *New York Times* that it failed to print. The strike proved bitter and costly, hurting workers and publishers alike. Reston was beside himself with anger at the unions but initially tried a light touch in his column, which was still appearing in the paper's western and international editions and in the hundreds of other newspapers that syndicated his work. "All I want for Christmas," Scotty wrote the day before the holiday, "is the *New York Times*. I don't ask for any of these new fur bed sheets, or electric socks, or automatic spaghetti winders, but a man is entitled to have old friends around at a time like this. . . . I've been

fielding the *Times* on the first bounce on my front stoop every morning now for 25 years, and it's cold and lonely out there now. Besides,
how do I know what to think when I can't read what I wrote?"

As the strike dragged on, he wrote a tough column criticizing Bert
Powers, the leader of the printers union. He charged that the printers' power to shutter a whole city's newspapers was equivalent to
censorship and suggested that the papers simply start publishing
with nonunion workers. When Orvil Dryfoos saw the column, he
asked Reston to withdraw it. The publisher thought that there was a
growing chance of an agreement and Reston's column would only
harden the resolve of the unions. Scotty agreed, marking the only
occasion in his entire career in which one of his columns was spiked.

Finally, after 114 days, the strike came to an end. It had cost the
Times millions of dollars, but the most severe price was paid by Orvil
Dryfoos. The publisher had fretted and anguished through the long
ordeal. He had to cut wages of those who were still coming to work.
He did battle with his haughty general manager, Amory Bradford,
who bungled the negotiations and displayed a calculated disdain for
Dryfoos. The publisher courageously approved an exhaustive investigative story by the paper's labor reporter that assigned no small
part of the blame for the strike to Bradford. The enlarged heart that
had plagued Dryfoos from his youth finally gave out. He died only
months after the strike at age fifty-two. He had been Scotty Reston's
friend and colleague and had replaced the ailing Arthur Hays as
Scotty's main support in the *Times'* corporate suite.

Marian Dryfoos asked Reston to deliver the eulogy for Orvil.
Reston was so proud of his words that he appended them in their
entirety to his own memoirs. They were delivered at Temple Emanu-
El, a bastion of upper-class Jewish worship on New York's Fifth
Avenue, before two thousand mourners. Scotty and Sally loved
Orvil and Marian, and Scotty made that quite clear on that sad day.
"The death of Orvil Dryfoos was blamed on 'heart failure,' but that

obviously could not have been the reason," Scotty began. "Orvil Dryfoos's heart never failed him or anybody else – ask the reporters on the *Times*. It was steady as the stars – ask anybody in this company of friends. It was faithful as the tides – ask his beloved wife and family. No matter what the doctors say, they cannot blame his heart."

Dryfoos's death immediately set off a nearly panicky search for his replacement. Despite his weak heart and extraordinary burden, the family had been operating on the assumption that Dryfoos would serve as publisher for at least another decade. That would have allowed Marian's younger brother, Arthur Ochs Sulzberger, a decent apprenticeship on the paper. Even his father wondered whether "Punch" Sulzberger, still just in his thirties, was up to the job.

The day before Orvil's funeral, Amory Bradford and his wife hosted Scotty and Sally at lunch in their huge townhouse on New York's East Side. Bradford knew the doubts about Punch but also knew he himself had no chance to succeed Orvil as publisher; the family felt too strongly about keeping that position in the family. But Bradford felt he could secure the position of president, the top position on the business side of the paper, if he could get Reston, who was almost Sulzberger family, to become publisher until Punch was thought ready for the job. Banking on Reston's intimacy with the family, he proposed that Scotty try to convince Arthur Hays of the wisdom of this arrangement. "It was a very uncomfortable lunch," Sally Reston remembered. Scotty was, as usual, careful in his responses. He didn't like Bradford but couldn't rule out the possibility that his plan might succeed. He told Bradford that it was he, not Scotty, who had the duty as the senior corporate executive to make the case to Arthur Hays. But he did not say categorically that he would not serve as publisher.

Some days later, Arthur Hays rolled his wheelchair by Bradford's office and summoned him to his own quarters. There, Sulzberger told Bradford that he was concerned about Punch's readiness and was considering resuming direct control of the company himself. Bradford countered with his plan: Bradford as president; Reston as publisher. The meeting ended inconclusively. Arthur Hays continued to agonize over the decision, but Iphigene saw the problem more clearly. She weighed in heavily on the side of her son Punch.

Others had their own opinions. George Woods, chairman of the World Bank and a New York Times Company board member, sent a private letter to Arthur Hays suggesting that Punch be teamed with Scotty as a way of helping the young Sulzberger learn the ropes. In early June 1963, Arthur Hays and Iphigene invited the Restons to their country estate to discuss the succession. By then Arthur Hays had decided he wanted to team Bradford and Punch as the top leaders of the company. He asked Scotty what he thought. Reston came down solidly for keeping the leadership of the paper within the family and Bradford out of the top position. "It's a bum arrangement," Scotty declared. "If you don't trust Punch now, you'll never trust him, and you'll cripple him." Arthur Hays continued to waver. When he offered Bradford the chance to remain as general manager working for Punch, Bradford decided to quit. Arthur Hays buckled and agreed to make Bradford president. But when Punch heard that news, he calmly told his father he would take the top job alone or not at all. His father reversed again and agreed to his son's terms.

Once the decision was made, Arthur Hays showed Reston Bradford's letter of resignation. Reston wrote to Bradford, trying to cover his own tracks. He had left Bradford with the belief that he would back the scheme to keep Punch out of the top job; now he said Bradford's resignation "depresses . . . [and] frightens me." He claimed not to know how the decision to give Punch the top job was made. "I do not know how it all happened. . . . Nobody on the paper outside the family was asked for an opinion. This is at least true in my case," Reston dissembled. Scotty was obviously worried that Bradford would spread the word either that Reston had sold him out or that Reston had tacitly conspired with him to thwart Punch. The embittered Bradford saved the letter and turned it over to Alex Jones and Susan Tifft for their definitive history of the Sulzberger family. It was Bradford's revenge for what he saw as Scotty's duplicity and dishonesty.

As Orvil Dryfoos was waging his fatal fight with the unions, his counterpart at the *Washington Post* was engaged in a life-and-death struggle with mental illness. By late 1962 Phil Graham's behavior had grown increasingly erratic. He had taken to phoning his friend the president of the United States to berate him for one thing and another. Kay Graham had discovered before Christmas that Phil was having an affair with a young researcher from *Newsweek*, the newsmagazine that the Grahams had acquired.

At a meeting of members of the Associated Press in Arizona early in January, Phil Graham went uninvited to the podium, ranted at the audience, and began taking off his clothes. Kennedy sent a government jet to take him home to Washington where he was admitted to a mental-health facility. He was treated and released, then left Kay for his girlfriend. He continued to manage the newspaper, since he alone, not the couple together, had been given controlling interest in the *Post* by Kay's father. The situation was excruciatingly uncomfortable for Phil and Kay's friends, especially the Restons, to whom each turned for counsel and guidance. On February 18 Scotty sent a "personal and confidential" letter to Orvil describing Phil's weird behavior. He noted that Graham had taken to bringing his girlfriend to the *Post* offices. "He is testing friends to see whether they will back him in this relationship," Reston explained. Reston told Dryfoos he had agreed to meet with Phil and his mistress, but not in the

Post building. Scotty went on to warn Orvil that Graham had become obsessed with surpassing the *Times*, so there would be expensive personnel raids coming.

At one point the desperate Graham approached Scotty to talk about the power of religious faith. When Kay Graham was preparing her memoirs, Reston described the conversation to her this way: "Phil thought my religious faith could help him. He thought, inaccurately as it turned out, that I had this deep faith of my mother and father, which I wish I did have, but I did not have at that time. I did not tell him that. I told him that I thought there were times in life when you go through all these things and did he have any feelings about religious faith that could help him through this period and he said no he did not. And I don't know what I said to him that time, but it obviously was a failure. I was not able to get through to him, probably because I couldn't define it myself in any persuasive way and then he just went away."

Since Phil Graham now lived apart from his family, Scotty counseled Kay to fight Phil for control of the paper. "It does not belong to Phil Graham. Your father created this paper. There is no room in Washington for two Graham families. You and I can't do anything about Phil, but we can start training Donny [the Grahams' eldest son] and I would like to take him as my clerk this summer."

Although he was younger than most of the news clerks Reston would hire over the years, Donald Graham, then a student at Harvard and now chairman of the Washington Post Company, spent the summer working with Reston at the *Times*. Scotty wrote to Phil, extravagantly praising the son's performance:

I have had two guys doing this job at the *Times* for me – one the editor of the *Tar Heel* in Chapel Hill, who is now on the News Review of the *Times* in New York; the other, a young Englishman finished at Oxford and half-way through his master's degree at the University of California. Don Graham, in his sophomore year at Harvard, is better than either of them. He has come in here very quietly and composed sometimes as many as 60 letters a day and written them simply and quickly and done a lot of other things on the side. Everybody likes him. Tony Lewis took him up to the court on closing day, when they sent God off to the minors [a reference to the Supreme Court's ruling banning school prayer] and he has been getting around a little more each day. I hope all this is useful to him; it certainly has been to me.

He still tried to be supportive of Phil too. "I don't know what to say to you except that we all love you and need you, and want to see you when you feel like it." Scotty didn't mention his reason for making Donald Graham a clerk at such a young age.

The young Graham found his stint with Reston exhilarating as well as comforting, since his own family was coming apart. "At a horrible time in my life, he was such a sympathetic and understanding guy," Graham remembered. He idolized Reston and recalled years later that a piece of research he had done on the right of free assembly appeared in one of Scotty's columns about Martin Luther King's huge civil rights march. Graham also noticed Reston's sympathy toward the whole civil rights movement. "I remember his saying on the day of the march," Graham said, " 'I'm going to go down there and march a few paces.' "

The Grahams saw the Restons as rocks of stability and balanced good sense. But to Phil those qualities seemed alien. He wrote, but did not send, a long letter to Scotty trying to rationalize his own irrational behavior: "I find it unendurable to believe that 'balance' or 'moderation' or 'middle-of-the-road' represent human approaches to living. Similarly we are told that all tough questions are a matter of degree, of simply drawing a line, etc. What nonsense. . . . The man who leaves life by the most violent suicide is still at least more honest than those who choose suicide-while-living by defining away all that is human in life."

In the summer of 1963, Phil Graham was hospitalized again. In early August he came home to spend a weekend with Kay at their Virginia farm, where the Grahams and Restons had been so happy together. On Saturday, August 3, he shot and killed himself in a downstairs bathroom of the elegant home. The Restons were in Europe and despite telephoned assurances that they need not come, Scotty and Sally immediately flew back to be with Kay and her family.

The immediate problem at the *Post* was who would run the privately held company now that Phil was gone. Though the paper had belonged to her family, Kay had never been much involved with its operations. Scotty's counsel to her was forthright: "Take over the joint." She did, nearly trembling with fear that came from her lack of self-confidence. At first she relied on the men from both the business and editorial sides of the enterprise to help her along. Scotty had asked her if she didn't want to leave her children "a greater paper than you inherited?" "That made me realize," she recalled in an interview, "that I could do things I hadn't envisioned." Like Phil some years earlier, she thought that Scotty Reston, good friend, great journalist, the stable antithesis of her manic-depressive husband, would be an enormous help.

One way to accomplish that goal, she thought, would be to bring Reston to the *Washington Post*. So, as Phil had some years before, she tried to lure Scotty away from the *Times*. The discussions between her and the Restons went on for months. In early 1964 Kay wrote to them both, knowing of course that any decision by Scotty to leave the *Times* would be made by the two of them. In her letter Kay acknowledged that discussions had not been terribly specific.

They have been indefinite only because I wanted to work out what was best for you, since what is best for us is to have you here advising me and advising us, and being part of the Washington *Post*. My hopes are that you can consider coming to us at this point in your lives. I fully realize your close ties and emotions binding you to the New York *Times*. They have meant a great deal to you and you have meant as much or more to them. You have given up a lot of the world's goods already as proof of what they meant to you, and your loyalty to them.

There is no record of what sorts of financial inducements Kay Graham offered — if she ever mentioned that issue. The generous precedent Phil had set some years before would indicate that she and the Restons understood that the Post Company would make the move profitable. Kay didn't rely just on her own blandishments; she enlisted Reston's mentor Walter Lippmann in the effort. Lippmann was then a regular columnist for the *Post* and counseled Reston to agree to the offer. Again, his reasoning, according to Scotty's account to Kay Graham, was that "the *Times* is made. There's not much you can do about the *Times* except carry on a tradition that is well established and you'll have trouble changing that because they think they're the greatest thing since pretty girls. You know you can't change them, but the *Post* is growing, just coming. It's in the capital, which is a very powerful argument."

Kay never quite offered Scotty the top editorial job at her paper, suggesting instead that he continue writing his column and stand next in line to succeed Alfred Friendly, the incumbent editor. When Lippmann continued to press Scotty, Reston responded that he had in the past chosen to stay in Washington rather than accept the top editor's job in New York, and thus it made no sense to leave the *Times* to become an associate editor at the *Post*. Lippmann nudged Kay to offer Reston the editorship of her paper. She refused. In the summer of 1964, Scotty wrote to Kay Graham turning down her offer. But he said he would offer his advice "for free" in return for her friendship.

"I remember weeping," Graham said years later as she and Scotty and Sally reminisced about her attempt to hire him, "when you said no, finally." She still worried that if she had agreed to make him editor, as Lippmann suggested, he might have consented. Scotty reassured her that it was his devotion to the *Times* that was decisive. "So it was just that you were married to the *Times*?" Graham asked. "It was a question of personal loyalty," Scotty replied.

Ultimately Mrs. Graham, with advice and consent from both Lippmann and Reston, brought Ben Bradlee over from *Newsweek* to run the paper.* Under his leadership, with the full support of Kay Graham, the paper won the Pulitzer Prize for its courageous, persistent coverage of the Watergate scandals. The *Post*'s pursuit of the story was so much more aggressive than the *Times*' that there has been much speculation: had Reston gone to the *Post*, would the paper have led the way on Watergate? By the time Watergate occurred, Reston was out of the management circle of the *Times*. But some of his disdain for muckraking had been inherited by his protégé Max Frankel, then the bureau chief in Washington, and their shared reluctance probably dulled the *Times*' ardor to probe the Nixon scandals. But even the Pulitzer the *Post* won for its Watergate coverage was due in large part to Reston. For some inexplicable reason, the Pulitzer jury making recommendations for the coveted meritorious public service prize did not include the *Post*. Reston and Newbold Noyes, editor of *Post* rival the *Washington Evening Star*, led the Pulitzer board to overrule its jury and award the prize to Kay Graham's newspaper.

*Bradlee, in his memoirs, recalled an incident in 1954 when he was a newly minted *Newsweek* correspondent. Bradlee had gone to Geneva to meet John Foster Dulles's airplane, hoping for a word with the secretary of state, or at least one of his aides. "My heart sank," Bradlee wrote. "There to meet Dulles was my hero, James 'Scotty' Reston, the New York *Times*'s best of breed. A few seconds later, Chip Bohlen — a critically important source . . . came down the ramp and greeted Reston, the way Damon must have greeted Pythias. 'How are you, you old Scotsman?' Bohlen asked, and cringed as Reston punched him playfully on the shoulder."

*   *   *

Like every sentient American, Scotty Reston remembered exactly where he was when he heard that John F. Kennedy had been shot in Dallas. He was in Winston-Salem, North Carolina, having lunch with the governor. He flew back to Washington immediately and wrote his column for the next day. That he was able to organize his thoughts, discipline his writing, and make his deadline under the emotional circumstances is remarkable, although his colleagues in news organizations across the country, like soldiers in battle, did their jobs with amazing grace and professionalism. As Scotty recalled in his memoirs, he wrote "not always quite seeing the keys on my typewriter."

"America wept tonight, not alone for its dead young President, but for itself," Reston wrote. "The grief was general, for somehow the worst in the nation had prevailed over the best. The indictment extended beyond the assassin, for something in the nation itself, some strain of madness and violence, had destroyed the highest symbol of law and order."

Despite the pain he felt for the loss of Jack Kennedy, Reston managed to include a bit of cool and prescient political analysis, suggesting that the gridlock that had stalled many of Kennedy's initiatives would be broken by the tragedy. He noted that Lyndon Johnson had already suffered heart problems and that the constitutional succession led to two old men in the Congress, raising the question of whether that process was sufficient to the twentieth-century needs of the country.

"President Kennedy," Reston continued, displaying his own changed feelings about the man, "was, even to his political enemies, a wonderfully attractive human being, and it is significant that, unlike many Presidents in the past, the people who liked him best were those who knew him the best."

CHAPTER 20

LBJ

ONCE KHRUSHCHEV'S BELLIGERENCE set the tone, the Kennedy administration firmly believed that the struggle in Vietnam was more than a civil war: it was, they felt, a proxy war between the United States and the Soviet Union. Although the president was cautious about the level of U.S. commitment, no one with any influence believed it was a fight America could abandon. But over time, as they witnessed the failure and frustration of the war effort, reporters representing U.S. publications and networks made that commitment increasingly difficult to sell to the American public.

Many correspondents based in Southeast Asia, men like David Halberstam of the *Times* and Neil Sheehan and Malcolm Browne, writing for United Press and Associated Press, respectively (both later became *Times*men), began their tours believing fully in the American mission. But as U.S. involvement deepened, their reporting started to reflect the difficulties of the war effort. The stories from "in-country" badly irritated Jack Kennedy and his administration.

In October 1963 Punch Sulzberger, then only a few months into his job as publisher, met with Kennedy in the White House. It was a bit more than a month before Kennedy would be killed. Halberstam's reporting was on the president's mind. He had taken the unusual step of asking the CIA for an analysis of Halberstam's work. The spy agency reported back that while Halberstam's facts were accurate, the analysis derived from them was consistently pessimistic. Kennedy explained to Sulzberger his own frustrations with the struggle in Vietnam, which had grown from six hundred to involve about 16,000 American soldiers. He complained that Halberstam had lost his objectivity. "I wish like hell that you'd get Halberstam out of there," Kennedy told the publisher. Punch had been anxious about meeting with the president alone, but Reston had reassured him the session would be occupied with small talk. Sulzberger did not know how to react to the presidential request, so he told Kennedy he would look into the matter.

When Punch called his editors in New York, he was told that Halberstam was already scheduled to end his arduous tour in Vietnam. But when Sulzberger told Reston of the president's request, Scotty immediately objected. He had brought Halberstam to the *Times*. (When Reston first called Halberstam at his desk at the *Nashville Tennessean*, Halberstam, suspecting that his editor, John Seigenthaler, a chronic practical joker, was playing a prank, shouted into the receiver, "Seigenthaler, I don't have time to fuck around," and then hung up. Reston had to call back to convince Halberstam to come to Washington to see him.) So Scotty felt a personal as well as professional reason to refuse the president's request. "Obviously we can't do what we were thinking of doing," Scotty told Punch. "We can't buckle in that kind of stuff." Halberstam was told to stay on in Vietnam.

*   *   *

In the early-morning hours of November 23, as the Washington bureau correspondents finished touching up their stories on the assassination and Johnson's succession, Reston called an impromptu meeting of the dozen and a half reporters still in the bureau to figure out what angles they would pursue the next day. They talked about the mechanics of covering the coming funeral and the like. Then the conversation turned to what an LBJ administration would be like. "In the large, everything that happened in the Johnson administration was foreseen that night," Eileen Shanahan recalled. "It was foreseen that he was an ignoramus in foreign policy and would probably make mistakes, that he would be blustering and overbearing in that area. It was specifically foreseen that he would run into trouble in another way because he understood Washington but he didn't understand the country. It was foreseen that he would coddle and nurture and do everything to please the press until he was elected in his own right and that then we would have all manner of trouble with access, with his rage, probably being cut off if we displeased him. I found it quite remarkable, and it tells you something about the quality of the people Scotty hired."

Reston had another, seemingly irrelevant thing on his mind that night. According to Shanahan, Scotty told the bureau: "I am not encouraging enterprise on the Bobby Baker story." The *Times* had lagged behind on the story about corruption involving one of Johnson's most important aides but was just beginning to catch up. "When he said that," Shanahan recalled, "nobody said, 'Why? What do you mean?' We all knew what he meant. He didn't have to say the country is in a state of trauma. It would not be the patriotic thing to undermine this new president who is coming into office in these horrible circumstances. I don't think I even formulated those sentences in my own mind at that time. I knew what he meant. I heard no word of disagreement. I do think he was right. Today's group of journalists will think he was wrong."

*   *   *

In those frightening, crushingly sad days after Jack Kennedy's murder, Lyndon Johnson struggled to find his footing as the inheritor of the presidency. He did what he knew how to do best: he talked and talked and talked to as many influential people as he could corral, asking for their support, urging them to put aside partisanship and move on with the agenda Kennedy had left. He swept through the upper echelons of the Washington press corps, talking to Walter Lippmann, Joe Alsop, Kay Graham, and, of course, Scotty Reston.

One of the first encounters with the new president that Scotty recalled was a few weeks after the assassination. A spate of stories had commented on the wealth of the new president, including his ranch and a television station in Texas. Reston wrote a column suggesting that Johnson sell the station to end the curiosity about how it was acquired. "My telephone rang shortly after seven the next morning," Scotty remembered. "The White House operator said the president was calling. 'Where are you?'" Johnson asked. Reston told him he was at home. "Didn't I tell you when I took this job that if you wanted to know anything about me all you had to do was call up?" LBJ demanded. Reston admitted the truth of that statement, but then Johnson went into high gear, shouting, "Then why do I have to get up and read this garbage in the *New York Times* about selling the television station? Don't you know that station belongs to Lady Bird? She's the one who went to college and worked for that station, and now you come along and tell me to ditch it and break her heart." The tirade lasted, Reston said, forty-two minutes, and included the usual Johnson dose of self-pity about his impoverished youth and the real wealth he had forgone by entering politics.

When he was ready to hang up, Johnson announced that he was not yet finished with Reston and summoned him to the White House for a session with his aide Walter Jenkins. There Jenkins laid out for Reston the books on the station, the bill of sale, and other documents to support the claim that the station had been acquired and was being operated legitimately. While Reston was going over the books with Jenkins, the president came in and, to soften the impact of his telephonic rant, invited Scotty to have dinner with him and Lady Bird. Reston remembered that Johnson took a boyish pleasure in a new battery-powered pepper grinder, which he proudly presented to Scotty as a memento of the evening.

On Christmas Day, 1963, Johnson and Lady Bird made a series of holiday calls from their ranch in Texas to cabinet members, aides, and several newspaper people. They phoned Reston at his home, and the president described in some detail how he and Lady Bird had spent the holiday; the always-earthy LBJ mentioned that he had eaten a good bit of cornbread stuffing and "had indigestion ever since." "I just called," the president added, "to tell you that I'm thinking of you and hope you had a merry Christmas, appreciate your friendship, and want your advice and counsel in the days ahead because, God A'mighty, I've got so much to do. I don't know how I'll ever do it. And I've got to have some friends who will speak with candor." He invited the Restons to come to the ranch right away, but Scotty explained that he was about to leave on a trip to Arizona, where Barry Goldwater was to announce his plan to run for president. "I just may go through there [Texas] on my way back," he added.

Then Lady Bird got on the phone to thank Scotty for a nice column he had written praising the way she had handled the transition. "God bless you in the new year," Scotty replied. She repeated her husband's invitation. "Sometime I would like to show you, quietly and serenely if possible, the wonderful country which has made our life, and which has made Lyndon whatever he is, because it is one of the Lord's blessedest pieces of real estate."

Just after New Year's, Scotty, Sally, and their son Richard flew out to Arizona for the interview with Goldwater. (Sally traveled now and then with Scotty, and the *Times* footed the bill; she was kept on the newspaper's payroll for years at an annual salary of less than $30,000, as a way to supplement Scotty's salary and compensate her for taking some photographs and helping him.) While they were there, press secretary Bill Moyers called to again invite them to the LBJ ranch on their way home. The ostensible purpose was to quiz Scotty about press reaction to Goldwater, but the visit turned into a classic Johnson "treatment." Over breakfast on a Sunday morning, Johnson lamented the difficulty of having to staff the government, and the problems of proposing a new budget that might exceed $100 billion. (As he frequently did, the omnivorous Johnson not only gobbled down his own meal but also helped himself to everything left on Scotty's plate.) Lady Bird, in a recorded journal she kept, remembered taking the Restons to a small log cabin church that morning in nearby Fredericksburg, along with Gerri Whittington, "Lyndon's attractive, Negro secretary." From there they went to Johnson City to see the old stone fort and commissary where the president's grandfather had lived after the Civil War. "We pointed out to the Restons the portholes in the commissary through which the settlers stuck their rifles to fire at the Indians," Lady Bird remembered. On they went to the small house where Lyndon grew up. As they drove back to the ranch, they passed a farm across the road from Johnson's land. The president picked up the radio-telephone in the car to tell his ranch manager to inquire about buying the property. Later the two couples helicoptered to Austin for coffee with Governor John Connally and his wife, Nellie. From there they were whisked into a reception held by Senator Ralph Yarborough. Then they flew to Washington on Air Force One with some of Lady Bird's relatives in tow for their first visit to the White House. The Restons thought their exhausting visit had ended when they landed in Washington, but LBJ insisted they come to the White House with the family group. The president took Scotty and Sally to his bedroom and, kneeling on the floor, pointed to an inscription on the keystone of the fireplace: "In this room lived John Fitzgerald Kennedy with his wife, Jacqueline – during the two years, ten months and two days he was president of the United States – January 20, 1961– November 22, 1963."

"Johnson nodded to it, looked at Sally and me, and raised his eyebrows but didn't say a word," Scotty recalled. The gesture would seem to have been designed to impress upon the Restons the awesome burden Johnson had been called to bear. At long last, they were ushered out of the White House.

But even as Johnson was acting chummy with the Restons, he was ready to play hardball with the *New York Times*. The following Tuesday he met with Secretary of State Dean Rusk to complain about a Tad Szulc story leaked by someone in the State Department. "There's somebody in that outfit that's leaking. I don't know who it is, but they're leaking awfully bad. We can't run a government unless we can stop it," the president said. "Right, well, we may have to put a tail on this man," Rusk replied, attempting to sound as tough as Lyndon and referring to Szulc. "But," Rusk added, "then if we get caught doing that, it's going to be rough." Johnson saw the point. "Yeah, I'd try to stop it some way. I don't know how I'd stop it."

Discussing the Johnson presidency in his memoirs, Reston recalled the iconoclastic journalist I. F. Stone's observation about the press "outdoing themselves in flattery of the new monarch." But, Reston wrote, "I didn't join them." That was eventually true but not immediately so. Like most of the nation, Reston was pulling for Johnson to succeed in the wake of the Kennedy tragedy. He had not much liked Johnson's crude powerfulness as a senator and had missed a big scoop at the 1960 Democratic convention when he was tipped that JFK would pick Johnson as his running mate the next day. Reston couldn't believe it and didn't write it. But after Johnson's moving address to the Congress immediately following the assassination, Reston saw a rough Texan transformed. "It is part of the mythology and even the history of the Presidency that no man is ever the same once he walks through the portals of the White House," Reston wrote on November 28, 1963. "Right or wrong, this pleasant fancy seemed already to be working on Lyndon Baines Johnson today. By the time he faced the Congress, he had taken on the gravity of the hour and the office. In his old Senate days, he slouched and mumbled, or when aroused raced his engine and whooped and bellowed, but shock and sorrow and responsibility have already toned him down. . . . He was both bold and restrained and never read a speech better in his life."

Right after his visit to the ranch but before the State of the Union speech in 1964, Reston opined that Johnson had already done "a remarkable job of maintaining a line with the Kennedy Administration while putting his own personal stamp on the Presidency." Invoking his weekend experience with the president, Reston wrote:

> The other day, walking around his ranch in Texas, he said, "The best fertilizer for a piece of land is the footprints of the owner," and he applies this doctrine not only to the LBJ Ranch but the conduct of the Presidency. . . . Mr. Johnson's qualities are energy, boundless confidence in his intuitive judgment about what men will and will not do, a shrewd gift of anticipating trouble ahead, and a tireless, almost nagging persistence in following things through to a decision. . . . President Kennedy's eloquence was designed to make men think; President Johnson's hammer blows are designed to make men act. . . . Maybe he will do more with his program in Congress than Kennedy did with his, and maybe he won't. But if he doesn't it won't be

because he has any doubts about the system or any lack of knowledge about how to make it work.

After the State of the Union speech, Johnson noted he had been applauded eighty-one times. He called Reston to crow about his triumph and how he had so successfully crafted his agenda that the Republicans would have no issues left in the coming presidential campaign. "You heard what the young Republican said to the old Republican senator, didn't you?" Johnson joked. "No," said Reston, playing along. "Said, 'Senator, he didn't leave much for us Republicans, did he?' And the old senator said, 'Oh yes, he did. . . . We can always declare war,'" the president said, laughing to himself. "God bless you," said Reston, never expecting that it would be Johnson himself who would become the war president.

By the spring of 1964, LBJ had begun to descend into a nearly paranoid state about his opponents, especially those in the press. At one point there was a series of stories claiming Johnson had been driving at high speed at his ranch, with a beer in his hand. Reston was in the White House with the president to talk about the coming campaign when an aide showed Johnson another of the drinking-and-driving stories. As Scotty remembered it, Johnson was "angry and sad." The question wasn't who might run against him, Johnson told Reston, but "whether I'll run, when they print things like that. I don't know that a southern president can ever unify this country. These big-city folk in the national press are against me. They're trying to make a hick out of me."

Reston was alarmed and upset by the depth of Johnson's resentment and tried to argue with him. Reston pointed out that many of the top people in the Washington press corps were just like LBJ, from small towns and land-grant colleges. "You've got it all wrong," Reston remembered telling Johnson. But Johnson kept pouring out his feelings of being picked on by the establishment. Reston wrote a column trying to explain to the president publicly that stories about his drinking and driving had not been meant to portray him as a bumpkin but rather had been written out of concern for his safety. When another story appeared in the *New York Herald Tribune* describing Johnson's anger at the drinking-and-driving stories, the president of the United States, in a conversation with his press secretary, called the *Trib* writer a "little, dirty son of a bitch."

Reston went a step further to try to mollify Johnson. He persuaded James Rowe, one of Washington's powerful alumni of FDR's New Deal team, to try to convince the president that his treatment by the press was not so bad. According to Johnson, Rowe's message was simple: as long as Reston and Walter Lippmann supported him, he would "get a good press" from the rest of the Washington corps. As if to reinforce the point, Reston a few days later wrote that "one of the vital natural resources of this country these days is the tireless negotiating skill of President Lyndon Johnson. . . . The emotional content of the Johnson appeal, the total absence of ideology, the passionate insistence on the general welfare, the willingness to talk endlessly through the night if necessary, the vivid earthy American language and optimistic faith that problems can be solved – all this is highly effective under Johnson."

Indeed, Reston and most commentators supported Johnson for some time. They admired his ability to get things done, backed his domestic initiatives, applauded enthusiastically his formulation of a "Great Society." Reston wrote in a column that spring that the country was getting over the Kennedy love affair and coming to terms with Johnson as a solid, political practitioner. "Washington is now a little girl settling down with the old boyfriend," he wrote. "The mad and wonderful infatuation with the handsome stranger from Boston is over – somehow she always knew it wouldn't last – so she is adjusting to reality. Everything is less romantic and more practical, part regret and part relief, beer instead of champagne, not fancy but plain, and in many ways more natural and hopefully more durable. This may not be the most attractive quality of the new Administration, but it works."

In May 1964 Reston went along on a political tour of the South with Johnson. He wrote of the president's firm insistence on the need for civil rights legislation in speeches across the old Confederacy. He approvingly quoted the president telling a Georgia audience, "I will never feel that I have done justice to my high office until every section of this country is linked in a single purpose, a joint devotion to bring an end to injustice, to bring an end to poverty." As Reston noted: "The South would probably hesitate to take this from anybody else, but even the most segregationist Southerner cannot wholly disown President Johnson." Even on the controversial issue of Vietnam, which Johnson was trying desperately to keep off the front pages, Reston wrote reassuringly about the president's intentions. When LBJ named Maxwell Taylor, chairman of the Joint Chiefs of Staff, as ambassador to Saigon, Reston said that the assignment did not signal the administration's intention to expand the war into North Vietnam.

But about a year after Johnson took office, Reston had tired of many of the same Johnson qualities he had earlier praised. In an especially biting column, Scotty teed off on LBJ's style of governance. He called the president "tyrannical with his personal staff, disorderly about his administration, thin-skinned about the press and inclined to regard criticism not as a duty in a free society, but a crime." At one point when Johnson grandly announced he was going to tone down his behavior, take up golf, and swear off whiskey, the native Scotsman couldn't help but kid the president in print. Didn't Johnson know that the Scots invented golf as a punishment for man's sins and that they invented whiskey as a consolation for playing the game, so that he could suffer another day? LBJ couldn't take a joke and furiously asked Reston who he thought he was trying to tell him how to run his life.

But later, when the Johnson legislative program barreled through Congress, Reston was lavish in his praise. "President Johnson is beginning to make Franklin Roosevelt's early legislative record look like an abject failure," Scotty opined. "He's getting everything through the Congress but the abolition of the Republican party, and he hasn't tried that yet. It's a political miracle. It has even surpassed his own expectations, which were not modest, and while he's still a long way from achieving a Great Society, he is at least making progress toward a more equal and compassionate society."

In 1964 Johnson campaigned as the president who would not send American boys to fight an Asian war. The specter of the more belli-cose Goldwater overshadowed criticism of Johnson's Vietnam pol-icy. In a phone conversation with Reston in mid-June, the president asked what the columnist thought about Vietnam. "Oh, I'd just depress you," Reston replied, carefully. "I've always thought, you know, that it's always unwise to assume that . . . other great nations would stand for things we couldn't stand for ourselves. . . . I've always believed that in the long run France's experience [in Viet-nam] is right – that nothing can be done there over a long period of time without the acquiescence of China. . . . We can't do anything about it except go on doing what we're doing now. . . . I don't think we have any easy options. We can't get out and we can't go smash-ing into China, à la Mr. Goldwater."

"Well," said the president, "that's exactly the way I look at it." He went on to lament how those who favored ending the war by neu-tralizing Vietnam couldn't explain how to get it done. "So the only thing you've got left is to make this thing more efficient and more effective and hold as strong as we can and keep this government as strong as you can and improve it as you can. And that we are doing day and night. Okay, my friend, come by and see me."

As the election approached, Reston remained on good terms with Johnson. When LBJ teased his party and the country – and tortured Hubert Humphrey – about whom he would choose as his running mate, Reston called Johnson from the convention in Atlantic City to wheedle the decision out of him. The *Times*, Reston pleaded, needed to know his choice so they could prepare an adequate profile of the veep. Johnson wouldn't play but did agree to say hello to Punch Sulzberger, who was sitting with Scotty as he talked to the president of the United States. LBJ got more news out of Reston than the newsman dragged out of the president. He pushed Scotty to say, in Punch's hearing, that the *Times* would surely endorse Johnson for reelection, although the paper was hardly likely to have backed Goldwater.

After the election Johnson moved steadily and inexorably to expand American involvement in Vietnam, sowing the seeds for the destruction of his presidency. As the war escalated, so did Scotty Reston's criticism, and soon Johnson regarded anyone who failed to cheer for his Vietnam policy as the enemy. In his memoirs, he singled out Reston and Walter Lippmann for special blame. "It was not long before these two reporters ceased to support me and began their tireless assaults on me and my administration," Johnson wrote. "When that happened, I could not help noting that it was hard to find many words of support anywhere in the Washington press corps or the television media." He had taken Jim Rowe's advice a bit too literally.

LBJ's resentment of Reston curdled into real anger after he left office. Speaking with his biographer Doris Kearns Goodwin, Johnson bitterly denounced "the columnists." Reston of course noticed and quoted this passage from LBJ's tirade in his memoirs.

They turned against me on Vietnam because it was in their self-interest to do so, because they knew that no one receives a Pulitzer Prize these days by simply supporting the President and the administration. You win by digging up contrary information, by making a big splash. Truth no longer counts so long as a big sensation can be produced. Every story is always slanted to win the favor of someone who sits higher up [one wonders who sat higher up than the president of the United States]. The Washington press are like a wolf pack when it comes to attacking public officials, but they're like a bunch of sheep in their own profession and they will always follow the bellwether sheep, the leaders of their profession, Lippmann and Reston. As long as those two stayed with me, I was okay. But once they left me in pursuit of their fancy prizes, everyone else left me.

Moreover, Johnson told Ms. Goodwin, the criticism was inspired by the Communists: "And isn't it funny that you could always find [Soviet ambassador] Dobrynin's car in front of Reston's house the night before Reston delivered a blast on Vietnam?"

Reston responded, noting that his two Pulitzers – he had won a second in 1956 for commentary – had come long before Johnson was president, and no Soviet ambassador or official had ever been in his house. "The significant thing about all these tragic imaginings is that they came from the mind of the man who had directed the war, yet we're told that reporters shouldn't be so nosy about looking into the character and characteristics of candidates who seek the presidency." Reston felt that Johnson's tragic blunders in Vietnam were fueled by a

combination of ignorance, vanity, and booze – increasingly from booze as his disappointments mounted. First, he knew little or nothing of the enemy or the guerrilla war he was fighting. Second, he had supreme confidence that the United States could do anything it set its mind to, and thought money and machines were the answer to any test of power, and third – a touch of racism here – that America was superior and that "these little brown men," as he called the Vietnamese, would run into the rice paddies at the sight of American troops and modern weapons.

(Reston had forgotten he had called the Japanese "little yellow men" after Pearl Harbor, but he had grown and learned over the years.)

Reston's passage from hope and admiration to despair and disgust with Lyndon Johnson perfectly mirrored the mood of America during his presidency. Scotty Reston was indeed the voice of America.

CHAPTER 21

VIETNAM

SCOTTY RESTON NEVER had much doubt that the American policy of "containment," in George Kennan's phrase, was the right and proper way to deal with the threat posed by a belligerent Soviet Union and its Communist client states. After the 1961 summit meeting in Vienna, he believed it was the Soviets' bullying that caused Kennedy to try to prevent the Communist takeover of South Vietnam. He even made that point directly to Aleksey N. Kosygin, the premier of the Soviet Union, in an argumentative interview in 1965.

But at the same time, Reston felt strongly that the French experience in Vietnam and the proximity and interests of China made the chances of American success in Southeast Asia small. He was not initially opposed to the idea of trying to bolster the South Vietnamese government. But as the difficulty of the job became apparent, Reston grew ever more critical of the conduct of the war. He could never quite believe in the application of containment theory to a jungle war, fought with American soldiers on the borders of another great power, especially when the third great power, the Soviet Union, was also heavily invested in the success of the north.

His opinions came from firsthand experience. Just as he was taking Arthur Krock's place as bureau chief in 1953, Scotty went off to Asia, a trip he described in his columns. He stopped in Korea to watch the signing of the truce ending the bloody war. He interviewed Syngman Rhee, the first president of the Republic of South Korea, and Chiang Kai-shek, the Chinese nationalist leader exiled in Taiwan.

In Saigon Reston interviewed a British brigadier, who proceeded to enlighten Reston about the Vietnamese conflict. The jungle, the soldier told Reston coolly, is "not an ideal place to fight a war." The French had controlled the air but still lost 150,000 men fighting the Communists. He wryly propounded a strategy to counter the jungle fighters: "If we give tanks and other military vehicles to the Communists, instead of to the South Vietnamese, then maybe we could get them up on the roads where we could fight them on our terms." Reston remembered that this was not offered "wholly as a joke."

Scotty asked the British soldier if it wasn't necessary to stop Communism in its tracks sooner rather than later to avoid the kind of all-encompassing war the Allies had needed to stop fascism. Vietnam, answered the brigadier, is essentially a civil war and Ho Chi Minh is not Hitler. American embassy officials conceded to Reston the validity of the British analysis, but they countered that allowing the Communists to expand into the south might lead to dangerous Red advances elsewhere. The premier of South Vietnam gave Reston the most discouraging news: the villagers in his part of the country thought they had a better chance of improving their lives under the Communists than with his own government.

Reston remembered all this through the years. The knowledge served him well when the agony of Vietnam began to eat away at the largely trusting relationship with the government that marked the Reston era in political journalism.

As early as March 1961, Reston was critical of those in the Kennedy administration who wanted to intervene in Southeast Asia. At issue was the struggle for control of Laos, and Scotty, sounding a theme he was to return to many times in writing about American involvement in the region, warned in a column that geography was the decisive factor in Cold War proxy conflicts: "We may by bold maneuvers influence events in Laos and even save its independence for a while, but the odds are against us." In the fall of that year, as the South Vietnam government demonstrated wild incompetence and the Kennedy administration anguished about how to solve the problem, Reston was ready to write a column calling for an end to our assistance to the corrupt Saigon regime. National Security Advisor McGeorge Bundy told his colleagues in the White House that he had barely managed to argue Reston out of the idea.

The immediate problem was ended later by an American-approved coup in which the president and his family were assassinated. After the coup, Reston raised the question of why, if the United States was willing to settle for a truce splitting Korea, Washington would not accept a similar solution in Vietnam.

> The official assumption here is that a negotiated political settlement in Vietnam is impossible and maybe even dishonorable, but how do they know? . . . A neat and tidy military conquest of the whole peninsula by the South Vietnamese backed by 15,000 American troops is not very likely. The French couldn't do it with 380,000 troops. . . . President Kennedy, however, is apparently not prepared to either expand the fight, or negotiate. . . . This [a negotiated split of the country] may not be possible now, but before we embark once more on the

purely military policy of "killing Communists," who in turn have a nasty habit of killing Americans, it would be interesting to find out.

Week after week, the official Washington version of success in Vietnam lost credibility against the somber stories American correspondents were filing out of Southeast Asia. The dissonance led to struggles in every major news organization that had reporters in both Washington and Vietnam, with the Washington correspondents tending to believe the rosy scenarios being spun out of the White House, the State Department, and the Pentagon, and the field reporters ever more skeptical. In many cases the chiefs of the Washington bureaus sided with their own reporters against the Saigon contingent. *Time* magazine, for example, lost one of its best reporters, Charles Mohr, when he resigned in protest over the magazine's refusal to heed the gloomy dispatches he was sending to New York. He went to work for the *Times,* with Reston playing a key role in his hiring, where he felt his work would fare better.

While Reston was certainly supportive of the reporters in his bureau, thinking they were accurately reporting what they were being told, he had huge respect for the war correspondents who were risking their lives and seeing quite a different picture. But even at the *Times,* disputes raged. At one point early in the war, Reston suggested New York simply print the Washington and Saigon stories side by side and let the readers decide. To some extent, the paper followed his advice, but as the argument over the war grew more heated and more ideological, the compromise satisfied no one. "His journalistic instinct told him it was not working, that it smelled bad," recalled David Halberstam. "So he played it rather cautiously with his sources. But he backed up guys like me and Neil and Charley vigorously. It was almost as if he knew it was going past him. Unlike many of his generation, he didn't turn on us. He knew we knew a truth he didn't know, and he didn't like it when those people took shots at us."

In 1965 Reston went out to Vietnam himself, in part to report back to Punch Sulzberger – the young publisher, a proud ex-marine, was nervous about his paper's role in questioning the war – and in part to see for himself exactly what the war effort looked like on the ground. By this time the American presence had reached 200,000 men.

"The *Times* office," Reston wrote in his memoirs, "was on the second floor of number 46 Tu Do, a street of shops, bars, and subsidiary services. In the daytime, it was full of happy squealing kids, newsboys, pedicabs, and Jeeps. At night, Tu Do was deserted after the eleven o'clock curfew, except for roving military police cars and bats, which wheeled in alarming numbers through the trees on either side of the street."

The Saigon office, Reston wrote, "was not as cushy as ours had been in the Savoy Hotel during the big war. The place reeked of disinfectant and vague seeping odors disinfectant is expected to banish. It had no air-conditioning, but it had a couple of lazy fans that often took the night off. It had a refrigerator full of beer, which was good, and a toilet that I will not describe."

The Saigon bureau chief was R. W. "Johnny" Apple. Charles Mohr, David Halberstam, and the newly hired Neil Sheehan were there as well. Like the Washington bureau, it was the best collection of journalists in the country and was heavily staffed with Scotty's boys. Apple had come to the *Times* from NBC, with Scotty doing the arranging. Apple first did a stint for the paper in New York, then in Albany, and in early 1965 was loaned to the foreign desk for a six-month tour in Vietnam. When the metropolitan desk asked for him back, Apple got Mohr to write to Reston to help him stay on. He spent three years in Vietnam. Sheehan was a similar case. He became a close friend of Halberstam's in Vietnam and made several attempts to get hired at the *Times*. In 1963 Reston had wanted Sheehan in Washington, but the stringency caused by the newspaper strike left no positions. So Reston had sent Sheehan to New York for a job inerview, where Clifton Daniel and Turner Catledge greeted him with great suspicion because he was a Reston recruit. "I walked in there with a great big *R* on my forehead," Sheehan said. In an interview with a personnel officer, Sheehan was asked if he drank liquor. Sheehan said that he had drunk liquor in college but that he had quit because booze "didn't agree with me." This raised a red flag with the personnel department, which apparently feared that he was either abnormal – a newspaperman who didn't touch booze – or more likely had a problem with too much alcohol. The latter was true; Sheehan had realized it early and quit drinking entirely. But New York used the liquor issue as an excuse not to hire him. Finally, with Halberstam lobbying hard from Saigon, Reston warned New York that Sheehan was about to be snapped up by the *Washington Post*. It was not true, but it broke the logjam and Sheehan was hired.

Even though Reston was the patron of Apple, Halberstam, Sheehan, and Charley Mohr, he was treated not as a visiting dignitary but as another reporter, albeit a revered one. In the early days of his visit, Reston wrote a little piece about something he had seen in the field. Apple, seeing the story before it was transmitted, told him: "Scotty, I don't think we want to run this. We've said this many times. Why don't you save it for a column." "I can't imagine what emboldened me to say such a thing," Apple recalled, "but I did and it was an honest judgment. He took it as such and said, 'Fine, that's what I'll do.'" Another night Sheehan recalls being alone in the bureau, typing by kerosene lantern, since the electricity had gone off, "sweat running off my fingers into the typewriter." Reston asked him to file his column for him when he had finished with his own piece. "And," said a still-mortified Sheehan decades later, "I forgot to file Scotty's column. I realized what I had done the next morning and called him to tell him. I asked should I send it now. A pause. Then Reston replied calmly, 'No, it's too late. They'll substitute someone else. It's all right, we all forget once in a while.'" Sheehan had been petrified with fear when he called Reston: "Most men of his stature would have reamed me." Reston showed the bureau other kindnesses as well. Sheehan's wife, Susan, was glum and missing home on her birthday, when Scotty showed up to share some celebratory cake with her. He wrote a happy piece about the Sheehans for the newspaper's internal newsletter, *Times Talk*, trying to boost their morale.

The bureau set Reston up with their best sources, men whose judgment they all respected: Dick Holbrooke, Peter Tarnoff, Tony Lake, John Negroponte, Pete Dawkins – all junior diplomats, intelligence, and military officers, not the Saigon-based top dogs. Recalls Apple: "They were out in the field and they saw it day in and day out. Reston saw a young major out in the delta whom I knew very well named Colin Powell. Those people were our sources. We got Scotty to them and to other diplomats and he was not brainwashed. It was an important trip for him, I think, in the sense of satisfying himself that we were getting it right and that we were not a bunch of gunslingers."

"The longer I stayed in Saigon, the more depressed I became," Reston wrote in his memoirs years later. "I admired and respected the officers in the field, who had been given an assignment to clear the Communists out of the south, but not the means to carry it out." He experienced the awful, bewildering, surreal world of the war and found it "almost beyond comprehension." Scotty realized it was not a war in the way he had known war in Europe, but

a series of violent actions, some rather like Al Capone's gang raids in Chicago, some like the frontier skirmishes in the

French and Indian War, still others like the savage encounters between the Americans and the Japanese in the Pacific island caves of 1945. . . . It really needed a new vocabulary. Vietnam was not a nation but a physical and strategic entity broken into conspiratorial families, clans, sects, hamlets, and regions. . . . The prime minister in Saigon was not prime. Nothing was as it seemed.

Most important, Reston caught the central, self-defeating paradox of the application of enormous American firepower. Writing from Saigon on August 28, 1965, Scotty called the vast destruction a "devilish dilemma," clearly hurting the Vietcong but also hurting the campaign to change the hearts and minds of the Vietnamese people who gave aid to the enemy. "We are chasing guerrillas with bombs and it is apparently having much more effect on the Vietcong than anyone thought possible, but in the process we are attacking and often destroying the areas we want to pacify. . . . Maybe nothing can be done about it, but somewhere in a corner of the mind, their tragedy must be remembered. For we could win the war and lose the people, and that would be the final irony of the story."

As a finale to his tour, Reston was flown out to the carrier *Independence,* from which American flyers launched their bombing runs. A German correspondent, Lothar Loewe, landed after Reston and was impressed by Scotty's generosity. The American commanders were giving Reston top-level briefings when he wasn't watching takeoffs and landings, and he invited the German along. "He was like a father figure," Loewe recalled. When it was time for Reston to be flown back to the mainland, he climbed aboard a Grumman C-1A twin-engine reconnaissance plane and asked Loewe to snap a few pictures of him as he departed. Off they went heading for Saigon. Not long after they were airborne, the plane's hydraulic system failed and the pilot headed for the nearest American base, at Da Nang. As Reston recalled, "We almost made it." The plane crashed within sight of the landing strip, into a housing development. The pilot screamed at his passengers to get out before the plane caught fire and they all crawled out through the roof, bruised but not seriously hurt.

Back in Saigon, Sheehan received an emergency message from a public information officer in Da Nang reporting the accident. "My heart was in my mouth," Sheehan said. But not long afterward, Reston called to say he was just a little banged up. Two or three hours later, the phone in the Saigon bureau rang again. This time it was a colonel from the National Military Command Center in Washington, wanting to talk to Reston. "I've been told to find out how he is," the colonel explained to Sheehan, who asked who wanted to know. The colonel refused to say. It was President Johnson, worried that the war that was going so badly had now claimed America's leading journalist. When Johnson found out Reston had survived, he called Tom Wicker, now bureau chief in Washington, in the middle of the night to tell him of the crash. "Tell Sally Scotty's all right," he told Wicker.

When Reston got back to Washington, President Johnson had a few other things to say to him. LBJ summoned him to the White House and laid into him about his negative view of the war. Reston had pretty much concluded that Johnson was doing exactly what he had said in 1964 he would not do: he was bombing the north and sending American boys to fight an Asian war. As Reston recalled in his memoirs, Johnson berated the very correspondents who had impressed Reston with their work and their courage, and then asked Scotty: "Why don't you get on the team? You have only one president." Reston said he thought perhaps the problem was that Johnson was too prideful to see the war clearly and was more interested in saving face than ending the war. Johnson showed him to the door. "I'm not trying to save my face," he told Reston, "I'm trying to save my ass." In the end, he saved neither.

Throughout the Johnson years, Reston remained a powerful skeptic of American strategy in Vietnam, but he never crossed over into absolute opposition to the war. Nor was he ever a cheerleader for the war. A few months after Reston returned from Vietnam, syndicated columnist Joe Alsop wrote a harsh letter to Scotty criticizing the reporting of Sheehan and Halberstam. Alsop was always a convinced hawk on Vietnam. After he read an account by Sheehan of a battle in which there were substantial American casualties, he wrote a letter to Reston lambasting the *Times*. "I can recall few performances by seasoned, battle-hardened American troops to equal the performance of our decidedly green troops in Vietnam in the last month. The fact that they are performing so magnificently should not only be a matter of deep pride; it is also a matter of the utmost political import," Alsop wrote.

In reply, Reston questioned the premise of Alsop's complaint. Scotty argued that the victories were more important than the casualties only if they were indicators of eventual success in the war. "You are always dogmatic about that," Reston wrote politely but pointedly, "but I cannot be. I have always respected your judgment and your courage in these matters, but for myself, I simply do not know, and frankly, I am very skeptical."

To close the letter, which appears to have been typed by Reston himself, Scotty quoted the French poet Paul Valéry's "Ultima Verba": "Stop conqueror. . . . Pause at this lofty moment of victory. Be silent for a time and reflect on what to think at this pinnacle. . . . Whenever you re-live this day, may there never come into your mind these cruel words: 'What Was The Use?'" "I do not question that we can have won 'victories,'" Scotty concluded, "but in the end, I cannot believe, try as I do, that we will have a satisfactory answer to Valery's terrible question."

As polite as his answer was, Reston was quite angry at Alsop's ideological assault on his Saigon reporters. Halberstam once asked Reston, as the two strolled back to the bureau from the Metropolitan Club, why Alsop had written such vicious things about Sheehan and himself. "I'm afraid Joe is a cruel man," Halberstam recalls Reston saying, apparently pained by the very bluntness of his own description of Alsop.

Scotty Reston was a man of the political center, always his virtue and his strength. But as the center began to erode, as the country divided ever more bitterly over the wisdom of the war in Vietnam, Reston scrambled to keep his balance, to hold to the center. He maintained excellent access to top policy makers in the Johnson administration but also kept his lines open to the few and very quiet dissidents inside the administration, like Undersecretary of State George Ball. In the spring of 1967, U.S. ambassador to India Chester Bowles wrote to Reston to support his repeated warnings that the Chinese might intervene in Vietnam. The letter was marked PERSONAL, PRIVATE, OFF THE RECORD because it was a sharp dissent from official American policy. "If our military efforts in Viet-Nam are successful enough to persuade China that it must enter the war, we would have a rough time on the ground, and as in the past we would find air retaliation less effective than experts anticipate," Bowles wrote, also worrying that a conflict with China might bring the Soviet Union into the war as well. "Once this ugly possibility begins to seep into our national consciousness, the pressures for a negotiated peace in Viet-Nam may grow significantly," he concluded. A postscript urged Reston: "Please treat this letter as strictly off-the-record." Reston did.

Reston showed how deftly he navigated the new divide not long after Neil Sheehan came to Washington after his tour in Vietnam. He was assigned to cover the Pentagon. (Sheehan almost didn't take the job because he wanted to be chief military correspondent, a post that went to another man. Reston wrote him saying he was being "a foolish young man" and Sheehan quickly changed his mind.) Sheehan produced a major, three-part series on U.S. arms sales abroad, accusing the Johnson administration of force-feeding weapons to client states. The pieces caused consternation in the government, which saw its arms supply program as a major weapon to counter Communism and as one of America's chief ways to support Israel.

After the first piece appeared, Sheehan remembers Reston telling him that Navy Secretary (and Reston's neighbor) Paul Nitze had called to say that Secretary of Defense Robert McNamara had wanted to fly to New York to talk the publisher into stopping the series. Reston told Sheehan he had asked Nitze if there were any factual inaccuracies. Nitze could find none. Reston advised him it wouldn't do any good for McNamara to see the publisher. Reston offered instead to write a column expressing the government's point of view, but meanwhile the series would continue. He then asked Sheehan if there were any questions he was having trouble getting answered. Sheehan gave him a list and Scotty called Nitze back to pursue the promised column. Casually, he got the questions answered. Sheehan was at his side, writing new questions as the two men talked.

"He suckered Nitze for about forty-five minutes or so," Sheehan said. "This was Scotty Reston doing two things. One, he backed reporters. You were expected to show loyalty up and he showed loyalty down. He also liked tough reporting. He wanted us to be tough. He once said to me, 'We don't have any friends in government. We're like the British Empire, we don't have any friends, we only have interests when it comes to government.' He didn't want to do this kind of reporting himself at this stage of his career. He wanted us to do it. A part of Scotty wanted to be part of the establishment, to be accepted by the Nitzes. But he passed along everything he heard and learned, unbeknownst to them, and he wanted us to use it."

Serious establishment critics of the war – columnists like Reston and Walter Lippmann, and politicians like Bobby Kennedy – were leaning on Johnson to move to the negotiating table. But the degree of their insistence varied. Much of the argument in 1967 centered around the question of whether the United States should stop bombing North Vietnam as an inducement for negotiations. In the spring of that year, Robert Kennedy began to increase his criticism of the president's war policies and gave a pair of speeches in which he made it clear that he was for an end to the bombing and for negotiation. Reston wrote in March that the Kennedy speech was good because it "expressed the conscience of the nation about the human tragedy of the war." At the same time, he criticized Kennedy's speech as diplomatically and politically fuzzy, "and maybe even opportunistic." He defended Johnson for having offered Hanoi a conditional bombing halt in return for negotiations and blamed Hanoi for demanding a permanent cessation of bombing without promising that negotiations would have a time limit and a definite purpose.

The column brought an angry phone call from Kennedy. He complained that Scotty was wrong to criticize his efforts to move American policy toward a negotiated settlement in Vietnam. Scotty promptly wrote back to say he was "puzzled and embarrassed" by Kennedy's irritation. "My quarrel with your two major speeches on Vietnam is not, God knows, personal or political. I agree with the spirit of both of them. I want our country to recognize and negoti-ate with the National Liberation Front. I don't see how we can end the fighting unless we talk to the people who are fighting us." But he continued the critique he had started in his column: "Your premise was that serious peace talks were blocked because we would not take one single, simple step, whereas the British, who are not hawks, were testifying that what blocked the peace talks were not Washington's obstructions but Hanoi's. . . . Anyway, I was not trying to cut you up. I agree with your objectives . . . but I still think your argument is faulty and not up to the position you have achieved in the country." He signed it: "Sincerely, Scotty Reston."

Reston never made the jump to the absolutist side of the antiwar movement. His devotion to the country, his respect for authority, his realistic sense of the evils of Communism, all made him critical of the mass unrest racking the country. He understood the feelings of those who were increasingly radicalized by their hatred of the war, but he never supported their tactics. He never forgot that if the United States simply quit Vietnam, the people there would be forced to live under a political system he despised. In the fall of 1967, after a spate of street demonstrations against the war, Reston criticized both the antiwar movement and the administration:

This has not been a very happy period. The sound of the billy club on youthful skulls has been heard across the land. The Secretary of State has been trying to scare people with apocalyptic visions of a billion Chinese armed with nuclear weapons. . . . The leaders of the Administration . . . are so busy rushing around the country defending the war that they have little time left to try to figure out how to end it. . . . The demonstrators . . . want to change Vietnam policy and "dump Johnson" . . . but they are not likely to do either by concentrating on mass demonstrations on television, which gives the country the impression that the President is fighting a two-front war – in Vietnam against the communists and on the home front against militant young radicals.

His ambivalence about the antiwar protests was perfectly captured in a column in early January 1968. The federal government had just indicted Yale University chaplain William Sloane Coffin Jr. and famous pediatrician Benjamin Spock and others for urging students to evade the draft. "It is important to be clear about what is *not* at issue in this case," Reston wrote. "The Government is not challenging the right of Coffin, Spock and the other defendants to speak out against the war. It is not challenging their right to say that the military draft is wrong or unfair. But it is saying there is a critical line between expressing an opinion and inciting and organizing young men to defy the law." Reston went on to argue both sides of the case: that breaking the law demands government legal action and that higher moral law demands more than conventional, democratic argument against the enormous evil of the war. Concluded Reston:

> Legally, the Johnson Administration obviously has a good case. It can undoubtedly prove that it went to war under the Constitution, legally, if by stealth. Legally, it has the right to draft its citizens, no matter how unfair the draft system may be to the poor, and legally, citizens can oppose all this under the freedom of speech clause of the First Amendment. But Coffin and Spock have gone beyond this, and in the process, with the help of the Government's indictment, they have raised the basic question: Is the war not only legally but morally right? Is it an offense to oppose the war or to support it? Whoever wins the legal case, the moral case will obviously remain.

In early March, Reston returned from a trip to the West Coast to write about the steadily declining morale of the American public. He remarked, as he often did, on the stark contrasts between wealth and poverty and decried, as he did frequently, the large indifference he found in middle-class white communities toward privations in the black ghettos. But he noted a deeper despair in the country.

> When the people turn to their institutions for help, they feel abandoned. The churches are divided about the war and even about the Negro revolution. The universities are in turmoil. The military draft is obviously unequal. The press is a confusion of advice between hawks and doves on the war, and the

pro-Negro and anti-Negro arguments in the cities. Finally, the Johnson Administration asks for confidence and trust for policies which are not succeeding either at home or abroad, so there is no trust or confidence and the people are left to their own doubts and suspicions.

It was an uncharacteristically bleak piece by Reston; he nearly always found some silver lining, some reason to cheer for America. The only thing he could muster was, "Despite all the doubts and the confusions and prejudices, there is also a lot of honest debate in America about the great issues."

Reston was deeply discouraged by the murder of Martin Luther King Jr. In 1963, the day after King's "I Have a Dream" speech on the steps of the Lincoln Memorial, Reston sat in his office and listened again to the moving cadences that had washed over the hundreds of thousands who had come to Washington with King. Tears came to Scotty's eyes. When King was assassinated in 1968, the capital city Reston had loved for nearly three decades went up in flames. Parts of the city where many white reporters from the nation's biggest and best news organizations had never been erupted in waves of arson, riot, and looting. Army troops marched in; a machine gun was mounted on the steps of the U.S. capitol. Borders with the suburbs were heavily patrolled to prevent the riots from spreading into the white enclaves surrounding Washington. Reston tried to strike a balance between understanding the rage of the black community, which he and most of respectable white America still called the "Negro" community, and preaching restraint.

"At least the extremists have kept their promises," he wrote.

The white racists said they would kill King, and the black racists said they would burn us to the ground. And we will not hear again that strangled cry or the rolling Biblical cadences of that magnificent voice: and the smoke is drifting this weekend through the cherry blossoms by the Jefferson Memorial, and the rest of us have not kept our promises to the Negro people. . . . The evidence is plain before our eyes. For violence, while it can destroy indifference, which is the curse of the moderate, middle class, cannot choose. It destroys good as well as evil. Brute coercion and savage intolerance of the Negro must be destroyed, but they cannot be burned away by raging demons intoxicated with illusion.

Two months later, Robert Kennedy was shot in a hotel kitchen in Los Angeles, just after he had won the California Democratic primary. Reston could barely find the words to express the shock he and the nation felt. It seemed increasingly that as hundreds of Americans died every week in Vietnam and American cities became tinder boxes of rage, the country was coming apart: "There is something in the air of the modern world: a defiance of authority, a contagious irresponsibility, a kind of moral delinquency, no longer restrained by religious or ethical faith. And these attitudes are now threatening not only personal serenity but also public order in many parts of the world."

The world that Reston knew, the world he had understood, the world that had appreciated his calm, rational approach to public issues and to public people, was ending. Later in the year, Reston got a direct message about where the radical opposition to the war placed him on its moral scale. He was to speak at New York University on the prospects for the just-elected Nixon administration. A few minutes into his talk, a group of about one hundred students used a couch to bash down the locked door of the auditorium. They flooded into the hall chanting the usual "Ho, Ho, Ho Chi Minh." (The second verse of the chant was usually: "The NLF is gonna win.") Reston still had the microphone and responded cutely, "He isn't here." Ever the gentleman, he invited the angry mob up to the podium to explain its message. They chose instead to rampage up and down the aisles shouting obscenities, dismantle the loudspeaker system, and eventually drive everyone, including Reston, out of the auditorium. The man who for nearly two decades had been a revered voice of reason and good sense had run up against the ugly realities of an America at war with itself.

CHAPTER 22

SCOTTY VERSUS ABE

THE RELATIONSHIP BETWEEN Punch Sulzberger and Scotty Reston was never as intimate and affectionate as were Scotty's ties to the elder Sulzbergers and to Orvil and Marian Dryfoos. Arthur Hays was nearly a father figure for Reston; Punch was younger than Reston by half a generation. After Punch became publisher in 1963, he ended Reston's direct line of report to the publisher's office, leaving him to answer to managing editor Turner Catledge, who was closer to Punch. Catledge had mentored Punch before he became publisher and the two often enjoyed a quiet drink together after work. In 1964 Reston chose to step aside as bureau chief and turn over the administrative chores to his protégé Tom Wicker. The struggle between New York and Washington never ceased; since Catledge had better access to Punch, Scotty wanted to get out of the line of fire. Besides, Reston still held editors in New York in mild contempt; he once told Catledge he was neither managing nor editing the *Times*. Punch found Reston a bit austere for his tastes. In an interview years later, he coldly described Scotty as "a resource which I inherited," as if he were in the same category as the building and the presses and the desks in Times Square.

Wicker, one of the earliest and most brilliant hires Scotty made when he took over from Arthur Krock, was Reston's handpicked successor. Although a gifted writer and reporter, Wicker, by his own admission, had not proved a particularly effective manager of the bureau. As early as the spring of 1966, New York was planning to replace him as bureau chief. In a memo to Punch about Wicker, Catledge wrote: "I know of no specific problem that has caused me more concern than this one has over the last year." Catledge blamed Reston for having "rather suddenly dropped" the reins of the Washington bureau, but he also blamed some new editors in New York for mishandling Wicker. "Making allowances for the latter," Catledge wrote, "I cannot escape the conclusion that Tom Wicker's uncertainty and lack of the particular equipment required for the job are essentially the problem." Catledge reported that he had considered sending Abe Rosenthal, one of the ablest and most aggressive of the younger New York editors, to Washington on a temporary basis so that Abe "would no doubt shake things up." But he rejected the idea and proposed instead that Wicker, come the beginning of 1967, be given a column and eased away from the bureau chief's job.

By the end of 1967, however, nothing had changed except that Wicker had been given a column on the editorial page. That work was superb, but he continued to limp along as bureau chief because there seemed to be no logical successor. Max Frankel was still relatively young and his administrative skills were suspect in New York. Tony Lewis, now the London correspondent, was a possibility, but he was not popular among the other reporters in Washington and giving him the job would certainly have led to Frankel's resignation. Rosenthal was disinclined to leave the executive track in New York but shared Catledge's desire to move Wicker out and, in the process, seize control of the Washington bureau. Finally a candidate emerged. Rosenthal proposed that James Greenfield, an old friend whom he had recently brought to the *Times*, become Wicker's replacement.

Jimmy Greenfield, as he was universally known, was a former *Time* magazine correspondent who had met Rosenthal when they were both posted to New Delhi. From the magazine, Greenfield had gone to the Kennedy State Department as a deputy press spokesman. Then he worked as a publicity man for Continental Airlines, a job he got through Pierre Salinger, before Rosenthal brought him to the newspaper.

The top editors had little trouble convincing Punch that this was a good idea. Rosenthal mentioned the scheme to Reston, who was careful neither to endorse nor to oppose the idea. Rosenthal misread Reston's noncommittal attitude as at least acceptance of the idea. Wicker, the New York group figured, would be relieved to have done with the administrative duties of bureau chief and would be easily convinced to join Reston as a distinguished columnist. Frankel and Lewis would be offered various consolation prizes. Greenfield was told he would be the next Washington bureau chief. He was, to put it mildly, elated. After little more than a year on the *Times*, he was now set to succeed some of the biggest names in American journalism: Krock and Reston and Wicker.

Why Greenfield? "Because he was an extremely sensitive man about foreign affairs," Rosenthal explained years later. "I knew this man and I knew his mind. He had shown himself very well at the *New York Times*. He wasn't just a guy I had known in India. He was also one of the few people on the *New York Times* who really understood how the government worked. I thought he would be a very good choice, people liked him. And I didn't want a writing bureau chief." All true, as far as it went. More important was Greenfield's absolute loyalty to Rosenthal and to New York, and the absence of any obligation to Scotty Reston.

When Reston learned that the Greenfield plan was about to be implemented (apparently from Lewis, who wrote from London to complain that he had not been considered), Scotty first urged that no change in the Washington bureau be made until after the 1968 election. Changes at the top of the Washington operations of major news organizations were in fact usually made in conjunction with election cycles. Reston wrote a three-page memo to Punch about the planned changes, warning the publisher, "We may be on the verge of making a serious mistake by insisting on a change at this time." Wicker, Reston assured Sulzberger, would not take the change well, and the effect on Frankel and Lewis would be quite negative. "I go back to what seems to me to be the primary problem before us. This is to be sure that we keep all the special talent we have, including Tom, Max, and Tony and Greenfield and the others." Reston's reference to his boys by their first names and to Abe's boy by his surname was not purely accidental, although Reston went on to assure Punch that he liked and respected Greenfield. No one, however, bought the idea that Scotty thought well of Greenfield, least of all Greenfield himself. "I knew Scotty from my days in government," Greenfield recalled in an interview, "but I was very far from what he had wanted or intended or hoped for [as Washington bureau chief]. He had a cadre of disciples, people who had come up under his aegis; many of them were very, very talented. This was really challenging his authority in the bureau. Scotty, who was a total product of Washington, never thought of me as a journalist. He had only known me as a spokesman. He regarded me as someone he had met in the government. Scotty regarded me only in the Washington context." In the bureau the notion of Greenfield's succeeding Wicker was anathema. Fred Graham, who was covering the Supreme Court at the time, put it this way: "The fact that Greenfield was so unqualified was seen by us as a way of Abe putting his thumb in our eye because he had the power to do it."

For a few weeks, Reston heard nothing from Sulzberger and assumed his advice had been taken. Then Sulzberger announced he was coming to Washington to dine with Wicker and Reston. When Punch strolled into Scotty's office, Reston was cool and formal and informed the publisher that he would not be joining the dinner group. "You'd better do it in private because it will be a rough night and things will probably be said that a third person should not hear," he told Punch. As predicted, Wicker was furious and told Punch he would quit if Greenfield replaced him. Punch asked him to hold off a few days so he could talk to Frankel and Lewis. Wicker agreed but remained intent on quitting. Soon the story of the putsch was being merrily displayed in rival newspapers and newsmagazines.

After a few days, Reston flew to New York to talk to Punch again. He fully understood the stakes. If the New York editors could impose their own man on Washington, then not only were Wicker and Frankel likely to quit, it would also mean that men who were indebted to Reston, devoted to his style of reportage, would be gone. Reston, by example and by suggestion, was still the most powerful figure in the bureau, and the bureau was still the most powerful counterweight to New York. Catledge was close to Punch, and if Greenfield answered to Rosenthal, Reston would be pushed well down the influence ladder. Some people at the paper saw the unhorsing of Wicker as a key ploy in the battle for the top editor's job. Catledge seemed to be grooming Abe for the job, while Reston seemed to hope Wicker would one day be the ultimate boss of the news operation.

The night before he was to meet with Sulzberger, Reston received a delegation of disgruntled Washington correspondents at his home. According to Neil Sheehan, Reston asked the group whether they thought he should offer his resignation. The correspondents offered no opinion and Reston suggested perhaps it wouldn't be necessary. Sheehan told Reston that if he decided to quit, he, Sheehan, would resign with him. Reston left the group with the impression that he was ready to resign if he couldn't change Punch's mind, but it is doubtful that he made such a threat or even seriously intended to. Sulzberger denies that Reston ever mentioned the idea. "It would have been difficult because when people threaten to resign, I accept," Punch said. But Reston did tell the publisher he was on the side of the younger men – Wicker, Frankel, Lewis – and not with Rosenthal, Catledge, and Clifton Daniel, an assistant managing editor who joined them in pushing the Greenfield scenario. All the brouhaha convinced Punch that the trouble the Greenfield appointment would cause was not worth it.

Greenfield was both eager and apprehensive about the Washington job. "I knew my introduction into the bureau would be very difficult, not impossible, but extremely difficult." He promised a writer from *Newsweek* that once the deal was official, he would sit for an interview. On the morning of February 7, 1968, he arrived at the *Times* and noticed a good bit of coming and going in the executive offices. Still, he expected to claim the prize as Washington bureau chief. "It was supposed to be announced at ten o'clock in the morning," Greenfield remembered, the disappointment still evident decades later. "At ten-thirty Abe told me it was off. I enjoyed everything at the *Times* except those few minutes. I suppose I stayed fifteen minutes. I remember looking for my sweater and I asked someone else to pack up my desk." Greenfield then walked out of the building. "It was embarrassing and I didn't like the way it was handled," Greenfield recounted. "I wasn't going to stick around and mope about it." Reston, knowing that he had hurt Greenfield, called him that night. "I said, 'I really have no desire to stay,'" Greenfield recalled. "He asked me to come on down and talk to him. And I said there was really no job I wanted as a consolation prize. I don't believe he cared one bit. I think he wanted to smooth it over. It had created a certain amount of confusion on the paper. There were stories about it and I think he wanted to stop that. I don't think for a moment he cared. As a matter of fact, later I heard a disturbing rumor that Kay Graham had asked Scotty about me and Scotty said, 'Oh, he's just a government flack.'"

Greenfield was not, in fact, a good choice by Rosenthal and the other New York editors. His journalistic credentials were thin compared with the Wicker-Frankel-Lewis set; his sojourn in the government and in private public relations made him suspect; and his brief tenure at the paper prevented him from gathering any powerful patronage beyond Rosenthal. Greenfield had become a pawn in a power game played by men in another league altogether. It was easier to embarrass Greenfield than buck Reston or frustrate Frankel and Lewis. As Frankel explained: "The main point of the Greenfield blowup was that Tom Wicker, even though he was not the world's greatest bureau chief, did not deserve to be treated the way he was treated. And the rest of us, Tony Lewis and me, who had aspirations for leadership, did not deserve to be trumped by a Greenfield."

Abe Rosenthal has a different take on those events. "I look back at how stunned and how innocent we all were in New York. You know, Tom Wicker had said the time was coming when he would no longer be a columnist and bureau chief. So I thought, well, if he's going to do it, let's do it, because an election was coming up. I hadn't the faintest idea. I was like a kid, because it turned out he really didn't want to go and Mr. Reston didn't want anyone he hadn't chosen to become the Washington bureau chief and he created an enormous fuss. I talked to Catledge and to Clifton Daniel. I don't recall talking to Scotty, although I probably did. If he was opposed, he cloaked it. It's inconceivable to me I didn't talk to him. We posted the notice about Mr. Greenfield. And then bang! If I had known he [Reston] was opposed, I certainly would have taken account of it. I would have gone another way or not told Jimmy. And Punch certainly wouldn't have done it if Reston was opposed. My attitude toward

Wicker was that he had said he wanted to leave [being bureau chief]. I was utterly astonished when he made such a big fuss. I really didn't understand that I was cutting across Mr. Reston's plans, not only for the Washington bureau, but for the *New York Times,* a plan which he never really gave up."

Wicker stayed on as bureau chief until the end of 1968, when he was replaced by Frankel. Lewis stayed in London and was to figure in a later New York confrontation. The reaction from Daniel and Rosenthal to Sulzberger's veto of Greenfield was angry and ill considered. Abe tried to call Punch to protest the mistreatment of Greenfield – and by extension himself – but was lucky enough not to reach the publisher right away. When he did talk to him, Punch finally calmed him down enough to keep him on the staff. When Daniel and Sulzberger tried to talk about the debacle, Daniel got so loud and abusive that the encounter dissolved what little regard Punch had for him. He was soon demoted and lost his chance to be a successor to Catledge. Two months after the incident, Sulzberger told Catledge rather abruptly that Catledge's retirement had been moved up and he was to be replaced by . . . Scotty Reston! Only Rosenthal survived, to fight another day, and that day came quite soon.

According to Catledge, Reston had been in Punch's mind as a potential successor as managing editor for some time. But Punch was not ready, prior to the dustup over Greenfield, to make a move. Rosenthal was not deemed ready to run the paper. That left Reston as the only choice in the time of crisis. Punch was likely hearing counsel from his mother and father to bring Reston in from Washington to help the paper navigate past the huge upset the Greenfield affair had caused. On June 10, 1968, James B. Reston came north to run the *New York Times,* the paper he had joined as a war reporter three decades earlier.

*   *   *

The Restons did not sell their big house on Woodley Road, nor did Scotty intend to give up his column. He believed he was only as strong inside the paper as he was outside it and the column was his signature product. He took the top editor's job with, at the very least, a certain ambivalence. For his part, Punch Sulzberger believed Reston wanted the job and had made it clear even before all the difficulty over Wicker. But whether Scotty took the most powerful editorial job in the world of journalism intending to stay for a long period is not entirely clear. By retaining his house in Cleveland Park and his column, he was at least hedging his career bets. The Restons were installed in a grand apartment on the East Side of Manhattan at the UN Plaza, sublet from philanthropist Mary Lasker. He was provided with a green Lincoln and a driver and given use of the company plane.

Reston clearly enjoyed at least the trappings of power. He occupied a separate office off the massive third-floor newsroom, but he also immediately commandeered a desk in the newsroom itself. He often worked there in his shirtsleeves to make himself accessible to the staff. The barons on the New York news staff had dutifully written him notes of congratulations, some with a jocularity that bordered on sarcasm. Theodore Bernstein was one of the bullpen editors who wielded power over the display and final editing of stories. His note began: "Dear Boss Man." It ended with a question: "Need I pledge my undying fealty?" Even Clifton Daniel, the biggest loser aside from Greenfield in the power struggle, sent a note, albeit a rather cool one: "I offer you my congratulations and my cooperation. I have some ideas, of course, about how things should be run in the future. When you want to hear them, I am at your disposal."

But Scotty's reception was chilly at best. He had immediately asked Richard Mooney to be his deputy. Mooney, a tall, blond Ivy Leaguer, had been hired by Reston to cover the economics beat in Washington in 1956 and was the only person on the New York staff who had ever worked for Reston. "He was coming to a hostile environment and must have thought, 'I have somebody up there who knows me and loves me,'" Mooney said. Mooney focused on personnel, interviewing potential employees, and sometimes went to meetings in Reston's stead. He was not involved in the editorial content of the paper, and the other editors tried to keep it that way to preserve their power in the face of the Reston takeover. Mooney remembers one late afternoon when someone came by his desk and showed him a copy of the page one layout. "Ted Bernstein came storming over, indicating I was not supposed to be screening page one," Mooney recalled. "I wasn't screening page one. Some stupid guy was just showing me what we were doing that night. Bernstein was very conscious of who had what authority and he sure as hell didn't want me having authority over him."

But the petty resistance was nothing compared to what Reston got from Rosenthal shortly after Scotty arrived in New York. Reston had some very distinct ideas about how to improve the *New York Times*. He believed that intellectual conflict was never covered, while conflict in the streets or between countries was always covered. He urged everyone to broaden the perspective of the paper, to try to make the daily report reflect some of the intellectual and emotional life of the country, not just the political and economic. He imagined that he could create, in the midst of the enormous bureaucracy of the New York office and alongside the veritable army of reporters — more than four hundred at that time — an elite corps of correspondents not unlike those he had hired in Washington. The super-reporters would work out of the New York office and would be called upon to parachute into stories anywhere in the world where their particular talents and expertise could raise the quality of the coverage. They would be paid better than line reporters and be offered perquisites like lengthy leaves during which they could write books. He even imagined they would have their own offices and assistants to help them in their work. He also thought he would loosen the rigid desk system, permitting a freer movement of reporters between foreign, national, and metropolitan staffs. In short, Reston wanted to create a group of reporters who would work under the same conditions he, Scotty Reston, had managed to create for himself in Washington.

Not long after he arrived in New York, he tried this set of blue-sky ideas on Abe Rosenthal, who, as an assistant managing editor, was now the second-most-powerful editorial person on the daily paper. Rosenthal hated the Reston vision then and hates it today. "Ridiculous," he snorted in an interview three decades later. "He was going to make two classes of reporters, his class and the others. It was not going to happen. We were not going to have two classes of reporters, one of them getting all the good assignments, special working conditions, money, and all the rest of it. We had struggled very hard to make this one newspaper instead of a collection of duchies. Scotty wanted to take us back where, in the same room, we would have duchies." According to Harrison Salisbury, at that time a deputy managing editor and later the author of a brilliant book on the inner workings of the *Times,* Rosenthal and Reston had dinner one night at which these subjects were broached:

As Reston talked Rosenthal grew more and more silent; a flushed look came over his face, the veins pounded in his temples. Finally he burst out. Enough! He was not going to preside over a second-class city room! He would not serve under a system in which he did not control his own men. He would not have *his* staff working alongside Reston's chosen few. It was impossible. Intolerable. . . . If this was what Reston had come to New York to do, he, Rosenthal, would get out. His resignation was available at any time. It would be on Reston's desk in the morning.

Salisbury saw Reston in the office early the next morning, and Reston recounted his experience at the dinner. He told Salisbury he had wound up trying to calm Abe down, to help him get himself under control. Rosenthal later claimed to Salisbury he had no recollection of the dinner. Whatever his memory, the fit he threw had its desired effect. Reston had come to New York promising Sulzberger he would smooth the troubled waters, not roil them. Reston knew if he provoked Rosenthal into resigning, there would be another round of chortling stories in the rest of the press. Punch, already mortally embarrassed by the Wicker-Greenfield contretemps, would not be happy. Reston quietly set aside his grand plans.

It was not just the big ideas that failed. Even the more mundane chores of running the paper eluded Reston. Perhaps the best description of his failure comes from Eugene Roberts, then the national editor of the paper and subsequently one of the best news executives ever to run an American newspaper when he took over the *Philadelphia Inquirer* years later. Roberts had a front-row seat as Scotty walked through his role as executive editor; he had been named national editor as a compromise candidate when Rosenthal and Reston couldn't agree on a choice, since Roberts did not belong to either man.

"There were divisions within the *Times* in New York that were even sharper than that between Washington and New York," Roberts explained. "The first was the dayside versus the nightside [the bullpen, where the copy editors worked] and also between the daily paper and the Sunday paper. On the daily paper, the dayside would leave before the first deadline and the bullpen would then actually control the shape of stories.

"The feeling in the office was that Reston was a brilliant newsman but that he had no experience as an editor. Many in New York felt that it was unjust that he had gotten that kind of promotion. Most of these people were used to being in chains of command, even the bullpen. Everyone believed in the procedures. But Scotty never really figured out what they [the bullpen] did or how to insert himself over them. The power of the bullpen was derived from the fact that the day editors wanted to get home for dinner. Many of the bullpen staffers had been put into their jobs by Catledge. Scotty started his day with a morning meeting at 10:00 A.M. and would complain about what the bullpen had done the night before, but he was the only one in the room who could do anything about it. He would fuss about the play of this story or that.

"The bullpen never came in until two or three in the afternoon. One day, walking out of the meeting, I said, 'You know everyone in the room agrees with you. Maybe you should start inviting them [the bullpen] to the meetings.' Scotty waved his hand and said, 'They are not like us.' I always felt he wouldn't know quite what to say to them. The nightside was a great mystery to Scotty. They took their mission seriously. Scotty never understood that he could walk in and tell them what to do. It was like Reston was still in Washington fighting them rather than being their boss.

"It was one of the most highly intelligent and bureaucratic systems ever created. But Scotty didn't know how to run that system. His meetings were like second-day discussions, and they were discussions rather than take-charge sessions. The place also went nuts with meetings. Scotty's meeting was in the morning. Cliff Daniel had one at four, which was the front-page meeting. Later Rosenthal had a five or five-thirty meeting. If you weren't careful you could spend all day shuffling back and forth between meetings or preparing for meetings. It was very touchy. If you started sending your assistants, people thought you weren't taking their meetings seriously."

While trying to navigate this complicated new terrain, Reston was also struggling to continue his column three days a week. The kind of reporting he had once done, moving from the White House to

Capitol Hill to the Department of State, lunching with officials at the Metropolitan Club, seeing someone for a drink early in the evening, was no longer possible. He would do some phoning around to his old sources in Washington, but he could no longer rely on his hands-on reporting experience and an almost sixth sense about what Washington was thinking. His philosophical musing had never been the stuff for which he was read. Rather, the best columns were Reston telling the nation what it should make of the bewildering machinations of their national government and the contrary posturing of their elected representatives. Writing his columns became a scramble. When he should have been in front-page meetings he was in his private office working on the column. When he should have been reporting for his column, he was busy in meetings. Often he would go to an editorial-board lunch with some luminary and do a column that simply ruminated on that discussion. This was not the way Reston had become Reston.

"It didn't work at all and I don't think he ever intended it to work," Rosenthal said. "If you're going to be executive editor, you've got to be one. I don't think Scotty ever had much respect for editors at all. They were not part of his life. He never gave up his column. He didn't give a shit about being executive editor. He certainly didn't have any idea what an executive editor did. He was not in the newsroom. He just was not an editor. He didn't know what editors did, how you run a paper like this, or at least how you try to run it."

The two men were in constant conflict. Rosenthal recalls one confrontation over the problem of editorializing in the news columns. Rosenthal had objected to the tone of a story, but Reston defended the piece. Rosenthal says he told Reston: "If you want to preside over turning the paper into a political journal, go ahead. But I won't." Scotty relented. "He didn't give up anything," Rosenthal concluded. "The column stunk. And the *Times* should not have permitted it."

*   *   *

Reston knew he was having little impact on the paper and so did Punch Sulzberger. The choice was between writing the column and being an editor. So thirteen months after he had arrived, Reston was set to leave New York to resume his old role in Washington. He recommended to Punch that Max Frankel, now Washington bureau chief, be named the top editor and that Rosenthal be named Frankel's deputy. But Punch ignored his advice and gave the top position to Rosenthal, the one person whom Reston wanted to prevent from succeeding him. It stung, but at least Reston was free to go back to Washington. He had never been happy in New York, and he, like everyone else, knew that his all-important column was suffering. Gene Roberts measured Reston's impact as executive editor this way: "He did buy some time for discussions about the future direction of the paper. And he was a soothing presence after a period of rancor, urging human and family considerations. But with the staff that most worried him, he never engaged. It was sad in a way that he didn't take more control of the paper. It would have become a much more civilized undertaking. Change might have been brought about in a nonrancorous, burn-the-village way."

After Abe was named top editor, Reston made one last, ill-advised attempt to maintain his influence in the high counsels of New York. He phoned Tony Lewis in London and offered him a job as Abe's deputy. Lewis remembers the offer vividly. He had gone to the opera, and phoned the office during an intermission to get his calls. There was an urgent message from Reston. Lewis phoned him immediately. When Reston offered him the number two spot on the paper, it was an easy decision for Lewis and he agreed to come to New York immediately.

"So I was managing editor," Rosenthal remembered. "And I went into Scotty's office. One of the first things I had to do was to decide who should be assistant managing editor. I passed over Arthur Gelb, a very close friend, because we were both emotional and excitable. I chose [Seymour] Topping. There were things I was very good at, and things I wasn't good at. Topping was very good. You didn't fuck around with Topping. He did not invite arguments. There was a quality of organization that he had. I thought we would be a very good team.

"Reston congratulated me. He asked me whether I had given any thought to my deputy and I told him, yes, I had picked one. He got very upset, I mean real upset. He said you can't do that. I said, 'What do you mean, I'm the managing editor. I always pick my own deputy.' He said to me, 'You're managing editor now and you want to pick up all the marbles.' I really was a jerk [about office politics], but I was becoming less jerky. He said, 'You can't do that. I just called Tony Lewis and he's going to be your deputy.' I said, 'What did you just say?' At first I laughed. I thought he was kidding. Not because Tony's a fool. I said, 'Tony, he's never been an editor for a day.' Reston didn't think you needed to be an editor to be a managing editor.

"He said Lewis was on his way over here. I thought that was the most atrocious thing I had ever heard of. Outrageous! Then he said, 'If that's the way you're going to be about this, you know I don't have to go back to Washington. I can stay here.' I said you're telling me that unless I do what you want, I won't be the managing editor and you won't go back. Well, I said to him, if that's the price of being managing editor, you can take it and shove it up your ass. I don't think anybody had ever said that to Mr. Reston. He didn't know how strong I could be. He looked at me and then I got up and walked out. I went home and told my wife that I had just had the shortest tenure of any managing editor."*

---

*Rosenthal later amended his recollection: "I was thinking about it and I can't be sure I actually told Reston to shove it up his ass. I know I told my friends that I had told him to shove it up his ass. I know I used some vulgarity, but I can't be sure I told him to shove it up his ass."

The very next day, Punch convened a meeting to mediate the deputy dispute. "As far as I was concerned," Rosenthal said, "I was not the managing editor anymore. That was it. And Reston was very un-Restony, I mean in the sense that he wasn't calm. He was very upset. He was very excited. He said, 'Now that he's managing editor, he wants to do everything himself.' Punch didn't say anything. I said, more calmly, 'Look, if I'm the managing editor, I will pick who I want. With Lewis, I'd be the laughing stock of the whole newspaper business. Not because Lewis is bad, but he hasn't been an editor.' You see that's a Restonian idea – you take a reporter and you make him an editor, you put him in charge. You put someone like him in charge. The meeting ended. I thought it was all over for me. Punch put an arm around my shoulder and said, 'You can be very strong, can't you?' And that was that."

The next day Lewis showed up in the New York office early and encountered Sulzberger. "There was Punch and he gave me a big hello," Lewis recalled. "He said, 'I know why you're here and I'm terribly sorry. It's been a terrible mistake. Abe has decided he wants Top, and if he wants Top he will have him. I know Scotty meant well, but it's terribly unfair to you to have made this trip and to have these expectations.' I said, 'It doesn't matter.' I meant it. Punch said, 'No, it's not right, we shouldn't have treated you that way. Tell me, would you like to write a column?'" Out of the ashes of the Reston-Rosenthal wars arose a columnist who occupied a part of the op-ed page for more than three decades.

Reston's measure of his own tenure as executive editor was naturally less harsh than Rosenthal's. But he did come to the same conclusion: "In short," he wrote in his memoirs, "I was not a successful executive editor." He added, "For the first time in years, I felt like an outsider again, and I asked to be relieved of the job." He joked that his one contribution had been to force the paper to print page numbers in slightly larger type. A second reform proposal, he wrote, was either to find ink that didn't come off on the hands of the readers or to supply a washcloth with each copy of the paper. "My colleagues didn't think this was practical or even very funny."

In the discussion with Kay Graham as she prepared to write her memoirs, he was more direct and more critical in assessing his brief stay at the top of the *Times*. He told her that his experience as executive editor proved that he would not have done well for Mrs. Graham at the *Post*: "I was in great turmoil myself at that time because I never wanted to be an editor. I'm not good at moving people and hurting people, and I just was never comfortable. I wasn't comfortable as Arthur Hays's assistant. I wasn't comfortable as executive editor, and I wasn't a good executive editor. You know, that just wasn't my particular gift. I thought I had the creative mind to do it, but trying to change a system which was all concentrated on the bullpen being in charge of the news . . . I thought it was a terrible system, but trying to change it would have been a life's career and I didn't want to spend my time fighting with my colleagues. I would not have been good on the *Post* as a managing editor. You did the right thing, exactly the right thing, when you got Ben [Bradlee]."

On December 6, 1974, when he formally retired from the paper, Scotty sent a handwritten note to Punch Sulzberger.

> I want to say something to you that I have never been able to say to another soul except my parents and my wife: Every promise was kept, every opportunity given, every kindness shown over the long years. It has been such a rewarding experience I seem to have mislaid 20 years somewhere, and none has been more reassuring than our last few years together.
>
> I wish I could say, what I almost said: that every hope had been fulfilled, but this would not be true. You gave me the greatest prize in your possession – to be executive editor of the

Times – and I let you down. . . . But all this is in the past, which is not important. I just want to thank you for giving me a chance to go on writing for the *Times*. That and our continued association mean more to me than I can express.

When Abe Rosenthal learned about that note, his reaction was harsh: "He owed Punch that apology and to a lot of others because he took the number one job on the *Times* and ignored it. He owed Punch an apology and he owed me one too, and he owed Greenfield."

When Rosenthal was replaced as top editor by Reston's old protégé Max Frankel, Rosenthal was permitted to write a regular column on the op-ed page. He was never a graceful writer and his opinions were as blunt as his management style. Asked what he thought of Rosenthal's column, Reston observed mildly: "It's a mistake to give people columns so they won't leave."

At the end of 1968, Arthur Hays Sulzberger died. "Mr. Gus," as Reston had called him, had been ill for years. Arthur Hays was upset and disappointed by the turmoil around the Washington bureau appointment and was especially unhappy when Turner Catledge was pushed into early retirement. The day Punch told Catledge he was going, Catledge met with the wheelchair-bound Arthur Hays and the two had a glass of sherry together. But if Catledge and the old man were close, Reston and Arthur Hays were closer. Indeed, Arthur Hays treated Reston with almost more respect and affection than he showed his own son. With Arthur Hays's passing, Reston lost his strongest patron, the man who had given him the keys to the kingdom.

It was Scotty Reston whom the family chose to give the eulogy, at Temple Emanu-El on Fifth Avenue, where he had spoken at Orvil Dryfoos's funeral years earlier. "Men went away from him feeling that they had been heard out and that they had been treated fairly," Scotty said. "For he had the gift of reminding us, by his gusto and example, of the decencies of life." Sometime after Arthur Hays's death, Reston received a letter from Iphigene, with a check for $1,000 signed by Arthur Hays. Her note explained that her late husband had asked that she send along the check after his death, with the message "It's been fun."

CHAPTER 23

THE *GAZETTE*

FOR MOST OF the 1960s, James Reston sat securely at the top of his trade and at the pinnacle of his influence in Washington and the nation. As the decade ended, however, the political turbulence all around him began to erode his position. Although it was not yet obvious, the increasing polarization of American politics was crowding out the moderate, establishmentarian approach that had made Reston such a powerful figure in the American press. Although he had prevailed in the first battle with Abe Rosenthal over the Washington bureau's leadership, the fallout from that struggle had pulled him away from his base in Washington and into a bureaucratic war in New York. He had, as a result, lost a good deal of his power and favor with Punch Sulzberger.

One of the few blessings of the period, Reston recalled, was that he and Sally bought the *Vineyard Gazette* on the resort island of Martha's Vineyard. It was and is one of the finest weekly newspapers in the country. But his pleasant memories of the acquisition were colored by the paper's ultimate success. In the years immediately following the purchase, it was just one more source of turmoil in Reston's life.

The *Gazette* was owned and edited by Henry Beetle Hough from the day the father of his wife, Betty, gave it to them as a wedding present in 1920. Hough was a Vineyard original, tall and lanky, full of opinions, gifted with the ability to write lyrically about any subject, and burning with a fierce love for the island and its natural beauty. He was revered by the summer people because they saw him as the defender of the island against rampant development. But he was equally detested by many year-round residents, who saw him as an impediment to the improvement of their economic lot. Just as a month on the Vineyard was a magic cure for the pressures of a successful off-island life, reading the *Gazette,* and especially reading Hough's ruminations on the simple pleasures of the place, was a tonic for the world-weary, high-powered doctors, lawyers, academics, and journalists who could afford to summer there. Many subscribed to the paper year-round, taking a few minutes each week to read about what was happening back on the island and to get a taste of the life they wouldn't experience again until next summer.

Hough built the *Gazette* from a hand-printed eight-page paper into an institution, albeit one that didn't often make money. His wife was his full partner in the enterprise; when she died he began to worry about the fate of the newspaper. The Restons first came to the Vineyard in 1965, vacationing on the western end of the island near Menemsha Pond. They naturally encountered the literary crowd: William and Rose Styron, Saul Bellow, John Updike. There were celebrity journalists as well: Walter Cronkite, Art Buchwald, Mike Wallace. There, in the homes of the famous, the Restons met Hough. In 1967 Hough out of the blue wrote to Scotty and Sally proposing that they buy his beloved paper. He admired Reston as a newsman and saw the Reston family as a way of extending the life and spirit of the paper he and Betty had built.

A great delusional dream of many journalists who work in news organizations of any size is to break free, to move to a small town and become the owner and boss of their own little newspaper. There, they like to believe, they would be their own masters, pillars of their communities, seeing the fruits of their work as the reforms they advocate were enacted. That fantasy appealed to Scotty, although he was entirely too cautious and realistic to embrace it fully. More important to him was the idea that the country newspaper might one day provide a safe haven for one of his sons. He wanted all of them to follow him into journalism, but he knew it would be difficult for them to match his own success.

After Hough's first offer, Scotty suggested that the old man continue to run the paper and that they would buy it from him when he was ready to retire. The Restons were concerned about what it would be like to own the paper while Hough was still active there, as he fully intended to be. They also worried about the price, which was a bit more than $100,000. But a Boston lawyer friend of Hough's named Don Hurley, who feared for the fate of the *Gazette* should Hough die suddenly, pushed both parties together. Scotty sold some *Times* stock to finance half the purchase. Scotty never anticipated running the paper himself because he did not intend to give up his column nor his role at the *Times*.

To share the risk and the cost, Scotty first asked his Washington lawyer, Lloyd Cutler, who was later White House counsel to Jimmy Carter and Bill Clinton, to come in with him as a partner. According to Cutler, Hough was adamantly opposed to the idea and told Scotty, "I'm willing to sell this paper to you but not to some damned Washington lawyer." Then, through the efforts of Hurley, Reston was introduced to Fairleigh Dickinson Jr., a wealthy philanthropist who summered on the Vineyard. Dickinson put up just under $50,000, becoming a member of the board of directors of the paper with slightly less than 50 percent of the shares. He told Scotty and Sally they were to pay him back as they could from the profits of the paper. For years Scotty would write apologetic notes to Dickinson saying the paper was either losing money or so close to breakeven that he could not return Dickinson's money. Dickinson never complained.

Far from being a romantic adventure in country journalism, the proprietorship of the *Gazette* was an immediate and major annoyance for the Restons. They bought a pretty house in Edgartown, near the newspaper's office, and, taking advantage of the *Times'* corporate plane from time to time, flew in and out as frequently as they could, including spending some portions of their summer vacations there. The visits were not fun. There were constant, if understandable, demands for Scotty to solve problems, raise wages, and mediate disputes between coworkers. Worse, Scotty was never passionately in love with the island. The ceaseless crashing of the ocean's waves made him restless, he said, and he much preferred the bucolic quiet of the pastures and forests around the Virginia cabin at Fiery Run.

The principal problem was that the Restons were absentee owners in a place that valued local roots and of an enterprise that needed constant attention. The people who ran the paper for the Restons were talented and eager but lacked full authority. Dick Mooney saw the strain that the *Gazette* added to Reston's burden during Scotty's brief run as executive editor. "He was in a brand-new job here," recalled Mooney, "with the responsibility of bringing order to the *New York Times,* and he had just bought this little country newspaper and was picturing himself as the new Henry Beetle Hough. To his great surprise, people had the knives out for each other in Edgartown too. He was caught between, say, the local druggist and somebody else and he'd say, 'Why do I have to be involved?' I just remember how forlorn he was that people on Martha's Vineyard didn't just all love each other."

In the summer of 1969, barely a year after Scotty and Sally bought the little paper, Martha's Vineyard became a famous place overnight. A young woman named Mary Jo Kopechne died one Friday evening in July when a car driven by Senator Edward Kennedy went off a bridge on Chappaquiddick. Reston was on the Vineyard at the time, attending to his newspaper property. He learned on Saturday morning that Senator Kennedy was being interviewed by the police. He tracked down the story and, naturally, called it in to the *Times*.

He dictated the first paragraph, the lead in which the essence of the story is usually conveyed, with this first sentence: "Tragedy has again struck the Kennedy family." The victim was not mentioned until the fourth paragraph. Later in the day, Abe Rosenthal called Sally Reston at home in Edgartown, asking her to advise Scotty that there had been a few changes made to Scotty's story. (In the edited version, the real victim was in the lead.)

It was not the job of the top editor to cover what was then a police story, albeit one with rather important implications for a potential presidential candidate. Rosenthal immediately dispatched Joseph Lelyveld, a young reporter just back from an overseas assignment and later himself the executive editor of the *Times*, to the Vineyard to take over coverage from Reston. Lelyveld arrived on the island late that Saturday afternoon and hunted up Reston. Scotty treated him like a weekend guest. Dinner came first – pasta, as Lelyveld remembers it. During the meal, Scotty opined that Ted Kennedy could still be president: time would pass and the incident be forgotten. Sally disagreed. "Scotty, how could you be so cynical?" she asked. Scotty was a bit surprised that Lelyveld had been sent. "The story is over," he told Lelyveld.

After dinner, Scotty took Lelyveld for a walk around Edgartown, not bothering to file any new material for the late edition. "Scotty was like the master of ceremonies in *Our Town*," said Lelyveld. "'This is our ferry, this is our newspaper.'" About 11:30 at night, the two got on the ferry that runs between Edgartown and Chappaquiddick. Scotty introduced his young colleague to the ferry operator as "Joe Lelyveld of the *New York Times*." He introduced himself as "Reston of the *Gazette*." The next morning the two men met where the accident had occurred. Two kids were fishing and said they had been there fishing the morning before; they described how they had found the car and called the police. Lelyveld took notes; Scotty took a fishing rod out of his car and began fishing with the boys. With that, he washed his hands of the story. Lelyveld, reflecting later on Reston's role that weekend, felt that he had operated for so long among the powerful in Washington that he saw the story as only about Kennedy. "He had no sense of how people outside Washington would see the story. He was not interested in the investigative angle," Lelyveld said. It initially eluded Reston that the story was not about something happening to Teddy Kennedy but about something a Kennedy did to someone else. A week after the accident, Lelyveld wrote a devastating story reconstructing the events that led up to the accident. Scotty called to congratulate him on the piece.

The *Gazette* struggled into the 1970s, still graced by Hough's writing and his sentimental journalism about the island. But Hough so irritated the commercial establishment of the Vineyard that they had backed a new rival weekly, which began to suck advertising away from the venerable *Gazette*. A series of hired editors and managers plodded along, none very successfully. At one point Reston used his stationery from the *Times* to write to the regional manager of the A&P grocery chain, complaining that their store on the island was advertising only in the rival paper. By the middle of the seventies, the old presses that had produced the paper for decades had worn out. It was obvious a major new investment was needed to modernize the production of the weekly, an investment the paper's scanty margins could hardly justify.

In the early summer of 1974, yet another general manager of the paper decided to move on. A young Brown University graduate named Steven Rattner heard there might be an opening, so he took the ferry to the island and hitchhiked down to the newspaper office. He talked to Reston and it was clear to both of them that Rattner was not the man for the job. The young grad was planning to go off to the London School of Economics in the fall and was really only looking for summer employment. Instead of the *Gazette* job, he signed on as a researcher at *Forbes* magazine in New York. But he soon heard again from Reston, now back in Washington writing his column. How about coming down to be his news clerk, Scotty asked. Rattner worked only one full day at *Forbes,* then went to Washington to see Scotty for a second time. They talked briefly and went to dinner at the Sans Souci, in those days one of the few good restaurants in Washington. There, Rattner knocked a glass of beer onto Scotty's lap. Reston took the assault with good grace, then hauled Rattner back to the house on Woodley Road. They talked some more until Rattner finally called a friend to come pick him up. The woman got lost and Scotty stayed up chatting with Rattner. When she finally showed up, her informal attire further embarrassed Rattner. But the next day he quit *Forbes* to become Scotty's clerk.

Rattner, as it turned out, had supervised the modernization of the Brown student newspaper's production from hot type to photo offset. He was almost immediately enlisted to look into the printing problems on the Vineyard. It was clear to Rattner that the same conversion was necessary at the *Gazette,* but when he told Reston the price tag – $120,000 – the Scotsman choked. Without asking Reston's permission, Rattner visited a bank in Edgartown and arranged for a loan to pay for the new presses. It was a surprisingly cheeky initiative by Rattner but one that foreshadowed his later move from journalism into investment banking. Scotty sputtered at the effrontery of his young clerk but finally went along. He still regarded debt as something close to sin, though, and had no real idea just how the debt was going to be paid.

Shortly after the Rattner deal bought them new printing equipment, Scotty and Sally found the real answer to their problems at the *Gazette*. In the summer of 1975, Richard Reston, the eldest of the three Reston sons, and his wife, Jody, decided to move to the Vineyard to take over the operation of the paper. It was a good move for both the senior Restons and the younger: it put a family member in permanent charge at the newspaper and offered a solution to personal difficulties faced by Dick and Jody.

Richard Fulton Reston was a few inches taller than his father and like his two brothers looked more like Scotty than like Sally. He had followed his father into the newspaper trade almost automatically. "I was sort of raised to go out and get my own job and to decide on my own career," Dick remembered. "Journalism was the only thing I really knew anything about, growing up. When it was time for me to look for work, all I could think about was a newspaper like the old *Washington Evening Star* or NBC when it was in the old Wardman Park Hotel. In my case it was also quickly very apparent to me that this was something I liked, something that was exciting." After studying for a time in Europe, Dick went back to Madison, Wisconsin, where he finished his degree at the university and worked on the state capital newspaper. He moved to Washington and eventually signed on with the *Los Angeles Times*. None of this, Dick insists, was his father's doing, because Scotty never once picked up a phone to ask anyone to help his son. So hands-off was Scotty, Dick says, that he often had to find other senior men in the trade to ask for advice on his career. While Scotty apparently never told Dick directly about his wishes for him to go into journalism, his very silence on the matter created a pull toward the trade.

Scotty was not really close to any of his three sons when they were young, and perhaps as a consequence of the emotional austerity of his own childhood, he was at times utterly oblivious to his sons' feelings. In the early 1970s, when Dick was serving as London bureau chief of the LA *Times,* Scotty and Sally went to visit for the Christmas holidays. Dick had undertaken to produce a full English feast, buying a goose and the plum pudding. But once in London, Scotty was phoned by Tony Lewis, the *New York Times* bureau chief there, and invited for Christmas dinner. Scotty unthinkingly accepted, devastating Dick with his rudeness. Jody warned Scotty and Sally that if they had dinner with Lewis rather than with their son, they would no longer be welcome in Dick's home. Scotty and Sally stayed for dinner with Dick and Jody.

Dick went on to become Moscow bureau chief, a tough assignment now and even more difficult then. It was doubly taxing for Dick, whose struggle with alcoholism could not have been made easier in the vodka-soaked Soviet Union. By the midseventies he and Jody were back in Washington and Dick was covering the diplomatic beat, just as his father once did. The job included trailing the overpowering secretary of state Henry Kissinger as he shuttled around the Middle East. The contrast between father and son was quite obvious: Dick was merely a beat reporter, while Scotty was an intimate of Kissinger's. Meanwhile, Dick's alcohol problem was hurting his career. The strains caused Dick and Jody to separate. In 1975 Dick and Jody were living apart in Washington when Scotty began to plead for help with the *Vineyard Gazette.*

"It was more accidental than anything else," Dick explained, minimizing the pressure from his father and his own need for a change of scene. "We had been on that merry-go-round in Washington for years and living out of suitcases overseas and traveling. We never seemed to have any time for anything other than what was next on our plate. So it was almost, 'Why don't we go in, try it, and see if there isn't something more to this profession, another dimension.' We didn't know anything about small-community journalism. We didn't even know much about living in small communities. We came here saying, 'Let's go and try it for a couple of years and if it doesn't work we can always go back to Washington or overseas.'"

The decision, according to Dick, was their own, not the result of overt pressure from Scotty and Sally. "I think they were hopeful that one of us [the Reston boys], and particularly me, because the others never really got themselves involved in journalism, that somehow on my own I would come to a decision to at least try this, take a crack at it. He never said, 'Help me out.' But it was very clear that he was very pleased when we made the decision."

Jody Reston remembers it somewhat differently. The senior Restons "just got more and more frustrated," she said. "They were putting great pressure on all their sons for someone to come up here and run it. Everyone was resistant to it. We were, too, for a while. Dick and his father went out to the cabin in the country for a weekend and talked and talked and talked, and somehow in that whole conversation Dick got convinced. I wasn't even part of the conversation. I'm pretty easy. Dick and I had gotten engaged on the Vineyard, so I loved the place."

Their decision to give the Vineyard a try was a huge relief for Scotty and Sally. But when Dick and Jody arrived on the Vineyard, they found all sorts of problems. The largest was that the paper made no money. "One year it would make one thousand dollars," Jody said, "the next it would lose twenty thousand dollars. No one [on the local staff] paid any attention at all. The whole concept of budgeting or anything like that seemed to be beyond them. No one here had any financial or budgetary concept. They would spend what was needed. No one really sold ads. They would accept ads that came in, but no one went out and did anything. We had to change the whole mentality here."

Dick was initially installed as the business manager to replace an incumbent marked for dismissal. Jody was planning to find a job of some sort outside the paper, but upon their arrival, the advertising manager quit. Jody got a call from her parents-in-law begging her to help them out. "I really didn't want to," she said. "I remember I cried, but not in front of them. I said to Dick, 'Please don't make me do this.' But I did it."

Jody thought it was not smart to make Dick the business manager, since his entire experience was in editorial work. Nor did she herself know much about business. "I didn't have any background," she said. "I really didn't want to work for my in-laws and I really didn't want to do advertising. Any interest I had in a paper was on the editorial side. I had done some writing. I worked for my hometown paper in Delavan, Wisconsin, and I was a freelance writer when we were in Moscow." Jody's parents warned her against the idea of working for her in-laws. "My father told me I was a fool," she recalled. Even though Dick and Jody were now almost totally responsible for the health of the *Gazette,* Dick, not Jody, actually held stock in the company; his parents and brother Tom owned the rest. James Reston Jr. went in and out of ownership positions, at least twice selling his shares back to his parents to raise cash for his own family's needs.

Scotty was a tough boss. "He made his opinions known very quickly and very definitely on the business side," recalled Jody, who soon became business manager while Dick became the editor. "I think he was always a little careful with Dick on the editorial side," she added, "because, after all, there was a father-son problem, that is, when you're the son of a famous father. Scotty understood that. But on the business side he wanted things to work and he wanted the paper to make money and he was tired of its losing. He didn't need it [the money] at all. He didn't care about it in that way. He just wanted it to succeed."

Jody especially remembers an incident early on when she and Dick decided, unilaterally, to raise the price of the paper. They simply announced the new thirty-five-cent price, up a dime from what it had been. Scotty learned of it for the first time when he read about the increase in the *Gazette*. A sharp telegram soon arrived, asking the couple: "Have you lost your manners or have you just lost your way?"

The more complicated problem was Dick's alcoholism, which continued to flare off and on. In a letter to a former editor of the *Gazette*, Scotty wrote in 1982:

> The outlook for Dick is now more hopeful. We thought we were doing the right thing by urging him to go to Dr. Ryback, the head of the NIH Alcohol Control unit in Bethesda, but they look at this problem from a psychiatric point of view, which may or may not be right, but in any event was not right for Dick. Now he is at Chit Chat Farm in Wernersville, Pa., which operates on the assumption that this is a physiological disease, requiring quite different treatment and this seems to be working more effectively.

In Dick's absence, Jody ran the paper by herself, but that therapy failed too, and Scotty began to doubt Dick's stewardship of the paper. About ten years after Dick had taken over the paper, Scotty sent him a telegram relieving him of his duties and telling his eldest son that he could not again be editor of the *Gazette* until he had been sober for a year. It was tough on father and son and tougher on Jody, who again took over sole responsibility for the newspaper's operations. This time, however, the intervention worked. Dick returned to the paper the next year, and he and Jody continued to build circulation and revenue. Twenty-five years after they took over, the couple had increased the circulation to 18,000, the annual revenue to more than $3 million, and the net profit to well over a million dollars a year, making the property worth, conservatively,

$10 million. And Dick, for all his struggles with his father and with his father's prominence, had brought much of Scotty's own good judgment and fine journalistic skills to bear on the *Gazette*. He and Jody produced as fine a small newspaper as is published in America. After Sally's death in 2001, ownership of the paper passed to the three Reston sons and Jody.

The burden of being a Reston was perhaps even more taxing for the second-born, the one who carried Scotty's name, with the weight of the designation "junior" attached. From the beginning, even though he had inherited from both his mother and father a love and facility for writing, he fought to stay away from newspapers. In 1964 and 1965, Jim Reston experimented briefly with journalism, working for eight months at the *Chicago Daily News*. There, under the inspirational editorship of Larry Fanning, he had a privileged charter to travel and write about the growing youth culture. He then joined the army, where he wrote his first novel. "Publishing that novel made me more committed to staying away from journalism," Jim Reston said. "But because I had made no money through that decade, he [his father] was constantly after me to give this thing up and do real work." Which, in Scotty's mind, meant newspaper reporting.

Scotty's first tactic was to make Jim and his wife, Denise Leary, understand how difficult life could be for someone who refused to accept conventional employment. "He was extremely Calvinistic about money," Jim observed. "In fact, when we bought land to build our house in Chapel Hill in 1977, instead of giving us money, they forced us to sell the shares we had in the *Gazette*. Denise thought this was not really fair to us. We had no money at all. Denise was struggling to get through law school at that time. It's been a hand-to-mouth existence, really, for most of our adult life. I was determined not to do what I viewed as copping out by falling back on the journalistic thing. It was partly to avoid Dick's problems." After building their house outside Chapel Hill, Jim wanted his parents to come see the work that had been done. Sally wanted to go, but Scotty couldn't find the time, and in the end neither parent ever visited. But Jim Reston did not avoid journalism just to avoid competing with his father. His ambition was higher, aimed at creating a more literary body of work than his father had. Scotty saw that ambition, according to Dick Reston, as "swanning about," a career without the strictures of working for a company. But for Jim Reston it was anything but an easy way to go.

When finances got very short, Jim and Denise would muster the courage to ask for help. But according to Jim, the process was "agonizing." A request would produce "little bits of money here and there, but not what you would think of as real money," he recalled. "I think that was not fair, because we went through unnecessary struggles for fifteen years, where now, knowing what I know now about the family situation, they could have been more generous than they were. And I think this goes back to that depression generation and not allowing the next generation to get soft. What was slightly bizarre about it is knowing now that there were multiple millions of dollars. I think Dad was excessively austere."

It was not that Scotty didn't care for his boys. He would regularly update his colleagues at the *Times* on what they were doing with their lives. But he had only two objects of total devotion: Sally and the *New York Times*. There seemed to be neither time nor energy left to pay much attention to anything else.

Scotty's second tactic to coerce Jim into the newspaper business was to arrange periodic job interviews for him with executives at the *Times*, hoping that an offer would be made that would entice him. While Jim would keep the appointments, he would subvert their purpose by letting the interviewers know he was really not interested in journalism. Jimmy Greenfield, the man Scotty had blocked from becoming Washington bureau chief, eventually returned to the paper as an assistant managing editor under Abe Rosenthal, handling personnel matters. Jim Reston was sent to see Greenfield. "Scotty wanted him to get on the paper to get the benefits," Greenfield recalled bitterly. "He [Jim] had no interest. Punch would call me saying, 'Please, you've got to interview him.' It would wind up with my telling Punch, 'He doesn't want to be on the *New York Times*. He has two books he wants to write.' Punch would say, 'Well, Scotty wants him to be settled.' Twice I interviewed him at great length. Jimmy [Reston] was absolutely frank about it. He said, 'I'm here because I was told to be here.'"

It wasn't until much later, after his frustrating experience writing his memoirs, that Scotty fully understood what James B. Reston Jr. had accomplished. When the memoirs were published, father and son wound up on book tours at the same time; in Kentucky they sat shoulder to shoulder signing their books. It was the eighth of Jim Reston's books, which by then included a brilliant reconstruction of the suicidal/homicidal madness at the cult settlement called Jonestown in Guyana, an examination of the ambiguous guilt and innocence of a young black woman in the South, an exegesis on the similarities between General Sherman's destructive march through the South and the war in Vietnam, several television specials, and a play based on the Guyana tragedy. By the time he reached his sixtieth birthday, Jim Reston had written eleven books. He had avoided his father's trade but not his craft. He had succeeded on his own terms, if not financially, then artistically. Still, it was difficult to forget the cost. Shortly after his father's memoirs were published, Jim Reston was enjoying a game of tennis one day with one of Scotty's former news clerks, Steve Roberts, by then a well-known political commentator. Roberts remarked on how nice it must be for Jim to have his father being noticed again. Jim did not feel that way. He was surprised that the resentments built up over the years had not gone away. "I thought I had put that behind me," he said.

*   *   *

In some ways, Thomas Busey Reston, the youngest of the three boys, escaped the heaviest undertow created by his father's importance. But not completely. He described his father as "not distant," but it was more a "hair tousling" relationship than one of real intimacy – not uncommon for fathers of Scotty's generation. Because of Tom's bad leg, he didn't share the interest in sports that both of his brothers had in common with Scotty. On the other hand, Tom was powerfully attracted to the world his father had written about and to those personalities he had seen firsthand in his father's home. At first Tom did head toward journalism. He was on the Saint Albans school newspaper and wrote for the *Harvard Crimson*. He worked one summer on a country newspaper near the Fiery Run house, and another summer on the *Atlanta Constitution*. In 1968 he was a volunteer for all three of the major Democratic campaigns, starting with Eugene McCarthy, moving on to Robert Kennedy, and ending with the nominee, Hubert H. Humphrey. Then he traveled around the world for a year and a half, writing as a stringer for the *Boston Globe*.

When the world tour was over, he had to settle on a career. He looked at journalism and at his father and decided, in his words, "I'm not going to compete in that." He felt a strong pull toward political activism, as the antiwar movement gathered force. Like many of his generation, he wanted to play a real part in the politics of his time, not simply watch and report. "I thought of journalism as a bank shot and I wanted a more direct effect," he explained. "I thought the law was the more activist pursuit."

Scotty had a habit of summoning his sons from time to time to dispense fatherly advice, often over a meal at the Metropolitan Club. When Tom told him at one lunch of his decision to go to law school, Scotty did not think it was a great idea. "Dad did not approve of law school," Tom remembered. "He wanted me to be a journalist. He loved his life and he said he thought I wrote well." To discourage Tom, he sent him around to visit Dean Acheson, by then a senior lawyer in Washington, and to Lloyd Cutler. He wanted Tom to hear firsthand just how boring life could be in the law. It didn't work. Tom enrolled in law school and Scotty and Sally paid the tuition.

The law and work in Democratic campaigns eventually brought Tom a rather visible job in the Department of State during the administration of Jimmy Carter. He was deputy departmental spokesman under Hodding Carter III. Oddly, that was the same job held by Jimmy Greenfield in the Kennedy years. After his stint with the department, he launched a solo law practice in Washington. But the lure of the life his father led still pulls on him. "He may have been right all along," Tom says.

All three boys, like their father, married strong, talented, independent women. To the extent that happened as a result of their relationship to their parents, it was a great blessing for all three. But a Reston childhood had proved a mixed blessing for the boys: lives filled with encounters with the famous and powerful, fine schools, interesting trips abroad, but also a youth pressured by high expectations and a father too busy to be a good parent, too rigidly involved with his own success to set his boys free to choose their own paths. The sad irony is that inside the *New York Times*, Reston was revered by a host of young reporters for his fatherly attentions. The hugely successful Reston hires such as Tom Wicker, David Halberstam, Max Frankel, Russell Baker, and Tony Lewis love the man dearly to this day. The young clerks who served one-year apprenticeships admired him enough to stage elaborate celebrations of his later birthdays and retirement. "When you were his clerk, you got all the benefit of his warmth, generosity, and advice, and he cared about you, but there wasn't that same weight of expectation," one clerk recalled.

CHAPTER 24

NIXON'S WASHINGTON

RICHARD NIXON CAME to Washington in the 1940s, only a few years after Scotty Reston. Although Reston was a few years older, the two men were of the same generation: they grew up in the depression, lived through World War II, and came of age as the United States struggled through the Cold War, and they both arrived in the capital brimming with ambition. There the similarities ended. Reston tended to be sunny and optimistic, forgiving and broad-minded, easy and confident in his dealings with others. Nixon was dark, full of self-doubt — even self-loathing — and afflicted with a self-fulfilling paranoia about the Eastern establishment press. He believed Reston was a charter member of that group, despite the Scotsman's humble origins.

Reston never liked Nixon. He thought the Californian was a small-bore, mean-spirited politician whom Eisenhower should never have put on the national ticket in 1952 and 1956. By 1957 Nixon had begun to separate himself ever so slightly from the Eisenhower regime, to prepare for his own run at the presidency. He asked Reston to put together a dinner group to discuss foreign propaganda and how the United States could counter it. Reston obliged. Afterward, in a memorandum for his own files, he observed that while Nixon seemed to be keeping his opinions open during the evening's discussions, the vice president was not "in any sense an original mind." Reston thought Nixon seemed "less at ease in a small group than in addressing a political rally or a news conference," a surprising observation, since Nixon seemed awkward enough in public. "He is a compulsive talker: seemed to feel that he had to take command, even when he had nothing to say," Reston continued. "In short, he seemed to me still to be full of vitality but shallow, a kind of symbol of the triumphs of techniques [over substance] in modern American life."

Over the years and for good reason, Reston's opinion of Nixon hardened. Nixon, Reston summed up in his memoirs,

> seemed false in whatever role he was playing. He knew that freedom in the world depended on the leadership of the United States, but he thought leadership was a conspiracy.... He was a sensitive man, personally shy and even generous, but he hid these appealing qualities behind a mucker pose of profanity and vulgarity. He was called Tricky Dick, and few would say he didn't earn the name.... He had a scowling face and fidgety smile.... He tidied up [Joe] McCarthy's tactics but retained many of Joe's vicious themes.

Along with most political columnists and commentators at the time, Reston took Nixon at his word in 1962 when he famously declared that the press would not have him to kick around anymore. Commented Reston in a column: "There was an element of tragedy in Richard Nixon's sour reaction to his defeat for the Governorship of California. Two years ago, he was within 100,000 votes of the American presidency and today, unelected and unmourned, he is an unemployed lawyer in Los Angeles. No wonder he slammed the door as he went out." Scotty noted that in the British system, there is a place for opposition leaders, but "our politics are more savage. The gap between victory and defeat is almost too wide. The winner gets more than he can handle and the loser more than he can bear. We put them in the White House before they are ready and retire them before they are ripe."

Nixon, Reston observed,

> came to power too early and retired too soon. He mastered the techniques of politics before he mastered the principles, and ironically it was this preoccupation with techniques that both brought him forward and cast him down. . . . No public figure of our time has ever studied the reporters so much or understood them so little. . . . He never seemed to understand the difference between news and truth. To him what he said was "news" and should be left there. Maybe he was right. It could be the "real Nixon" was the one on-stage, but that is beyond journalism now and will have to be left to the historians and the psychological novelists.

A few years later, as the defeated politician began to retool his public persona into the "new Nixon," Reston noticed the change. In 1966 Nixon was campaigning for Republicans running for Congress to rebuild his base for another go at the presidency. Scotty wrote that Nixon was "a little more relaxed, a little wiser, and a lot richer than the tense and painfully suspicious young man who served two terms as Vice President."

The next year, as it became clearer to Reston and everyone else paying attention that Nixon was now a major contender for the Republican nomination, Scotty's tone turned a bit more acidic.

Nixon was lurching around the world, meeting foreign leaders, trying to impress the nation with his expertise on international affairs. "He is proving," Reston wrote, "that he not only knows all the Republican county chairmen of the United States, but all the Prime Ministers of the world as well . . . [but] there is absolutely no evidence that travel has given him any new or deeper visions of America's problems in the world. . . . Few candidates have ever seen so many new things or had so little new to say about them." Notably, this was written at the same time that Reston's relationship with President Johnson had deteriorated into one of hostility on both sides.

At the end of 1967, Reston was sure the next year's campaign would pit Nixon against Johnson. "Why Johnson and why Nixon?" he asked in a column that perfectly caught the country's poisonous disillusion with America's politicians. "The answer to this is not easy to find, especially if you think about it for at least two minutes," Scotty wrote. The pair, he noted, "happen to be the two politicians who inspire more distrust among more people in this country than any other two men in American political life." After Nixon was nominated, Reston misjudged the effect his choice of the obscure Maryland governor Spiro Agnew as his running mate would have; he guessed it cast Nixon too strongly in a "minority" conservative position, against the "majority" liberal views of the country.*

Reston criticized Nixon through the 1968 campaign, especially on his unspecified plan to end the war in Vietnam. After he won the election, Nixon called on Johnson and his full cast of national security advisors in the White House for a briefing. Nixon was alone at the meeting. Johnson was accompanied by Defense Secretary Clark

---

*Agnew became one of Nixon's heavy weapons in his war against the press. But when Agnew was forced to resign in 1973 for taking bribes while in office, Reston wrote a sympathetic column about the vice president. "Thanks for not piling on," Agnew wrote to Reston.

Clifford, Secretary of State Dean Rusk, Chairman of the Joint Chiefs of Staff General Earl Wheeler, and Central Intelligence Agency head Richard Helms. Helms remembered the meeting vividly, recalling that Johnson asked Wheeler and Helms to sit with Nixon on one side of the Cabinet Room conference table to ease the president-elect's isolation in the group. One of the first questions Johnson asked Nixon was whom he intended to name as secretary of state. Nixon, not wanting to tip any of his plans, replied sarcastically that Scotty Reston obviously wanted to be secretary of state. It was an echo of something Dwight Eisenhower had said years before: "Who the hell does Scotty Reston think he is, telling me how to run the country?"

At least one person in the room was not able to grasp what passed for Nixon's bitter sense of humor. A few months later, Helms told Mel Elfin, the Washington bureau chief for *Newsweek*, that Reston had been promoting himself as a possible secretary of state. Elfin dutifully reported the tidbit to Osborne Eliott, *Newsweek*'s managing editor, who forwarded the intelligence to his boss, Kay Graham. Because she knew Reston so well, Kay found it unbelievable. It is astonishing that the man charged with running U.S. intelligence operations could so misapprehend Nixon's crack – and when asked about it again thirty years later, continue to believe the accuracy of his interpretation. Reston had in some ways come to be seen as so much a part of the governing establishment that it seemed plausible to Helms that the journalist would seek a cabinet post – even in an administration led by a politician Reston did not respect. As much as Scotty did come to see himself as part of the ruling apparatus of the United States, he never thought of crossing over into government itself. "It would have been a betrayal of his whole life," Tom Reston observed.

* * *

It was Richard Nixon's Washington to which Scotty Reston returned after his failure as executive editor. It was thus a very different Washington and a very different Reston that were reunited. Reston was, like almost everyone else who had watched Nixon over the years, astonished to see him become president. ("He was elected president twice," Reston wrote later, "which said more for the indifference of the people than for their judgment.") It was a different place from the one Reston had left thirteen months before. Although the venomous debate over the war had not waned, the people who ran the government had changed. The new men were by and large not people who knew or trusted Scotty Reston.

The new president, having learned too well from his defeat by the telegenic Jack Kennedy, was not interested in an intellectual dialogue with the voters through columnists and writers like Reston. He and his aides believed that only television pictures mattered, and those could rather easily be controlled. Rather than appoint seasoned former newspaperman and campaign press secretary Herbert Klein as presidential spokesman, Nixon instead named a twenty-nine-year-old advertising man, Ronald Zeigler, to the post. It was immediately clear to everyone that he was a mere mouthpiece, not a knowledgeable source for what was really happening in the Nixon administration. Soon the regulars in the White House press room nicknamed him "Ron Zigg-liar."

Nor was there anyone else Reston could rely on for inside information. He knew Secretary of State William Rogers, who had been in the Eisenhower administration, but Rogers was deliberately excluded from the inner foreign policy deliberations at the White House. He knew Melvin Laird, the defense secretary and former member of Congress, but Laird, too, was a second-tier figure in the grand diplomacy that Nixon began to play. The powerful people close to Nixon, like H. R. Haldeman and John Ehrlichman, completely shared the president's contempt for the writing press. They

understood their boss's aversion to his advisors' speaking to reporters, so they made themselves virtually inaccessible to the press. In
his own memoirs, Nixon professed to believe that the press was
more powerful than the president in shaping public opinion. With
that mind-set, he came to the presidency, as he wrote, "prepared to
have to do combat with the media in order to get my views and my
programs to the people."

Even without many great sources, Reston by early 1970 had managed to annoy the Nixon White House enough to prompt Alexander Butterfield, a Nixon aide who later disclosed the existence of the
elaborate White House taping system, to order an FBI report on
Reston. Classified "Secret/No Foreign Dissemination," the six-page
document opened by stating that "there is no information in the
files of this Bureau that shows any association on the part of Reston
with the Communist Party or Communist Party front groups." The
bureau then summarized for Butterfield the kind of paranoiac busy-
work that occupied the FBI in those years. There were citations from
Whittaker Chambers's book *Witness* charging that Reston had once
been asked by John Foster Dulles about Alger Hiss's suitability to
become president of the Carnegie Endowment: "Reston stated Hiss
would be a very good choice," the FBI report noted.* There was a
reference to a 1953 article in an anti-Communist publication called
Counterattack in which Reston's cabled questions to Stalin were
called "journalistic bumbling." The bureau also recounted that in
the Washington records of the official Soviet news agency, Tass,
there were citations of "numerous articles written by James Reston
and forwarded to Moscow during the period 1948 to 1951."

Had Butterfield bothered, he could have perused the three-
quarter-inch-thick file the FBI had already accumulated on Reston.

*According to Chambers, Reston was also a member of the *Meet the Press* panel
when Chambers made his first television appearance. It was during that show that
Chambers first directly charged that Hiss "was a Communist and may still be one."

It is full of even more nonsense. In 1953 J. Edgar Hoover demanded to know, "What do we know about James Reston?" He got back a six-page, single-spaced typed report recounting Reston's life story to that point. The report noted that in 1948 the State Department had suspected that Reston had been the recipient of a secret report and had demanded a fingerprint check of the document. "The document was chemically treated but no fingerprints of value were developed," Hoover was told. The bureau turned up the fact that a Sunday edition of the *Daily Worker* had criticized Reston "as a cynical insider" of the State Department, hardly a damaging assertion coming from the newspaper published by the American Communist Party. In a summary report supplied to a lesser bureau official, agents reported that a prominent Republican "believes he has Reston 'pegged for being a New Dealer, and one who is not pro-Russian but would get great delight out of embarrassing the administration.'" Later the bureau did an internal document search to check on allegations that "Fabian socialists and communists" had infiltrated "high policy-making areas of Government service." Reston was one of some 122 people on whom the bureau checked. "No subversive derogatory information" was found.*

The Butterfield inquiry to the bureau led to nothing, but a year later Nixon went to war against the media and his prime target was the *New York Times*. The legal combat later came to include other news-

---

*Digests of this information flowed back and forth through the government, especially to the Secret Service as they did routine checks to issue White House press credentials. But the bureau was always alert to new tidbits, no matter how irrelevant. In 1963 the police in the District of Columbia notified the bureau, which in turn notified the "military authorities," that Reston had reported a telephoned bomb threat to his Woodley Road home. "An unidentified female . . . spoke in a Latin American accent," the bureau reported, "and stated 'We're going to blow you up. This is not a practical joke.'" The police searched the Reston home and found no bomb.

papers, but the fight began over the *Times'* publication of the Pentagon Papers, the Defense Department's secret, exhaustive study of the origins of American involvement in the Vietnam war. The study had been ordered in 1967 by Secretary of Defense McNamara in his last months before Lyndon Johnson booted him out of office for not being a staunch enough supporter of the war McNamara had helped expand. The study was a devastating indictment of the evolution of the war policy, documenting the levels of deceit and secrecy successive administrations had employed to gain support for and prosecute the most disastrous foreign adventure in American history.

The documents were classified, but one of the participants in the study, Daniel Ellsberg, by 1971 a research assistant at the Massachusetts Institute of Technology and a convert to the antiwar movement, decided to make the study public. He hoped to build opposition to continuing American prosecution of the war. Although he offered the papers to a number of reporters and congressional staffers with vague descriptions of their contents, it was Neil Sheehan of the *Times'* Washington bureau who first read the study. He quickly set about convincing his editors to publish the papers. When Ellsberg offered the papers to Sheehan, he wanted some guarantee that the *Times* would print them, if not entirely, at least comprehensively. Sheehan approached Reston, who made inquiries in New York, then told Sheehan to accept the secret papers.

It took the *Times* almost three months from receipt of the documents until their publication in June 1971. The time was consumed with arguments inside the *Times* about the legality and propriety of publishing classified government material and about the proper way, if the paper decided to publish, of treating the voluminous collection of analysis and documentation. Scotty Reston was not the dominant figure in the internal arguments, but he was heavily consulted about whether or not to publish. Arguing forcefully against publication was the paper's longtime outside legal counsel, Louis Loeb, whose firm had represented the newspaper since long before Punch Sulzberger became publisher. Loeb regarded the documents as stolen property that should by law be returned to the government. He warned Punch that the government would sue to prevent publication and that he and his firm would refuse to represent the newspaper in any legal action stemming from publication.

On the other side stood most of the paper's editors, most forcefully and important, Abe Rosenthal, but also including Reston; Scotty joined with his editorial colleagues in strongly urging publication. If the *Times* refused, he joked, he would publish them himself in the *Vineyard Gazette.* "Then you will go to jail," Louis Loeb warned him. But countervailing legal advice came from James Goodale, the *Times'* in-house lawyer, who firmly believed it was the paper's duty to publish the documents.

On Friday, June 11, Sulzberger, after some last-minute reassurance about the wisdom of publishing from Reston and other editors, gave the go-ahead. The next evening the presses were ready to roll with the first installment of the Pentagon Papers. Scotty Reston was out at Fiery Run, where his son was about to wed Denise Leary. Early in the day, he quickly filed a column entitled "The McNamara Papers," but failed to mark the column with an embargo to prevent the 360 newspapers around the nation that syndicated it from scooping the *Times* on its own story. Fortunately, the copy desk warned Rosenthal, and Reston's piece was withheld from distribution until just before the *Times* went to press. The same weekend, President Nixon's daughter Julie was marrying the grandson of former president Eisenhower, so much of high-level Washington was preoccupied with happy family matters. Reston, out of his long friendship with Kay Graham, felt he at least owed the *Post* a warning that they were about to be hit by one of the great scoops of the twentieth century. He dropped an oblique warning to Don Graham at the Fiery Run festivities. Don passed the tip on to his mother, who called managing editor Ben

Bradlee to warn him that the editors at the *Post* would have to spend their Saturday evening chasing a *New York Times* scoop. Bradlee, she said later, "went ape."

It took the Nixon Justice Department a while to respond. But by Monday evening, after the second of the series of articles had been published, Attorney General John Mitchell dispatched an official telegram to the *Times* requesting that no more pieces be published and the documents be returned to the Department of Defense. *Times* editors began frantic consultations among themselves and by phone with Sulzberger, who was in Europe: How should the *Times* respond? Goodale crafted an answer declining to cease publication. Reston happened to be having dinner that night at Robert McNamara's home. When New York reached Scotty to ask for his reaction to the paper's statement, he wrote the statement down word for word. Then he showed it to McNamara, the very originator of the war study, seeking his advice on the newspaper's proper reaction to the Justice Department's request. The Goodale statement said the paper refused to stop publication and vowed to oppose an expected request for an injunction, but it promised that the *Times* would comply "with the decisions of the courts." McNamara advised Reston to tell New York that the statement should make it clear that the newspaper would comply only with the final order of the Supreme Court, not lower-court rulings. The *Times* changed the wording to the more ambiguous phrase "final decision of the court." (It is interesting that McNamara, whose misguided judgments about the war were exposed in the Pentagon Papers, was trying to strengthen, not weaken, the *Times'* resistance to the government's position. It was perhaps the beginning of his lifelong attempt to apologize for his role in the Vietnam disaster.)

Louis Loeb made good on his promise to walk away from the case. Goodale scrambled to hire First Amendment experts, bringing in Alexander Bickel, a professor at Yale Law School, and a young lawyer named Floyd Abrams, later to become the country's most prominent First Amendment attorney. As part of Abrams's preparation for the looming legal struggle with the government, he decided to seek sworn affidavits from present and former government officials attesting that the papers did not of themselves compromise national security. Abrams's first choice was McNamara. At a meeting with the editors, Abrams asked who might approach the man who ordered the study in the first place. Reston piped up that he would call McNamara. Abrams also wanted Maxwell Taylor, chairman of the Joint Chiefs of Staff during the Kennedy administration. As Abrams remembers it, Reston again volunteered. Next on the list was the commander of the North Atlantic Treaty Organization. Reston said he would make that call too. In the end, none of the three executed the affidavits, although McNamara agreed that he would if it looked like any member of the *Times* staff was headed for prison. But what stayed in Abrams's memory was the direct access Reston had to these officials and the acknowledgment by Scotty's *Times* colleagues that it was he who was most likely to get help from the powerful in a high-risk situation.

The government did go to court, and ultimately the Supreme Court upheld the position of the *Times,* finding that there was no security risk to justify overturning constitutional precedent against prior restraint of the press. Reston's role was to support the editors and offer sound counsel to the publisher. Yet Reston bravely argued for embarrassing the very sources on whom he had relied for years, and by doing so steadfastly opposed the government he had covered so intimately for decades.

Of course, at the time, not everyone believed the Nixon administration would go to court to fight publication of the Pentagon Papers. The study, after all, had ended before Nixon took office, so its indictment of policy and policy makers was focused on the previous, Democratic, administrations. Nixon could simply have pointed to the papers as proof of the policy failure he had inherited. But the papers case offered the administration a great opportunity to bash the press, to paint the fourth estate as an enemy of the common good, and thus to further discredit media critics of Nixon and his policies. Nixon's legal challenge only made his position weaker. The monumental government deceit exposed by the papers, combined with the subsequent legal assault on the press, eroded further the trusting relationship that had so long characterized much of the commerce between the press and the government. It now seemed only good common sense for any reporter to approach the government and its leadership with the most deep distrust. That attitude profoundly affected the younger reporters coming of age during the early 1970s.

The Nixon administration had one other concern, if not a major one, in fighting the press over the Pentagon Papers. Nixon and his national security advisor, Henry Kissinger, were engaged in legitimately secret diplomacy at the time and had some reason to worry about how their potential failure to protect national secrets would affect their negotiating partners. Kissinger was a leading advocate of trying to stop publication of the papers. He was secretly negotiating with the North Vietnamese over terms for a possible end to the war. He was also quietly nudging the Chinese to break the long Cold War freeze in the two countries' relations to create a diplomatic triangle that would complicate the bipolar competition between the United States and the Soviet Union. The Nixon administration's conduct of the war in Vietnam, and especially Kissinger's role in it, was to be a subject over which Reston damaged his own standing. But the opening to China provided the backdrop for the crowning reportorial achievement in Reston's long career.

*   *   *

Only a few days before the publication of the Pentagon Papers, Nixon and Kissinger had received a diplomatic message from Chinese premier Zhou En-lai saying Kissinger would be welcome in China to prepare for a visit by the president during the election year of 1972. Long negotiations toward a rapprochement had been going on since Nixon took office. They had finally reached the point where Kissinger could go to China to finalize plans for Nixon's trip. As part of China's preparation for its new status in the world, Chinese leaders invited Scotty Reston to pay a visit. He was not the first American correspondent given entry under the Communists; Seymour Topping, who was married to the daughter of the Canadian ambassador to China, had been there before him. But to reintroduce the People's Republic to America, the Chinese wanted someone with unparalleled prestige, and that could only be James Reston.

Scotty naturally took Sally along, as he often did on his big foreign trips. They crossed from Hong Kong to the mainland on July 9, 1971. On the same day, Kissinger had flown into Pakistan under the guise of conferring with that country's leaders. He put out a cover story that he was suffering from a stomach upset and would be unavailable for the next few days. He flew straight to Beijing in a Pakistani military plane. The White House was quite upset that Reston, who knew nothing about Kissinger's trip, was lurching around China just as the security advisor arrived in secret. But Chinese authorities simply stuck Scotty and Sally in the Canton area, on the pretext that their plane to Beijing was unavailable. Scotty protested, but as Kissinger cracked in his memoirs, "The *New York Times* did not inspire the same terror in China as in Washington." Two days later, the Chinese put the Restons on a slow train that deposited them in the Chinese capital after Kissinger's departure.

Reston dutifully reported to the Chinese foreign ministry, where he naturally requested an interview with Mao Zedong. But just as he was making his pitch, Scotty was handed the announcement that

Kissinger had been in town and had successfully arranged a trip for the president. "I was not scooped. I was skewered," Reston lamented in his memoirs, still smarting from the fact that one of his best Nixon administration sources had managed to slip in and out of the city without Reston's ever suspecting his presence.

"It was then, I think, that I felt the first stab of pain in my groin. By evening I had a temperature of 103, and in my delirium I could see Henry floating along my ceiling and grinning out of a hooded rickshaw," Reston joked. The next day he was rushed to the hospital, where he was greeted with a sign proclaiming, in wonderfully Maoist fashion: "The time will not be far off when all aggressors and their running dogs in the world will be buried. There is certainly no escape for them." Reston took the sign as a bad omen for his illness. But a better sign soon appeared in the person of Zhou En-lai. Zhou was apparently concerned that the first major journalist visiting from the West would expire on Chinese soil and came to check on Reston's care. To speed Reston's recovery, Zhou promised to meet him for an interview.

Scotty had his appendix extracted by conventional surgical means. But the second night after the surgery, the Chinese doctors sought to relieve some of his postoperative discomfort by inserting acupuncture needles into his elbow and below his knees. They also burned some incense. Scotty, with Sally's considerable help, filed a surprisingly laudatory story to the *Times* about the unfamiliar procedures. He was quickly inundated with cables and letters asking how Americans might avail themselves of this miraculous treatment. Soon the popular imagination transformed this experience into surgery without anesthetic and with only the needles as painkillers. It set off a huge fad in the United States to revive all manner of traditional therapies. Scotty was besieged for years by pleas from individuals and groups asking him about the wonders of acupuncture. Some of these entreaties were the sad and desperate pleas of people who had exhausted conventional medical treatment and were looking for miracles.

Scotty and Sally attacked China with a natural appetite for the strange and forbidden. They were "minded" and shepherded at every turn and never saw much of the dark side of China: its shattering rural poverty, the repression of ethnic populations whose territory China had absorbed, its horrible treatment of political dissidents. The Chinese had deliberately invited Reston, whose fame and good name far exceeded his knowledge of Asia, rather than a serious expert on the country. In discussing the trip afterward, Reston acknowledged his own limits and said it was somewhat embarrassing that he did not know more about the place before he went. But while he was there, he gamely tried to introduce his readers to the country, painting word pictures of what he saw, while making it clear that he was being led about by the hand. While the Restons cooled their heels in Canton, unknowingly waiting for Kissinger's departure from Beijing, they were taken by car to an agricultural community about fifty kilometers outside the city. "All the way out and back, we never saw a single passenger car other than our own," Scotty wrote. He was amazed by the industry of the people and their obvious lack of modern machinery. "The extraordinary thing about this oldest civilization in the world," he wrote, "is that it seems so young. . . . China's most visible characteristics are the characteristics of youth: vigorous physical activity despite some serious health problems, a kind of lean, muscular grace, relentless hard work, and an optimistic and even amiable outlook on the future." Reston saw in the Chinese many of his own best qualities, but he took time to kid himself in print about his inability to master some of the country's customs: "China may have the answer to America's problem of overeating and over-weight. Having unsuccessfully tried every slimming formula from Lenten repentance to Joe Alsop's drinking man's diet, I have switched to chopsticks and reached the scientific conclusion that it is impossible not to lose weight if you rely on these slippery implements. . . . But after a few days of desperate experimentation with chopsticks, my problem now is not how to lose weight but how to avoid starvation." But he obviously loved the food. During their travels, Scotty and Sally typed pages and pages of notes about the exotic dishes they were served. They interviewed chefs on trains, recording their recipes and their claims that they were cooking "according to the teachings of Chairman Mao to serve all the peoples of the world."

Reston may not have been a China scholar, but he was undaunted by the task of interviewing any statesman. When he finally sat down with Zhou En-lai, the interview lasted five hours, interrupted only by an enormous banquet held in the Great Hall of the People. In typical Chinese Communist style, Reston and Zhou sat side by side in upholstered armchairs separated by a small table, with the requisite porcelain spittoon on the floor under the table. They addressed each other with heads cocked to the side as translators whispered simultaneously in their ears.

The interview text ran in full, taking up two pages of the *Times*. (The Chinese demanded that the complete transcript be published, including the entire text of Reston's questions. The usual journalistic practice is to pare down the questions, both to save embarrassment from poorly worded questions and to save space in the newspaper.) It was clear from his questions that Reston was surprised by the depth of China's persistent distrust of Japan, but he was fully briefed on the controversy surrounding Taiwan and handled Zhou's answers well.

What stands out now in the interview, with the benefit of three decades of hindsight, is the degree to which the Chinese were critical of the U.S. role in Vietnam yet still willing to overlook such an enormous problem in pursuit of rapprochement with the United States. The Chinese historically distrusted the neighboring Vietnamese, but even the presence of the American war machine in Southeast Asia was not enough to dampen their desire to open a more normal relationship with the West. During the interview, Reston freely explained his own opposition to the war. He suggested to Zhou that one reason Nixon was seeking a rapprochement with China might be his own guilt at having smeared so many of his political opponents as being soft on Communism, especially denigrating anyone who might think Red China should be admitted to the family of nations.

"I think he [Nixon] sees an historic opportunity here to repair the damage that has been done and even the injustice that has been done to China," Reston opined, "and also perhaps, in his own sense, a certain rebuke to his own past and a feeling that the role he has played in the cold war is something that might be altered by a great and generous move to unify the people of the Pacific before he ends his term."

"Thank you for providing us with this information," Zhou responded politely.

The Restons stayed in China for seven weeks, but the fallout from their trip lasted into the next year. When Nixon read Reston's interview, he immediately concluded that Scotty had reminded the premier of Nixon's sorry Red-baiting history to sabotage the success of his own trip. On August 11, the president dictated a memo to speech writer Pat Buchanan and his bulldog deputy H. R. Haldeman demanding that a "highly sophisticated, nasty letter" be drafted for signature by "someone in a high position" pointing out that "Reston is virtually guilty of treason in the comment that he made regarding the President's lack of courage, etc."

"This letter," Nixon continued, "should be written in anger, not in sorrow and should make the point that Reston's comments are not worthy of an American correspondent. . . . It is important not to let the TIMES get away with this attack." A draft bounced around the White House for a while, accumulating side notes about the difficulty of getting anyone to sign it. In the end, the revenge for insulting Nixon was an order from the president to make sure no reporter from the *Times* was included in the massive press corps sent to travel with him to China. Like many of the extreme orders Nixon issued during his periodic rages, this one was modified to make it less ridiculous. Max Frankel, the Washington bureau chief, had expected that he and his colleague Robert Semple would both make the trip, forming a tag team for what promised to be a grueling assignment. Instead, only one *Times*man was given a seat on the press plane. Frankel was furious but could do nothing about the slight. So he went alone, worked nonstop all day, writing well into the night to make each morning's deadline. He accomplished such masterful solo reporting on a breaking story that he won the Pulitzer Prize for his work. Frankel was, in the end, sarcastically grateful to Nixon for having set him up to win daily journalism's biggest award.

CHAPTER 25

KISSINGER

"IT WAS THE sweep of his mind, so often lacking at the top of the government, that I admired most," Scotty Reston wrote of Henry Kissinger in his memoirs. The two first met in the early 1950s when the German-born professor invited Reston to speak to his seminar on international affairs at Harvard. It was perhaps a prescient early courting of Reston. Kissinger was in touch again later, after Reston wrote a column questioning the wisdom of Jack Kennedy's decision to send thousands of "advisors" to Vietnam. Kissinger phoned to praise the column. But no courtship was necessary for Reston to hold Kissinger in high esteem. He was exactly the sort of public figure Reston most admired: well educated, well connected, well spoken. Kissinger's service as a paid foreign policy advisor to Nelson Rockefeller put him squarely in the center of the moderate political universe that Reston inhabited. When Nixon named Kissinger as his national security advisor, Reston called the appointment "reassuring."

Yet Reston was not blind to Kissinger's flaws. "[He] was a difficult man," Scotty also wrote, "inconsiderate of his staff, intolerant, often contemptuous of less brilliant but more practical men, and devious in his relations with the Congress and the press." That Kissinger was then, and still is, both brilliant and devious is beyond argument. One of his senior aides described him amusingly, saying Kissinger was exceptional not because he could tell ten different lies to ten different people but because he could remember precisely which lie he had told to which person. Even more remarkable, the aide could have added, was that each of the ten would likely have believed him.

Kissinger was the embodiment of much of what Scotty admired and longed to be. He was a true intellectual, and Reston knew and admitted that he himself was not. Kissinger was a professor from Harvard, the quintessential Ivy League institution. Reston had always held those schools in awe. And Kissinger, like himself, was an immigrant who became a powerful force in the political life of his adopted country. Kissinger was important to Reston not just for *who* he was but for *what* he was: the second-most-powerful person in government during the eight years of the Nixon and Ford administrations. In diplomacy, where the most interesting policy maneuvers of the Nixon administration were taking place, Kissinger was by and large the only person other than the president himself who knew what was actually afoot. Nixon and Kissinger effectively cut out the other usual sources of foreign policy information, such as cabinet secretaries and their staffs, and that was especially true on dramatic initiatives such as the opening to China, détente with the Soviets, and the secret machinations, both military and diplomatic, in Vietnam. Some cabinet members were bold enough to be seen on occasion speaking with reporters, but they rarely knew what Kissinger knew and were often deliberately lied to by Nixon and Kissinger to maintain secrecy. White House and administration officials were so cowed by Nixon's antipathy to reporters that they avoided any press contact at all. Reston had always talked to the most powerful men in government, right up to the president. Nixon confided in no one in the fourth estate. This made Kissinger the most powerful man willing to talk to Scotty Reston during the Nixon years. And that made Kissinger a powerfully fatal attraction for Reston.

Kissinger was confident he could withstand Nixon's disapproval if he talked to the media. He had a private agenda that required active cultivation of journalists: he wanted to maintain his reputation among his former academic colleagues, most of whom despised Nixon and his policies. It was an obvious necessity for Kissinger to try to cultivate the good opinion of Reston, who was revered and read religiously by those very people with whom Kissinger wanted to maintain his standing. But Kissinger had more nefarious purposes, too.

An incident during the 1970 invasion of Cambodia, retold by Max Frankel, illustrates how the Nixon administration and Kissinger worked to deceive the press and the public. The government announced the invasion, setting off huge and vociferous antiwar reaction protests, which led to the shooting deaths of four demonstrators at Kent State University. But the administration withheld the fact that it had simultaneously resumed heavy bombing of North Vietnam, which abrogated the promise Lyndon Johnson had made to suspend bombing to induce Hanoi to begin bargaining over terms to end the war.

The first word of the new bombing came from an Associated Press report that quoted Radio Hanoi's account of a raid conducted by more than a hundred American planes. Bureau chief Frankel asked his Pentagon correspondent to look into the story. The reporter was told Hanoi's account was an exaggeration. Kissinger's military deputy, General Alexander Haig, laughed at the reporter's question, calling it the "usual Radio Hanoi stuff." Haig stopped laughing later, Frankel reported, when the *Times* found a military source who confirmed the raid. Soon Kissinger was on the phone to Frankel, telling him it was a Defense Department matter and the

Pentagon would have to deal with it. His refusal to deny the facts left Frankel knowing the *Times* was right. Kissinger called back to tell Frankel the Pentagon would soon respond. When Frankel asked whether the story was wrong, Kissinger answered obliquely: "I would prefer you not to use the figure [of 128 airplanes involved in the raid] because the numbers in these things are always conjectural." Frankel recalled that he again asked Kissinger whether the number was incorrect. This time Kissinger replied that publishing the exact number "would not be right." Frankel interpreted the tortured locution as meaning something other than "incorrect."

Realizing the story was out, the Pentagon spokesman finally confirmed that the raids had occurred and then concocted a wonderful piece of newspeak to portray the bombing of the north as a "reinforced protective reaction." The spokesman was a former newsman and could not resist telling Frankel that he was "obviously onto something."

Kissinger made one last try with Frankel. He asked if he could make a "private" comment. Frankel, his Kissinger early warning system on full alert, agreed. The security advisor tried to convince Frankel that printing the story would constitute a nearly unpatriotic act, damaging to the national interest and the ongoing peace negotiations in Paris. Just how telling the American people what the North Vietnamese already knew from direct experience would hurt the talks, Kissinger didn't say, but instead of telling Kissinger to get lost, Frankel said he would pass the request on to his superiors. When he told Reston of Kissinger's request, Reston's response, as Frankel remembered, was curt. "Nuts," Scotty said. He straightaway picked up the phone and "chewed out" Kissinger for trying to censor the news. Then he wrote a column for the next day exposing the White House's attempt to cover up the bombing raid.

The matter didn't end there. After Reston's column appeared, a reporter from another newspaper tried to pursue Kissinger's attempt to suppress the story. Frankel says he refused to talk to the inquiring reporter, since his own agreement to let Kissinger speak privately on the phone made the conversation off the record. But Kissinger tried to deny he had done anything to suppress the story. He read the reporter his notes of the conversation with Frankel, revealing only his statement about the exact number of aircraft involved in the bombing raid. The reporter published a story disputing Reston's claim that the White House had been pressuring the *Times* to kill the story.

Dealing with Kissinger was as treacherous as it was necessary. As Frankel put it nicely: "Kissinger's gift with words was formidable. He persuaded adversaries on every continent that he understood their true interests and knew how to promote and protect them. He disguised selfish national interests as beneficent concessions to others and crafted statements and agreements that satisfied so many diverse audiences they seemed to reconcile the irreconcilable. He believed that in a lawless, nuclear world, survival was ethic enough for a diplomat." A less elegant description of Kissinger would portray him as a brilliant, lying, conniving, manipulative, power-hungry opportunist of the first order.*

Scotty Reston periodically expressed impatience with efforts to end the war, but he was supportive, in general, of the direction of Nixon's early policy. Reston wrote in his column in the autumn of 1969, after a belligerent speech by the president, that "the guess here is that he is determined to get out of the war, and like de Gaulle in

*When Frankel was ready to leave Washington for a new posting in New York, he relented on his policy of never inviting Kissinger to his home and had him to a farewell dinner. Frankel's wife sat herself next to Kissinger and explained that he had never been invited before because Max felt Kissinger had repeatedly lied to him. Before the evening was out, Kissinger confronted Frankel with that accusation, demanding to know when, exactly, he had lied to Frankel.

Algeria, is covering his retreat with clouds of brave rhetoric. . . . Our guess is that the President . . . is acting for peace." Shortly after that, Reston wrote, "The war is winding down in Vietnam, not winding up. What we are arguing about now, in the main, is not so much the direction of policy as the pace of policy."

Through it all, Reston was often openly admiring of Kissinger. He was not alone in that. The attitude was not unusual among reporters who were in Kissinger's sphere. In the spring of 1972, when Kissinger went to Moscow and managed to arrange a summit meeting between Nixon and Leonid Brezhnev despite a fresh wave of American attacks against North Vietnam, Reston was dazzled. "How he performs this delicate and dangerous role is a miracle," Scotty wrote. Kissinger's performance was often more dazzling than was known at the time: a jealous Nixon, abetted by Kissinger's ambitious military deputy, Alexander Haig, and the White House palace guard of Bob Haldeman and John Ehrlichman, constantly second-guessed Kissinger's diplomacy and denigrated his abilities. Kissinger's bureaucratic diplomacy was nearly as complicated as his negotiations abroad; he used Reston and other journalists to shore up his efforts on both fronts.

In the fall of 1972, only weeks before the presidential election Nixon would win in a landslide over the hapless but principled antiwar candidate George McGovern, Kissinger concluded the semblance of a peace deal with the North Vietnamese. Shorn of the niceties, the agreement traded a final American withdrawal from Vietnam for the return of U.S. prisoners of war. It left North Vietnamese troops in place in South Vietnam, dooming the Saigon government. Nixon recognized that he would win the election no matter what happened in the peace talks and believed that once he had been reelected, his negotiating position would be stronger. So he was not eager for Kissinger to accept the accords. But Kissinger did so anyway. He believed that since the north was ready to sign, it would be shortsighted to miss the moment. The fact that the South Vietnamese government would never agree to the terms did not deter him.

When Kissinger returned from the Paris negotiations to Washington that October, Nixon seemed to pay little attention to the difficulties involved in implementing the peace agreement. The president was more concerned with keeping the deal secret until after the election. But Kissinger wanted to cement the accords by making public the news that an agreement had been reached. He lunched with Max Frankel on October 25, and the next day the *Times* ran Frankel's story quoting anonymous official sources who said a cease-fire could come very soon, if neither Hanoi nor Saigon did anything stupid to undermine the arrangements. Nixon was furious when Kissinger told him he had talked to Frankel and immediately began to worry that Kissinger would reap all the credit for peace.

The next day Kissinger held a press conference in which he proclaimed "peace is at hand." His purpose was to reassure Hanoi that the agreement was on track and to let Saigon know that the United States was going to proceed even without their agreement if necessary. Instead, critics charged that Kissinger and Nixon were using the announcement to influence the imminent elections (as if Nixon needed any additional help in burying the McGovern candidacy).

Kissinger's announcement set off a wave of premature euphoria in the national press. Reston wrote a column called "The End of the Tunnel," playing off the shopworn phrase constantly used as metaphor for victory in Vietnam. "It has been a long time," Reston gushed, "since Washington has heard such a candid and even brilliant explanation of an intricate political problem as Henry Kissinger gave to the press on the peace negotiations." Reston wrote two more columns that week praising what he called "the Kissinger compromise." *Time* magazine produced a special issue recounting the history of the war in Vietnam as if the war were in fact over.

Newsweek and the *Washington Post* and just about every other news outlet joined Kissinger in proclaiming that peace had arrived.

Some reporters managed to mention that there were still some troublesome details. But few understood the depth of the resistance Kissinger and the administration were encountering from the South Vietnamese government. Reston did not mention the problem at all in his columns after the Kissinger press conference. Some skeptical pieces were printed, based on sources in other parts of the Nixon administration or from the North Vietnamese in Paris, saying that major problems had arisen with the prospective peace. Those stories were often watered down or killed because they conflicted with the optimistic line Kissinger was busy propounding. In mid-December the *Times'* Pentagon correspondent wrote that the negotiations had come apart because of intransigence in Hanoi and Nixon would soon resume bombing North Vietnam. The story was killed, based on Reston's reporting from Paris, where he had gone with Kissinger, who had resumed talks with the North Vietnamese. Reston wrote a story published December 13 based on several conversations with Kissinger, reporting that South Vietnamese resistance was the last obstacle and if the south could not be persuaded to sign, the United States would go ahead without the consent of its ally. Both stories were correct in part. The South Vietnamese were resisting the deal, but Nixon had decided to bomb the north as a demonstration of the U.S. commitment to help the south in the future, hoping that would persuade them to sign. Kissinger failed to tell Reston that part of the story. Seymour Hersh, in his scathing biography of Kissinger, *The Price of Power,* cites a member of Kissinger's staff in Paris who noticed that Reston was sharing occasional breakfasts with Kissinger in the American embassy. Invariably Kissinger would assemble his staff after those meetings, the aide told Hersh, and give them all hell about leaking, even as he predicted that the *New York Times* was going to break this or that story. "Every damned time there'd be a breakfast with Scotty, Henry would gather the staff to warn about leaks," the aide told Hersh.

Three days after Reston's December 13 story, Kissinger announced that the talks had come unglued. But he did not mention that in two days American B-52s would unleash a torrent of bombs on Hanoi, Haiphong, and other populated areas of the north. The bombing campaign lasted twelve days, with a pause for Christmas. Nearly sixteen hundred civilians in North Vietnam were killed, and ninety-three American flyers were lost.

Although Kissinger harbored some doubts about the bombing, he had recommended the assault to Nixon before he told Reston in Paris that it was the South Vietnamese who were holding up the peace. During the final deliberations on the bombing, Kissinger recommended using smaller fighter bombers against the cities and that the lumbering B-52s be used only for supply routes close to the demilitarized zone separating North and South Vietnam. Even though the big bombers were used against the population centers, Kissinger approved. In his memoirs, Kissinger owns up to the fact that he supported the bombing. Nixon noted in his diary that "Henry talked rather emotionally about the fact that this was a very courageous decision."

The bombing was met by outrage in the American press. Reston called it "war by tantrum." Diplomats and foreign leaders denounced it as well, some comparing it to Nazi atrocities, declaring it "a crime against humanity." Immediately, Kissinger scurried to distance himself from the decision to bomb the north, repeatedly characterizing it as Nixon's decision. And Reston was listening.

At the very end of December, the day after the bombs stopped falling but before the halt was officially announced, Reston wrote a column that enraged Nixon and his aides in the White House. The piece was headlined "Nixon and Kissinger" and depicted Kissinger as an opponent of the Christmas bombing. "The capital is buzzing these days with rumors about a split between President Nixon and his security advisor Henry Kisssinger over the terms of a cease-fire in Vietnam, but as usual in this gossipy town, the facts are less dramatic than the rumors," Reston began. The column went on to portray a patient and forbearing Kissinger tolerating the Nixon bombing strategy for the time being. "It may be, and probably is, true that Mr. Kissinger as well as Secretary of State Rogers and most of the senior officers in the State Department are opposed to the President's bombing offensive in North Vietnam," Reston continued, calling the aerial assault "the President's" alone, exonerating Kissinger.

"Mr. Kissinger is a servant of the President and has never pretended he was anything else. He has carried out the President's instructions in Paris to the letter. He has put all the blame on Hanoi for the impasses in the Paris cease-fire negotiations, and has said nothing in public about the bombing in North Vietnam, *which he undoubtedly opposes*" [italics added]. It was not the sort of thing Reston ever got wrong. But in one paragraph he was wrong three times. Kissinger did not precisely follow Nixon's instructions in Paris. Kissinger told Reston that it was the South Vietnamese who were holding up the peace. And Kissinger recommended and did not oppose the bombing. The column was the result of masterful manipulation by Kissinger. But more than that, the column carried a veiled threat to Nixon as a way of emphasizing Kissinger's innocence. Kissinger, Reston wrote, was "avoiding a break with the President." But if there were to be an open split, "Mr. Kissinger will be free to resign and write the whole story of the Paris talks and why they broke down, and this would probably be highly embarrassing to Mr. Nixon."

Charles Colson, Nixon's loyal and combative political hitman, read the column to the president at his retreat in Camp David. Nixon was utterly furious. He told Colson to order Kissinger not to speak to any reporters and not to call Nixon, because he wasn't going to speak to his security advisor. After getting his orders from Colson, Kissinger immediately called Nixon anyway. Nixon refused the call. Kissinger next phoned political columnist Joseph Kraft. Colson, who had been authorized to obtain Kissinger's phone logs to track down which reporters Kissinger was talking to, apparently had someone monitoring Kissinger's calls, even though the security advisor was on vacation in California. When Kissinger hung up with Kraft, Colson immediately called to remind him that the president had forbidden press calls. Colson claimed later that Kissinger responded by saying of Kraft, "I wouldn't talk to that son of a bitch." Kissinger was working to save his reputation in the press, but Nixon was trying very hard to shut him up.

The day after the Reston exculpatory column appeared, Nixon and Colson were back in the Oval Office. Nixon was still obsessed with the way Kissinger had been portrayed by Reston. Colson, captured on the White House taping system, reassured the president that they were now logging all of Kissinger's calls. From then on, they would know everybody Kissinger talked to. Nixon was not satisfied. He wanted to know whether they had found out if Kissinger had talked to Reston. Colson said they hadn't but were still looking for evidence. Nixon suggested that perhaps the leak to Reston went through someone else. Said Nixon: "There is another possibility, that he could have called Frankel. Frankel is not writing . . . he's gone upstairs. But Henry is compulsive about Frankel. He's Jewish. . . . The *Times* works that way. . . . They pass it around. You could check the Frankel calls." The obsequious Colson responded, "Mr. President, I just thought of that."

By the following week, they had tracked down a record of Kissinger talking to Reston before the bombing column was written. In a conversation with H. R. Haldeman, Kissinger first denied having had any conversation with Reston. Haldeman confronted him with the damning evidence. "Yes," Kissinger answered lamely, "but that was only the telephone." A couple of weeks later Reston repeated his exculpation of Kissinger: "His views of power, diplomacy and politics are well known to his large company of friends in the press and the university and political communities, and it would be hard to convince any of them who have known him over the last two decades that he approves of the recent bombing of North Vietnam."

In the first volume of his memoirs, Kissinger denied he had misled the press about his role in the Christmas bombing. But as ever his denial was carefully worded. "I did not indicate to any journalist that I had opposed the decision to use B-52s," he wrote, narrowing considerably the scope of Reston's claim that Kissinger had been against the bombing itself, not the choice of airplanes. "But," Kissinger continued, "I also did little to dampen the speculation, partly in reaction to the harassment of the previous weeks, partly out of a not very heroic desire to deflect the assault from my person. Some of the journalists may have mistaken my genuine depression about the seeming collapse of the peace efforts for a moral disagreement. Though I had much provocation and *thought* I acted *mainly* [italics added] by omission and partly through emotional exhaustion, it is one of the episodes of my public life in which I take no great pride."

Reston had been pursuing Kissinger for an on-the-record interview since before the "peace is at hand" press conference, but Kissinger had repeatedly turned him down, fearing further backlash from the president given how angry Nixon was about the favorable publicity Kissinger was receiving. (Kissinger had tried to talk *Time* magazine out of making him Man of the Year with Nixon at the end of 1972. He wanted Nixon on the magazine's cover alone, to avoid further charges that Kissinger was hogging the limelight.) At the end of January 1973, after a cease-fire had been achieved in Vietnam, Kissinger finally agreed to give Reston an interview but then got cold feet and refused. Nixon and his entourage were off in Key

Biscayne, Florida, so Kissinger felt comfortable enough meeting secretly with Reston at his home on Woodley Road. He tried to explain why he had again refused the on-the-record interview but did agree to talk on background. Reston wisely left his tape recorder off during the conversation. But after Kissinger left, he typed up four pages of notes.

According to those notes, Kissinger complained about the atmosphere in the White House; their attitude toward the Congress and press was even worse than it had been before. He claimed that he had asked permission to give an interview to the *Times* but had gotten a "very negative reaction." Nobody was giving Nixon credit for the cease-fire, Kissinger explained, and the president's anger at the slight was so great that Kissinger felt it was impeding Nixon's ability to govern effectively.

Kissinger told Reston, as he had told others, that most likely he would not stay through Nixon's second term. (Although the Watergate case was beginning, no one imagined it would lead to Nixon's resignation.) Kissinger's ploy was designed to spark a sympathetic anxiety in the liberal press as they imagined what a Nixon White House would be without Kissinger. The length of his continued service, Kissinger said, was dependent on "how long he could really add creative thought" to the policy-making process. Kissinger portrayed himself as lonely and unappreciated. He claimed that during his four years in the White House, he had been drawing on ideas shared at Harvard with other professors, cleverly citing the particular importance of a pair of dovish professors. Now, he complained, he was cut off from that source of guidance and inspiration. "He had very little time to think," Reston noted,

and his colleagues in the university community were so angry about Vietnam that they were no longer able to contribute objective thought. They were simply against the Administration, he seemed to be saying, and against him for cooperating with it, and he didn't know what to do about this: There was something sad about this: He needed the help of his old university but couldn't go back to it, wanted to stay in Washington, but feared, I thought, that he would be destroyed if he did.

Poor Kissinger. Caught between his old university colleagues and his enemies in the White House, Kissinger at least had Scotty's sympathy. The *Times* was trying to reconstruct just what had happened between the time peace was "at hand" and the bombing and then the cease-fire. Reston inquired, but Kissinger refused to discuss it. "Kissinger doesn't like to talk about the bombing," Scotty recorded, "because he is clearly ashamed of it as we are." Ashamed, perhaps. Responsible, certainly, but that's not the impression he left with Scotty Reston this time either.

And Kissinger talked about Nixon. Sally Reston joined the two men and asked whether Kissinger thought "there was any Quaker faith left in the President." "Kissinger said yes," Scotty noted, "he thought there was, but when we pressed him for an example, he never found it." Kissinger claimed he still did not know Nixon very well but told Reston he thought that "if he [Nixon] had more confidence in himself, maybe he could deal with the deeper philosophical questions before the country." The talk went on for hours before Kissinger left the Reston home.

Scotty Reston was certainly not the only reporter in Washington taken in by Kissinger's antibombing pose. But he was the most conspicuous and soon others began to notice. Had he been, like Lippmann, a columnist purveying just analysis and opinion, there might not have been much fuss. But the strength of Reston's column had always been its reliable reporting and so the Kissinger relationship provoked widespread dismay. In the February 1973 issue of the now-defunct journalism magazine *[More]*, former Kissinger deputy Anthony Lake and future *Times* correspondent Leslie Gelb wrote a tough analysis of the press coverage of the bombing; they cited the *Times'* decision to spike the Pentagon reporter's piece predicting the bombing and mentioned Reston's role in that decision. In the May issue of the same magazine, J. Anthony Lukas, whom Reston had recruited to the *Times* but who had left the paper the previous year, wrote a devastating piece about Reston's coziness with power. Speaking for a whole generation of reporters, Lukas recalled that when he was a young man "Scotty Reston was the man I most wanted to be when I grew up. . . . Reston was the apotheosis of the Washington Correspondent: scrappy but eminently respectable; brassy yet reflective; tenacious and still charming, irreverent but responsible. That marvelous moniker, 'Scotty,' conjured up the image of a tough little terrier, trim, well-groomed and welcome at the best tables in town – where he claimed, not the bones, but the choicest morsels – yet alert, unmuzzled and never hesitant to nip at even the best-booted heel."

Lukas praised Reston's accomplishments over the years, his scoops, his prizes, the loyalty shown him by the men he had hired. He rehearsed Scotty's rise at the *Times,* including his 1970 salary ($96,395), his "supplemental remuneration" that year ($30,000), and his deferred compensation in company stock ($857,648), as well as outright company stock ownership ($170,000). "He is certainly, as the *Saturday Review* puts it, 'a journalistic statesman who has arrived,'" Lukas wrote. "Richly deserved as these rewards may be, they have taken their toll. A Journalistic Statesman does not have much time or energy left for reporting."

Lukas went on to accuse Reston of two sins: lapsing into irrelevancy and being taken in by those in power, especially by Kissinger.

"Perhaps he was right to trust William Fulbright, Mike Mansfield or John Gardner," Lukas wrote, using examples of powerful Washington figures considered trustworthy. "But what of Robert McNamara, William Rogers and Henry Kissinger?" Reston, oblivious of the attack that was coming, made things worse during his interview with Lukas. When Lukas sat down, Reston said to him, "Henry Kissinger sat in that chair just the other night."

Lukas quoted devastating remarks from David Halberstam, one of Scotty's boys, the man Reston had recruited out of Tennessee and defended against John Kennedy and inside the *Times* on his Vietnam coverage. "Scotty was pretty good on the war itself," Lukas quoted Halberstam as saying. "But he wouldn't take what he knew and carry it the whole way. He kept saying 'the war is bad, but America works, the system works.'" That was a true description of the way Reston thought and lay at the root of the disenchantment with Reston settling in among even those like Halberstam who had long admired him. Reston still trusted power. He still believed in the essential goodness of America. But those sentiments were rapidly disappearing all around him.

Lukas had an explanation for the disenchantment with Scotty. "There are those who feel Reston's evolution of late is a bit like that of his friend Hubert Humphrey. . . . Both men were symbols and spokesmen for the great American liberal center in the 'fifties," he wrote. "But, largely as a result of the Vietnam war, the liberal center shifted during the past decade and their constituencies shifted leftward with it. . . . Some of those who have worked for and with Reston over the years may wish that he were a little less cozy with power, a little less reverential toward the System, a little more outspoken about the evils they detect in American society." Lukas was careful not to claim those sentiments for himself, although his own feelings were plain in the article. Rather, he let Halberstam carry the freight. "Those of us who honor and love him wish that he were still walking with us," Lukas quoted Halberstam as saying. "It's like what Chicago fans felt in 1919 about Shoeless Joe Jackson. Say it ain't so, Joe. Say it ain't so, Scotty."

When the piece appeared, Halberstam was furious with Lukas, to whom he thought he was speaking on a not-for-attribution basis. "He took all the good stuff and put it in his own voice and used all the negative stuff in mine. Devastating," Halberstam remembered. "Here's the man who hired me. Hired four or five people I had recommended. Fought for me for the Pulitzer when the *Times* wasn't even going to put me up. If anybody had ever reached out to me and helped me, it was him. It felt like you had just whacked your father." But Reston never reacted to the piece. "The last time we saw each other," Halberstam recalled, "we just hugged and he said, in front of my wife, 'I love him too.' He was just a wonderful man."

Nor did Reston alter his relationship with Kissinger after the *[More]* piece appeared. He continued to see him privately, and as Nixon's position began to erode under the weight of Watergate, Kissinger's power and freedom of action increased. Yet another of his and Nixon's foreign policy initiatives – the pursuit of détente with the Soviet Union – was attracting vocal opposition from some in Congress, especially Washington Democrat Henry M. "Scoop" Jackson. Senator Jackson was insisting on a commitment from the Soviets for freer emigration for Soviet Jews before any accommodations were set. Whether or not Jackson's role was misguided – many believed it was mostly a political ploy to position himself for a run at the presidency – Reston took Kissinger's side. In a phone conversation on April 25, 1974, Reston lectured the senator on his opposition to Kissinger's policy. "And what I don't understand is why you don't sit down, really, and talk about this," Reston said. Jackson, his voice sounding like a chastised schoolboy, told Reston that he was to breakfast with Kissinger on the coming Friday. Concluded Reston: "But it seems to me that you're getting into an avoidable conflict with Kissinger, but maybe I'm wrong about that."

Alexander Cockburn, a baroquely liberal columnist for the *Village Voice*, lambasted Reston for criticizing Scoop Jackson in print. The senator had been alleging that Kissinger had made secret agreements as part of the Vietnam peace accords and this had drawn Reston's disapproval. "One often feels James Reston has plumbed the nethermost pit of pompous idiocy," Cockburn wrote,

> only to discover that he has found some new abyss in which to immerse himself and his typewriter.... The most evidently depressing thing is that Reston has long ceased to regard himself as a journalist, dedicated to publishing important facts, or at least discussing whether such facts be true, but has rather become – in his own mind – an equerry for the administration, a sort of village elder lounging beside the well of inside knowledge, judging what is and what is not meet for the locals to know.

There was some truth to that. In 1975, with Kissinger now secretary of state in the administration of Gerald Ford, Reston visited the secretary in his office. Scotty wanted to discuss his forthcoming trip to Cuba. In his notes of the conversation, Reston wrote that Kissinger "made the following points and authorized me to repeat them to Castro if I saw him." The "points" were basically designed to explore the idea of beginning some talks to normalize the relationship between the two countries, while noting that it made "no sense" that the United States had "practical communications with every communist state except Albania and Cuba."

Reston had an audience with Castro, along with Pierre Salinger,

Jack Kennedy's former White House press secretary and at the time a correspondent for *Paris Match*. As Salinger remembered the encounter, about two hours into the interview, Reston said to Castro, "Mr. President, do you mind if I change my hat. I'd like to put on my diplomatic hat, because I have a message for you from the secretary of state, Henry Kissinger. He wants to begin negotiations to normalize relations with Cuba." Castro, according to Salinger, responded that the first thing the United States had to do was drop its economic embargo. "Well," Reston said, "that was the first thing Kissinger told me you would say, but we have to have talks first. What about some lower-level talks to start with?" Reston the diplomat and Castro the autocrat discussed the matter for about half an hour and decided perhaps there could be meetings between the American and Cuban ambassadors in Madrid to start these talks.

Reston carried Kissinger's water on other occasions. In the winter of 1976, Kissinger used Reston to send a message to Daniel Patrick Moynihan, the administration's very outspoken ambassador to the United Nations. Kissinger felt Moynihan was out of control – he was to some extent – and wanted him out. Reston wrote a column saying that the place for Moynihan was the U.S. Senate – where he eventually sat – and suggesting that Kissinger felt Moynihan was overplaying his hand. "Now Mssrs. Ford and Kissinger support him in public and deplore him in private. Having put him in the job, they can neither tame nor repudiate him. He has always been the enemy of his best ideas, always used the most provocative phrases, but Mr. Kissinger knew all that before and is now having to deal with the consequences of his own regrets." Moynihan, recognizing an official message when he read it in Reston's column, resigned his post the next day. It was and is often the way bureaucrats and politicians work, taking action by leaks rather than by direct conversation.

The Reston-Kissinger relationship was not, however, a one-sided affair. Reston got a lot in return. In March 1975 he had a long phone conversation with Kissinger about the Middle East. Kissinger was candid, describing an action by the Israelis as "one of the most reckless, dangerous things that I have ever seen. . . . They have wrecked our Middle East position." Speaking of the future prime minister Yitzhak Rabin, Kissinger said, "I can only draw two conclusions about Rabin. Either he's the most treacherous bastard I've ever met, or he can't carry his own government."

Even after Kissinger left government, he continued to be a good source for Reston. During the 1980 Republican convention, Ronald Reagan's staff attempted to avoid making George H. W. Bush vice president. They proposed a bizarre power-sharing scheme to make former president Gerald Ford both vice president and secretary of defense. Kissinger was in the middle of the negotiations between the Ford and the Reagan camps. Nothing came of the discussions and Bush was given the veep's job. But there was much speculation about the proposed deal and about Kissinger's role in promoting Ford. Reston got a full briefing from Kissinger over the phone, including the details of the various offers.

Not long after the piece in *[More]* appeared, coauthor Les Gelb joined the Washington bureau of the *Times*, where he watched Reston work close up. "Scotty never hid where he was coming from, the fact that he was a player," Gelb recalled. But while Reston had been a "player" for two decades, his best role was as a reporter and commentator on the game, not as a fully uniformed member of the team. That had altered dismayingly with his relationship with Kissinger, when he had come off the bench and onto the field. He was no longer an outsider with superb connections on the inside. He was a full-fledged insider, the wrong place for a respected journalist to be.

It is so often the case that what we do in the final lap is all that is remembered. More than twenty years later, the weekly editorial board meeting of the *Times* was convened in a conference room on the tenth floor. In the hallway outside, where photographs of the paper's Pulitzer Prize winners hang, there were two portraits of Scotty Reston. A question was raised about one of the paper's reporters' being too close to a source. "Oh no," groaned one man too young to have known Reston's finest work firsthand, "not another Reston." Present at the meeting was a young intern journalist, Maeve Reston, Scotty's granddaughter.

CHAPTER 26

DEADLINE

THE ASSASSINATION OF John Kennedy reverberated for years, leading to a series of accidental presidents. It is most doubtful that on his own Lyndon Johnson would have succeeded to the Oval Office after a two-term Kennedy presidency. Richard Nixon became president in 1968 because Johnson's prosecution of the war in Vietnam so discredited him and his party that Nixon was able to squeak by Hubert Humphrey. Nixon's depredations in the Watergate scandals drove him from office, made Gerald Ford a brief – and underappreciated – interim president, and resulted in the election of the preacherly Jimmy Carter, whose own failures set the stage for Ronald Reagan.

For a long period, tragedy seemed to be followed by catastrophe, followed by constitutional crisis, and the sorry sequence fundamentally changed the relationship between the government of the United States and its people. What had been a largely trusting, if skeptical, view of politics and politicians was transformed into an attitude of cynicism and distrust. The way the press and the government had worked together over the decades of James B. Reston's career changed just as profoundly. In his prime, Scotty Reston was the most admired journalist in the world. He won virtually every prize in his trade. Colleges and universities around the nation awarded him honorary degrees. He was made a commander of the British Empire, which honor, he was assured by a colleague from the BBC, "was particularly useful for eliminating warts on the back of your neck."

Young journalists coming to Washington, especially in the Kennedy and Johnson years, aspired to be Scotty Reston. But then, as those in power fell under suspicion and Reston came under attack for defending the powerful, it was Bob Woodward and Carl Bernstein, the relentless reporters who helped expose the Watergate cover-up, who became the role models for young journalists everywhere.

Whether or not he understood that he had been displaced as the standard of excellence for American journalists, Reston knew the tenor of the trade had changed. And he didn't like it one bit. At the end of 1979, he wrote a column criticizing Woodward for the book he and a collaborator wrote about the Supreme Court, in which they detailed the personal animosities among the justices. "We are living in an age of destruction," Scotty wrote. "Nothing is private now. . . . Criticism in this country is going too far, and . . . in the process we are harming the institutions we need the most. The press itself is now in confusion on this point. It is determined, for good reasons, to expose the weakness and corruption of government at all levels, but in the process tends to dramatize the worst in everything and everybody."

Reston continued to write his column and to interview the mighty, even after his formal retirement in 1974 as a vice president of the *Times*. He had an easy, old-fashioned relationship with President

Ford, both men throwbacks to a more civil time. In the spring of 1975, he had a chat with Ford in the White House, two aging pipe smokers behaving in the old way, trusted reporter talking to a balanced and benevolent president. Ford borrowed a pipeful of tobacco from Reston during the conversation and later repaid him by sending a leather tobacco pouch stamped with the presidential seal. Scotty penned a note to Ford to thank him for the gift. "Dear Mr. President," he wrote in longhand, "as you know the Scotch are tighter than a Pullman window, but that's the best deal any Scotsman ever made. One lousy pipeful of dry tobacco out of a paper envelope for a lovely English pouch. . . . I thank you most sincerely and will keep this as a memento of your kindness."

In the 1976 presidential race, Reston, like many Washington insiders, was dismissive of Carter as an outsider who didn't really understand the way Washington worked. He was right about Carter but wrong in thinking he could not be elected. For a while during the campaign, Reston joined the effort to pump up the possible candidacy of his friend Hubert Humphrey, hoping to put an old Washington operator on the ticket. After the Democrats nominated Jimmy Carter as their candidate for president, Reston scrambled to get access. On August 4 he took Sally along to interview the nominee in Washington. The interview was remarkable: it reads now as a chat between equals, the presidential nominee on the same footing as the veteran correspondent, both in awe of the greatness of America. Said Scotty: "Yes, there's something about this country. Every time I get in a plane and vault those ranges of mountains and there she lies. And it looks as if it's the way the world was when it began. Its not old. It's young . . . it's empty." Carter agreed: "It's unbelievable. Fly from Dallas to San Francisco, you can fly for just hours and see nothing but desert."

Scotty did ask some good, disarming questions of the nominee. "Why does the man of faith in America have to explain his faith,

when the man of no faith, no religion, is not called upon to explain?" he inquired of the Baptist Sunday school teacher from rural
Georgia. Carter observed that his public faith had become a curiosity in an era of uprootedness. (Since then attitudes have reversed, so
that no contemporary politician could admit to any religious doubt
and hope to win office.) Reston meditated on the theme of the sea
change that had overtaken Washington. "The poison in this town
over the last fifteen years, really since, even in the Kennedy period,
right straight through Johnson, was really terrible because of that
awful feeling that 'All right, that's what the president says, but what
is back of that?' It's an awful thing where you feel you can't trust the
president. It just poisoned the whole town." Carter assured Reston,
"I have a fairly easy relationship with the press . . . and I would open
up the government as much as possible." He did for a time, especially compared with the Nixon years, and he and his staff did pay
attention to Reston. They invited him to state dinners and sent him
the occasional briefing paper. Scotty conducted reflective year-end
interviews with Carter in 1977 and 1978. In April 1980 Scotty and
Sally had Carter's national security advisor, Zbigniew Brzezinski, to
lunch at their home. The meal took place shortly after the failure of
a commando raid to rescue the American hostages in Tehran and
right after Secretary of State Cyrus Vance resigned to protest the
decision to use military force. Brzezinski told Reston that both he
and Secretary of Defense Harold Brown had offered to resign to take
some of the heat off Carter. "The president laughed at this,"
Brzezinski told Reston.

The next month, after what he described as "a long evening with
the president," Reston wrote a column in which he called Carter "a
formidable candidate for re-election, especially considering his
opposition." Then and later, Reston never understood the appeal of
Ronald Reagan, a shortcoming he shared with many pundits. Over
the years, beginning with the Truman-Dewey race, he had rarely

been a good political prognosticator. But he was prescient in predicting in the same column that the coming battle with Ted Kennedy at the Democratic convention would be badly damaging to Carter. And as he got to know him, Reston was much more respectful of Carter and his presidency than most of the Washington journalistic establishment, which mercilessly pounded the Georgian as his troubles deepened. Such patience and reluctance to dismantle American leaders was quintessential Reston.

Scotty remained a director of the New York Times Company even after retirement and was paid a director's fee for that role and a consulting fee for his occasional columns. But the company's willingness to provide for him and Sally as they had in the past began to wane. In a 1977 letter to Punch Sulzberger, Reston tried to convince the publisher that Sally should continue to be carried on the company payroll. His argument was that he needed Sally to perform secretarial services. She was not employed, he wrote, as "it was presumed in New York," for merely representational purposes.

"My problem now is simply how to reconcile my professional and personal responsibilities," he continued, a bit lamely. "I can either go where the news takes me or continue to have Sally along to help. But I can't, if I lose her, afford to do both." Punch reluctantly agreed to a fee-for-service arrangement to compensate Sally for work she did for Scotty.

The publisher also sought to reduce Scotty's business spending. In an undated letter, Reston wrote to Punch that he had gotten the message about lowering his expenses. "Accordingly," he wrote,

I have gone over them very carefully, and some things I think are clear. Expenses at the Metropolitan Club and the F Street Club in Washington and the Century in New York are used for business purposes, but the National Press Club, which I would be obliged personally to join in any event, and the Chevy

Chase Club are not essential to the *Times* and will be eliminated. It takes years to get into the Metropolitan Club and since I happen to be the only resident member in the bureau, it is used not only when I take official characters there, but also when Daniel [Clifton Daniel was then Washington bureau chief] or Kovach [Bill Kovach was Daniel's deputy and later succeeded him] and the others want to have a business dinner, all of which are charged to my account. . . . Travel abroad is another and an expensive item, and here I have a bit of a problem. For example, when I went to Mexico and did an interview with the President in the *Times,* this was on the invitation of the Mexican government with no charge to us, but though I am no longer a staff member of the paper, I wonder whether this is a proper thing to do.

Without doubt, it was not the proper thing to do and it is surprising that Reston accepted a government-sponsored trip. But this was not the Scotty of old.

In 1980 he objected to Punch's request that he give up the office he retained on the executive floor of the *Times* building in New York. He rarely used the office, but he had the services of an assistant there who often paid bills and did other personal tasks for Scotty. He wrote Punch that the office was his continuing tie to the "engine room" of the *Times.* "I would feel vaguely amputated without it," he said, pointing out that he was about to begin writing a book about his years on the paper. But the office was cleaned out and someone else moved in.

Retirement didn't sit easily on Scotty Reston. He relinquished all his ties to the *Times* in 1989. But like many men of accomplishment, he had become his job, and without it he was restive, often cranky, and unhappy. One former clerk who saw him during this time described him as depressed. On a single day, he wrote to resign all his club memberships, although the Century in New York invited him to stay on as a non-dues-paying honorary member. He and Sally would have bouts of bad temper with each other, fueled to some extent by what one of his sons described as "a little bit of booze."

He did begin work on a memoir of his life, but he did not find it an easy task. "The book goes along fairly well," he wrote to Wally Carroll, "but it's my first experience with a long project of this sort and I find that my mind is adjusted to the length of a column and not the story of a lifetime. I would be less than candid if I didn't say it makes me think about the end of this long journey, but it has been such a joyful return ticket adventure that I have actually liked it much more than I expected."

Many of his former colleagues had urged him to write his memoirs. One was Jonathan Yardley, the first young man he had hired as a clerk. "I felt like others that in the early eighties his column had fallen apart, that it was nothing but bromides," Yardley explained. "You couldn't say it to him. It would be too cruel. There was too much of real accomplishment to go up and say something like that. I started prodding him, urging him to write his memoirs. I had two motives, the first was to get him away from that damn column. He was in his early seventies. The other was that I felt there was really the stuff there for a wonderful memoir. I don't pretend that my urging got him going."

Like every one of the clerks Reston employed over the years, Yardley remained a devoted Reston fan. He named his son James after Reston and asked Scotty to be the boy's godfather, though he was "inattentive" in that role. Then Yardley and Reston had something of a falling out when Yardley and his first wife divorced. Scotty was very disapproving, as he was with other colleagues whose marriages fell apart. He never imagined that all marriages were not like his to Sally. So there may have been a bit of resentment fueling Yardley's reaction to the first draft of the memoirs.

"It was awful," Yardley recalled. "What he had done was seven or eight very nice, short chapters about his boyhood. Then he had simply rehashed columns for about six hundred pages. It was boring and unrevealing. I think my letter kind of knocked him for a loop. He called me up and said we've got to talk. I went over and we spent about a day together. . . . He said, you know if I had known that this is what a memoir is supposed to be, I would never have done it because I don't believe in putting myself in the story. And that's true. He really did believe that, unlike some of today's reporters. He rather waspishly thanked me in the acknowledgment."

His family wasn't much happier with Scotty's book. Dick Reston remembers being in San Miguel Allende, Mexico, on holiday with his mother and father. "One night he gathered everyone around the fireplace and said he was going to read some of the early chapters and see what we thought. This happened two or three nights. And it was apparent to me right away, and I said to him, 'I hate to tell you this as a son, friend, colleague, journalist, what have you, but I think you got it all wrong. You are writing outside in, instead of inside out. You are Scotty Reston being an outside observer of Scotty Reston and of the events that caught you up in your life. You ought to be writing this the other way. You are writing columns. You are writing along principles you used to hammer me on, that is, "Hold on to your detachment, don't get in too close." The trouble with this book is that you are detached from yourself and there is no feeling that you were personally involved.' He took it rather well. . . . He might as well have been an actor standing onstage talking about somebody else, almost as if he didn't know."

Random House bought the book, with an advance against royalties of just under half a million dollars. But even editors there could not get Reston to stop being Reston. His editor, Kate Medina, put it this way: "What he had trouble doing was putting himself in front of the story. He believed history was more important than he was, and of course in a way he was right. Scotty was a very elegant man about his sources and his claiming credit for things. He didn't want to tell secrets. He was a gentleman. . . . He could not be a star of the show. He just wasn't going to blow his own horn."

After a couple of years, despite the many suggestions, the book did not change much. Its early chapters about Reston's life were delightful and somewhat revealing. But when he wrote about his professional life, the tone was that of the kindly columnist, making some judgments but always pulling his punches. Very little of the real story of his struggles with Arthur Krock or Abe Rosenthal appeared in those pages. The strength of his column had always been the reporting that went into it, but he left out most of the reporting of his own story. The tone of the book was the same as his column had been. But the restraint and balance that made his columns so valuable made much of this memoir, in a time of self-revelation and personal vendetta, seem dated and pale. The prose had the familiar Reston ease and rhythm, laced with an unfailing good humor and wit. But, recalled Medina: "There was a kind of fatigue. I think he was frustrated by it. It was publishable and it was okay, but it just wasn't a satisfying kind of okay." Random House printed forty-eight thousand copies of *Deadline,* but a large number were returned.

Scotty asked Henry Kissinger to contribute this blurb for the dust jacket: "Scotty Reston has been an invaluable public conscience and witness to history for much of this century. His perceptive memoir recaptures the turmoil and hopes of the times." It was the least Kissinger could have done, since the book never detailed the storm of criticism that resulted from Reston's dealings with Kissinger. Old friend Arthur Schlesinger Jr. also wrote a paean to Scotty: "A great newspaperman looks back on our times in a splendid memoir salted with humor, insight and meditative wisdom." In an interview some years later, after Scotty's death, Schlesinger summed up Reston a bit differently. "The great thing in life is to know when to leave the stage," the historian said. "Lippmann had that. He left. Reston stayed too long. Scotty wound up being not very interesting and bland, an acquiescer in things as they are."

In the fall of 1991, Scotty appeared on the government-watching cable channel C-Span with Brian Lamb to discuss his book. He looked slightly rumpled, his silver hair combed over from right side to left, flopping down over his face now and then. He was not trained for television. He mumbled a bit, didn't look at the camera as one is supposed to, and was just Scotty Reston, delightfully telling stories from his life.

Lamb asked Reston why he had appeared so rarely on television, a question that any viewer, seeing Scotty's discomfort on the screen, could have answered. "I'm of two minds about television," Scotty answered. "First of all, as a profession to be in, if you'll excuse my saying so, it frightens me because it makes you think about yourself. I do not think thinking about yourself is a formula for happiness. In print journalism, we're always writing from the outside in. That's been one of the problems of writing this book, because in a book of memoirs you have to turn it around and write from the inside out. The other thing about it that I want to make clear is that as an instrument of education in a time of revolution like this, there is nothing to compare with it. TV and civil rights. TV and Vietnam. We wrote about the dangers of Vietnam endlessly. It had no effect on policy. But when people saw on television our own lads setting fire to straw huts with Zippo lighters and saw the carnage of that war, then the country rose up against it." His observation was a fitting epitaph for his kind of journalism.

Reston noted that the title of his memoirs implied he was facing his ultimate deadline. "I'm not really happy about '*Deadline*,'" he said. "There's a paradox about that I think. *Deadline* is a pessimistic word, it suggests the end, even the end of life. Actually it is an opti-mistic book. It is a book believing in morality, believing in marriage, believing that our country can cope, can bring peace to the world."

He had just turned eighty-two years old when he spoke with Lamb. He was dreading what lay ahead: "I always wished I had had my parents' faith. My parents always thought of death as a reward. When our days were over and our work completed, we would be rewarded with everlasting life. Unfortunately, I have not been able to have that faith. But it was a wonderful solace and comfort to them. They were sure all their lives that at the end of their lives their family would meet again on the other side."

Over the next four years, Scotty's health failed precipitously. He had heart problems and a stroke, which disrupted his speech. During a visit in January 1995, he told former clerk David Dunlop that he hoped to live as long as Sally. That was not to be. He contracted bone cancer, which he sardonically called polio. On December 6 of that same year, after the first edition of the *Times* had gone to press, Scotty Reston died at his home. Sally and Jim and Tom were at his side. Jim was reading aloud to his father sections of Scotty's mem-oirs about his boyhood and his love affair with Sally.

The next day President Bill Clinton, the only president since Her-bert Hoover that Scotty hadn't known personally, called with his condolences. There should have been condolences, too, for the lost world of Reston's best journalism, his precarious and artful walk along the high wire between distance and intimacy, a balancing act that is so difficult that in the end even Scotty Reston could not sus-tain it. Clinton's presidency perfectly expressed the new world: sys-tematic lying from the highest official in the land, hounded by a mean and destructive press.

Reston's funeral was held on a cold and snowy Saturday in the gothic chapel of Saint Albans School, where his sons had gone to high school and the very symbol of the Washington upper class. It was a long way from the little Scots Presbyterian chapel he and his parents had walked to twice each Sunday when he was a boy. The sanctuary was filled to capacity. His former clerks were his pallbearers. The luminaries of American journalism, many of whom Scotty Reston had discovered as kids in the provinces, were among the mourners. Punch Sulzberger spoke, returning the favor for the eulogies Scotty had delivered for the Sulzberger family over the years. Kay Graham spoke too, telling stories from the times when she and Phil and Scotty and Sally had spent happy days together.

At the last came Tom Wicker, the man for whom Scotty had gone to war with the power structure of the paper he loved. The mourners wept as he spoke: "If it were possible, as I wish it were, I still would work for Scotty Reston for nothing, or even pay for the privilege. In 1957, nearly forty years ago . . . , that was a scared young man's fantasy. Now it's an old man's sorrow – for a newspaperman I admired, for a friend I loved, for a time of hope and faith I doubt I'll ever know again."

AFTERWORD

IT WAS OF course not just the selfish duplicity of Henry Kissinger and the particular vulnerability of Scotty Reston that ruined the tense but essentially trusting relationship between government and the press. The war in Vietnam and Watergate reinforced in profound ways the view that neither the people nor the press could fully trust their own government.

For a quarter of a century, the press and the government have been more often adversaries than allies. Reston's philosophy was that while trying to pry every last bit of information possible out of naturally self-protective politicians, the reporter had to practice his trade with a core notion that those in government, more often than not, were trying to do the right thing for the United States of America. Today, that is a difficult attitude to hold. Politicians have been on the defensive for so long, battling public and press cynicism, that their overriding attitude toward the press, and by extension the public, is a corrosively reciprocal cynicism.

The instincts of the politicians and statesmen in the Reston era were to at least try to explain, perhaps off the record, their positions and their understanding of national problems. Today's leaders' first instinct is to "spin," which is a nice way of saying that they refuse even a modicum of candor. As a friend of mine from Mississippi puts it: "They lie when the truth would do." This contempt for the intelligence of the electorate merely reinforces the syndrome of cynicism.

Is there any hope that a decent public dialogue between American leaders and the American people can be restored? The terrorist attacks of September 2001 might have resulted in a stronger sense of common national purpose, but instead it seems only to have provided a new rationalization for secrecy and new weapons to quash dissent.

The press itself doesn't provide much reason for hope. The ethic of disbelief in politicians and their pronouncements is still powerful. Much of the press is now part of huge corporate enterprises. This often produces coverage that is either sycophantic, to protect those corporations' relationship with the government, or stupidly sensationalistic, in order to pump readership and revenue.

The presidential campaign of 2000 did, however, provide two rays of hope. The candidacy of Senator John McCain of Arizona was almost totally a product of his candor, with the press and with the electorate. Although he failed to win the Republican nomination, his campaign was a throwback to the old days when politicians said what they thought and permitted the press to know them as they were. That McCain did as well as he did for as long as he did offers hope that a politician like him may one day succeed.

Perversely, the other moderately hopeful sign was the failure of Vice President Al Gore's campaign for the presidency. Gore was once a relaxed, relatively candid politician of high intelligence and easy discourse with the press. The more successful he became, however, the less he trusted himself and the public's ability to evaluate him fairly. He became a wooden, often condescending, and utterly ineffective candidate. That he lost perhaps carries the message that a politician who distrusts the people he seeks to lead will never succeed.

I concede that these are thin reeds to grasp. But I do firmly believe that this nation would be better served if there were again Scotty Restons mining the inner workings of the government and telling us the truth about what they pry loose.

NOTES ON SOURCES

CHAPTER 1. *The Reporter and the President*

The account of the summit meeting and of Reston's private session with President Kennedy relies on Reston's rather cryptic description in *Deadline: A Memoir*, by James B. Reston (Random House, 1991), and more important, on the reconstructions done by David Halberstam in *The Best and the Brightest* (Random House, 1969) and by Richard Reeves in *President Kennedy: Profile of Power* (Simon and Schuster, 1993). Both writers based their accounts on interviews with Reston. See also David Kaiser's *American Tragedy: Kennedy, Johnson, and the Origins of the Vietnam War* (Harvard University Press, Belknap Press, 2000) for a discussion of the importance of Kennedy's remarks to Reston about Vietnam.

CHAPTER 2. *The Outsider*

The recollections of Reston's youth are recorded in the early chapters of *Deadline*.

Reston's oral descriptions of his mother and his boyhood were tape-recorded by James B. Reston Jr. The tapes themselves are in the possession of Thomas Busey Reston. My notes from the tapes are with the other source materials for this book, at the University of Illinois library.

Johanna Reston's comments on the family's history, here and in the next chapter, are from an interview done for a *Time* magazine cover story on Reston that appeared in the issue dated February 15, 1960. The research for the story is contained in the magazine's research library. Photocopies of those files are deposited with the James B. Reston collection at the University of Illinois library.

Entries in Reston's sporadic diary are in the collection at the University of Illinois.

The account of Reston's father transcribing his column comes from the author's interview with Scotty Reston.

The quotation from Si Burick, the editor for whom Reston worked on the *Dayton Daily News* while he was in high school, is from a *Time* magazine interview for the 1960 cover story, as are Reston's sister's memories of their youth.

Reston's letter to his sister is at the University of Illinois.

The tape recording of Reston talking with his mother is with the collection at the University of Illinois. Sally Reston's description of her mother-in-law is from an interview with the author.

CHAPTER 3. *Scotty and Sally*

John Clifford "Fuzzy" Evans was interviewed for the 1960 *Time* magazine story.

Reston's threatened expulsion from the University of Illinois for failing to pay his tuition is treated in some detail in *Deadline*.

Both classmate Bertha Enger and professor Bruce Weirick were interviewed by *Time* magazine.

Many of the details of the courtship are from *Deadline*.

The accounts of the college years given to his son are on the tapes done by James B. Reston Jr.

Sally's recollections of their college years, and of subsequent events in their lives, are from the author's interviews with her. Tapes and notes from those interviews are in the Reston collection at the University of Illinois.

Quotations from the publisher in Springfield, Ohio, are from the *Time* magazine interviews.

The letter to Professor Fred Seibert is in Seibert's papers at the University of Illinois.

Milt Caniff and Associated Press editor Herb Barker were interviewed for the *Time* cover story.

CHAPTER 4. *Big Cities*

Reston's remarks about interviewing Maugham and about his abstinence from alcohol and sex are on the tapes made by his son James B. Reston Jr.

Milt Caniff's comments were made to a *Time* magazine reporter.

Quotations from letters to and from Sally Reston are from *Deadline*. At this time, the personal correspondence between Scotty and Sally is in the possession of the Reston family.

Sally Reston's recollections of her childhood in Sycamore, her early years in New York, and the move to London are from her interview with the author.

Ralph McGill was interviewed for the 1960 *Time* cover story. Reston recorded the Grand National incident in *Deadline*.

CHAPTER 5. *War*

The letter to Fred Siebert is in the collection of his letters at the University of Illinois library.

Reston described prewar and wartime in London in *Deadline* and in his first book, *Prelude to Victory* (Knopf, 1942).

Sally Reston's comments on their residences in England are from her interview with the author.

Ferdinand Kuhn and Raymond Daniell were interviewed for the 1960 *Time* magazine story.

Gay Talese's *The Kingdom and the Power* (World Publishing Co., 1966) contains a brief account of the coded report on the torpedoing of the *Belfast*. The University of Illinois collection has, apparently from Talese's own notes, the fuller report of the coded message and its contents.

The letter to Richard Reston is in the University of Illinois collection.

CHAPTER 6. *The Sulzberger Adoption*

The lives of Arthur Hays Sulzberger and his wife, Iphigene, are described in great detail in Susan E. Tifft and Alex S. Jones's *The Trust: The Private and Powerful Family behind the* New York Times (Little, Brown, 1999), and also in Mrs. Sulzberger's own memoirs, *Iphigene: My Life and the New York Times*, written with her granddaughter Susan W. Dryfoos (Times Books, 1979). Reston recounts the post-Christmas dinner party with the Sulzbergers in *Deadline*. His early days in Washington are also described in his memoirs.

The Krock correspondence regarding Reston is in the archives of the *New York Times*.

Reviews of *Prelude to Victory* are with the Reston papers at the University of Illinois.

Lester Markel's reaction to being forced to retire was recounted by Arthur Ochs Sulzberger in an interview with the author.

Reston's letter to Arthur Krock is contained in the collection of Krock's papers in the archival section at the Princeton University library.

CHAPTER 7. *Mr. Gus*

Descriptions of Arthur Hays Sulzberger rely on Tifft and Jones's *The Trust*.

Either Reston or Sulzberger had Scotty's extensive diary of their trip to the Soviet Union carefully retyped. The full text is with the Reston papers at the University of Illinois.

Sulzberger's comment to his wife about the troop train incident is recorded in *Iphigene*.

Many of the letters between Arthur Hays Sulzberger and Reston using the affectionate names derived from their Russian trip are in the archives of the *New York Times*.

CHAPTER 8. *Scoops*

Reston's memoir, *Deadline*, describes his working relationship with AHS, his opinion of Jimmy James, and his early opinion of Senator Vandenberg.

Krock's correspondence with Sulzberger is in the archives of the *New York Times*.

Turner Catledge recounts the story of the weekend at Cliveden in his memoirs, *My Life and the* Times (Harper and Row, 1971).

Arthur Krock's comment about Reston's not being a "cultivated man" was made to a *Time* magazine correspondent for the 1960 cover story. Krock's *Memoirs: Sixty Years on the Firing Line* was published by Funk and Wagnalls in 1968.

Dean Rusk's memoirs, *As I Saw It,* in which he tells the story of being invited to call on Lippmann and Krock, were published by W. W. Norton in 1990.

Reston's correspondence with Lippmann is with the collection of Lippmann's papers in the archives at the Yale University library.

The letter correcting Reston's identification for his source for the Dumbarton Oaks documents is with the Reston collection at the University of Illinois. The *Times'* own misidentification of Reston's source was in *The 1940s: Decade of Triumph and Trouble,* by Cabell Phillips (Macmillan, 1975).

Reston's lecture on Vandenberg was delivered in May 1968 at the University of Michigan. The text of the lecture is in the Reston collection at the University of Illinois. Reston's comment that "it must have been some other reporter" was reported in the *Toledo Blade* in 1946. Walter Lippmann's assertion that he and Reston wrote the Vandenberg speech is reported in *Walter Lippmann and the American Century,* by Ronald Steel (Atlantic–Little, Brown, 1980). Steel's explanation of the origins of that assertion was in a conversation with the author. The note from Arthur Schlesinger Jr. warning of Vandenberg's alleged affair and Reston's inquiry about it years later are in the Reston papers at the University of Illinois. Schlesinger told the author in an interview that he had no recollection of the note nor of Reston's inquiry about it. Reston's denial of having written the speech came in a conversation with the author.

CHAPTER 9. *Wise Men*

The text of the William Allen White lecture is with the Reston papers at the University of Illinois.

The Acheson correspondence concerning Reston is from *Among Friends: Personal Letters of Dean Acheson,* edited by David S. McLellan and David C. Acheson (Dodd, Mead, 1980), and from the Acheson papers in the archives at the Yale University library. Sally Reston's note to Acheson is in the Yale collection; his response is with the Reston papers.

Reston's dealings with John J. McCloy are described in *Deadline.*

William Coleman's recollection of Reston's visits with Frankfurter are from an interview with Barbara Gamarekian. Sally Reston's account of meeting with Frankfurter are from an interview with the author.

The story of Reston's work at the San Francisco conference is from an interview for *Time* magazine's 1960 cover story on Reston.

Arthur Krock's letter to Arthur Hays Sulzberger is contained in the archives of the *New York Times,* as is Jimmy James's explanation to Sulzberger of the Reston matter.

Krock's letters to Catledge and James are with his papers at the Princeton University library. Sulzberger's letters are in the archives of the *Times,* as is Reston's letter to Sulzberger.

CHAPTER 10. *The Restons of Woodley Road*

The story of James B. Reston Jr.'s bus accident is from an interview with him by the author. Subsequent quotations from him are from the same interview.

Reston's and Arthur Hays Sulzberger's correspondence concerning financing the Woodley Road house is in the archives of the *New York Times.*

Memories attributed to Richard and Tom Reston are also from the author's interviews, as are the recollections of Sally Reston.

The fragments of Reston's typed diary are in the University of Illinois collection.

The clerk's observation about not wanting to have been one of Reston's sons is from an interview by Barbara Gamarekian.

Copies of *Reston's Weekly* are at the University of Illinois.

CHAPTER 11. *High Politics*

President Truman's "knuckle-head" comment to Stevenson is quoted in David McCullough's *Truman* (Simon and Schuster, 1992).

Eric Severeid's endorsement of Adlai Stevenson is from David Halberstam's *The Fifties* (Villard Books, 1993). Halberstam was in turn quoting from Porter McKeever's *Adlai Stevenson: His Life and Legacy* (William Morrow, 1989).

Reston's comment to Kay Graham about Stevenson occurred during her interview with the Restons for her memoirs.

Stevenson's note to Tom Reston is quoted in *Deadline*.

The written exchanges with Arthur Hays Sulzberger over the Stalin questions are in the archives of the *New York Times*.

CHAPTER 12. *The Great Fear*

The McCarthy period in America is described in great detail in David Caute's *The Great Fear* (Simon and Schuster, 1978).

Reston recounted the story of his Yalta papers scoop in *Deadline*.

The *Times'* struggle with McCarthyism is described in Harrison Salisbury's *Without Fear or Favor* (Times Books, 1980) and in *The Trust* by Tifft and Jones.

CHAPTER 13. *The Other Newspaper Family*

Copies of Reston's confidential memos to Sulzberger and Lippmann are with his papers at the University of Illinois.

Reston's note to Lippmann is contained in the Reston correspondence file with the Lippmann papers at Yale.

The tribute to Lippmann was published by Harcourt, Brace and Co., 1959.

In addition to Reston's own account in *Deadline*, the relationship between Philip and Katharine Graham and the Restons is described in Mrs. Graham's memoirs, *Personal History* (Knopf, 1997). Additional details are from the author's interview with Mrs. Graham and from documents supplied to the author by her, including the transcript of an interview with the Restons conducted by Mrs. Graham and her book researcher Evelyn Small, as well as a copy of Philip Graham's handwritten contract proposal to Reston.

Arthur Krock reported his encounter with Richard Reston to a *Time* magazine correspondent for the 1960 cover story.

CHAPTER 14. *Bureau Chief*

Wallace Carroll's comments are from an interview with the author. Max Frankel, Anthony Lewis, Tom Wicker, Russell Baker, and Richard Mooney were also interviewed by the author. Baker wrote about his hiring by Reston in his memoir *Growing Up* (Congdon and Weed, 1982). Reston related Frankfurter's comments about Lewis in *Deadline*.

Edwin Dale and John Finney were interviewed for this book by Barbara Gamarekian.

Russell Baker's account of Allen Drury's unhappiness appeared on the op-ed page of the *Times*.

James Sterba was interviewed by the author.

Mary McGrory, Eileen Shanahan, and Nan Robertson were interviewed by Barbara Gamarekian.

CHAPTER 15. *What's Good for Reston Is Good for the* Times

Copies of the notes exchanged between Arthur Hays and Iphigene Ochs Sulzberger and Reston are in the archives of the *New York Times* and in the Reston collection at the University of Illinois. Reston's letter to Orvil Dryfoos urging that his column be extended to the daily paper is also in the collection at the University of Illinois.

Records of Reston's compensation are in the *Times* archives.

Marian Sulzberger Dryfoos Heiskell was interviewed by the author. Her note urging Reston to stay at the *Times* is in the Reston collection at the University of Illinois.

CHAPTER 16. *JFK*

The account of the relationship between the Grahams and the Restons is drawn from Mrs. Graham's autobiography and from the author's interview with her. See also *Deadline.* The story of Jack Kennedy's coolness in the face of Phil Graham's drunkenness is from Mrs. Graham's autobiography.

The story of Reston handling his first presidential election as bureau chief is drawn from *Deadline.*

Pierre Salinger was interviewed for this book by Barbara Gamarekian.

Ted Sorensen's thoughts on Reston's protest are from *Kennedy,* by Theodore C. Sorensen (Harper and Row, 1965).

David Halberstam and Tom Wicker and Max Frankel were interviewed by the author.

Arthur Schlesinger's report on Gilbert Harrison's agreement to drop the Bay of Pigs story from the *New Republic* is from Richard Reeves's *President Kennedy.* Harrison Salisbury wrote about the supposed JFK phone call to Orvil Dryfoos in *Without Fear or Favor.*

CHAPTER 17. *At the Summit*

For accounts of the Vienna summit, see Halberstam's *Best and the Brightest,* Richard Reeves's *President Kennedy,* Ted Sorensen's *Kennedy,* and *Deadline.*

Reston tells the story of his visit to Hyannis Port in *Deadline.*

John Kennedy's reaction to news of a Soviet bomb test is reported in Reeves's *President Kennedy.*

CHAPTER 18. *Missile Crisis*

Evan Thomas's biography *Robert Kennedy: His Life* (Simon and Schuster, 2000) contains an excellent reconstruction of the Cuban missile crisis.

President Kennedy's characterization of Senator Keating was passed on by Reston to Richard Reeves.

Max Frankel's autobiography is entitled *The Times of My Life and My Life with the* Times (Random House, 1999).

Reston's notes of his briefing by Robert Kennedy after the missile crisis are in the Reston collection at the University of Illinois.

CHAPTER 19. *A Bleak Year*

Tifft and Jones discuss the maneuvering to succeed Orvil Dryfoos in *The Trust*.

George Woods's letter suggesting Reston as a partner with Punch Sulzberger is in the Reston collection at the University of Illinois.

Reston's letter to Dryfoos about Phil Graham is at the University of Illinois, as is Reston's letter to Phil Graham about Donald Graham's internship. Donald Graham was interviewed by Barbara Gamarekian.

Phil Graham's unsent letter to Reston is from the *Washington Post* archives, as is Kay Graham's letter to the Restons urging Scotty to join her paper. The transcript of Kay Graham's conversation with the Restons was provided by Mrs. Graham.

Benjamin Bradlee's memoir, *A Good Life: Newspapering and Other Adventures*, was published in 1992 by Simon and Schuster.

CHAPTER 20. *LBJ*

President Kennedy's request that David Halberstam be removed from Saigon is detailed in Reeves's *President Kennedy*.

David Halberstam was interviewed by the author.

Eileen Shanahan was interviewed by Barbara Gamarekian.

Reston's account of his encounter with Lyndon Johnson over the issue of the television station is from *Deadline*, as are some details of the visit Reston and Sally made to the White House.

The taped telephone conversation between President Johnson, Lady Bird Johnson, and Reston is from the Lyndon Baines Johnson Library in Austin, Texas. Lady Bird Johnson's taped journal is also in the LBJ Library.

Sally Reston's compensation from the *Times* was declared annually after Reston became a director of the company.

The taped conversation between Johnson and Dean Rusk is in the LBJ Library. The transcript is quoted in Michael R. Beschloss's *Taking Charge: The Johnson White House Tapes, 1963–1964* (Simon and Schuster, 1997).

Johnson's conversation with Reston after the State of the Union address is also among the tapes at the LBJ Library. LBJ's comment about the *Herald Tribune* is reported in Beschloss's book.

Johnson's recollections of his relationship with Reston are from his memoirs, *The Vantage Point: Perspectives of the Presidency, 1963–1969* (Holt, Rinehart, and Winston, 1971).

The recorded conversation between Johnson and Reston on Vietnam is from the LBJ Library, as is the conversation that took place while Reston was attending the Democratic convention in Atlantic City. Johnson's assertion that Reston's criticism had been influenced by the Soviets is from Doris Kearns Goodwin's biography _Lyndon Johnson and the American Dream_ (Harper and Row, 1976).

CHAPTER 21. _Vietnam_

David Halberstam and Tom Wicker were interviewed by the author. Neil Sheehan, R. W. Apple, and Lothar Loewe were interviewed by Barbara Gamarekian.

The letters exchanged between Reston and Joseph Alsop are in the Reston collection at the University of Illinois, as are the confidential letter to Reston from Chester Bowles and Reston's letter to Robert Kennedy.

CHAPTER 22. _Scotty Versus Abe_

Arthur Ochs Sulzberger was interviewed by the author.

Turner Catledge recounts his role in the attempt to replace Tom Wicker in his memoirs, _My Life and the_ Times.

Abe Rosenthal, Tom Wicker, and James Greenfield and were interviewed by the author.

A copy of Reston's letter to Punch Sulzberger objecting to the change in the Washington bureau leadership is in the Reston collection at the University of Illinois.

Fred Graham and Neil Sheehan were interviewed by Barbara Gamarekian.

Max Frankel was interviewed by the author.

The notes congratulating Reston on becoming executive editor are at the University of Illinois.

Richard Mooney was interviewed by the author.

The account of the Reston-Rosenthal dinner confrontation is from Harrison Salisbury's _Without Fear or Favor._

Eugene Roberts and Anthony Lewis were interviewed by the author.

Reston's observations to Kay Graham about his failure as executive editor are from the transcript of Mrs. Graham's interview with Scotty and Sally Reston for her memoirs.

Reston's letter to Punch Sulzberger is from the _New York Times_ archives.

Reston's comment about Rosenthal's column was made during a conversation with the author.

Reston reprinted his eulogy of Arthur Sulzberger in _Deadline._

Iphigene Sulzberger's note to Reston after her husband's death is at the University of Illinois.

CHAPTER 23. *The* Gazette

Lloyd Cutler was interviewed by Barbara Gamarekian.

Richard Mooney and Joseph Lelyveld were interviewed by the author.

Reston's letter to the A&P manager is in the Reston collection at the University of Illinois.

Steve Rattner was interviewed by the author.

Richard and Jody Reston were interviewed by the author.

Reston's letter concerning his son's health is at the University of Illinois.

James B. Reston Jr., Denise Leary, and Thomas Busey Reston were interviewed by the author.

James Greenfield was interviewed by the author.

CHAPTER 24. *Nixon's Washington*

Reston's memorandum on his dinner for Nixon is at the University of Illinois.

Reston told his colleague Tom Wicker, who was interviewed by the author, about the note from Agnew. The note itself does not appear to be in the Reston collection at the University of Illinois.

Richard Helms was interviewed by the author, as was Tom Reston.

Nixon discussed his aversion to the press in his presidential memoirs, *RN: The Memoirs of Richard Nixon* (Grosset and Dunlap, 1978).

Reston's FBI file was obtained by the author under a Freedom of Information Act request.

The Whittaker Chambers accounts of his dealings with Reston are in *Witness* (Random House, 1952).

For various and complementary accounts of the Pentagon Papers story, see Halberstam, *The Best and the Brightest;* Salisbury, *Without Fear or Favor;* Tifft and Jones, *The Trust;* Graham, *Personal History;* Frankel, *The Times of My Life;* Ben Bradlee, *A Good Life;* Nixon, *RN;* and Reston, *Deadline.*

Floyd Abrams was interviewed by the author.

Reston's own account of his China trip is in *Deadline.*

Kissinger's comment about the *Times* is from the first volume of his memoirs, *White House Years* (Little, Brown, 1979).

The order from Nixon demanding a letter be concocted to criticize Reston is from H. R. Haldeman's *The Haldeman Diaries: Inside the Nixon White House* (Putnam, 1994).

Max Frankel's account of the consequences of Reston's reporting is told in *The Times of My Life.*

CHAPTER 25. *Kissinger*

Frankel's account of his pursuit of the Hanoi bombing story is from *The Times of My Life.*

The Reston-Kissinger breakfasts are reported in Hersh's *The Price of Power: Kissinger in the Nixon White House* (Summit Books, 1983).

Nixon's diary notes about Kissinger and the bombing are reproduced in *RN*.

The White House reaction to Reston's "Nixon and Kissinger" column is recounted in Walter Isaacson's *Kissinger: A Biography* (Simon and Schuster, 1992).

Kissinger's admission of his support for the bombing and his assertion that he never indicated to the press that he opposed the bombing are contained in *White House Years*.

Reston's notes of his secret talk with Kissinger are in the Reston collection at the University of Illinois.

David Halberstam was interviewed by the author.

A transcript of Reston's phone conversation with Senator Henry Jackson is at the University of Illinois, as are the notes of his conversation with Henry Kissinger before interviewing Fidel Castro and the transcript of his conversation with Kissinger about the Middle East.

Pierre Salinger was interviewed by Barbara Gamarekian.

Leslie Gelb was interviewed by the author.

The "not another Reston" comment was relayed to the author by a person present at the meeting.

CHAPTER 26. *Deadline*

A copy of Reston's note to President Gerald R. Ford is in the Reston collection at the University of Illinois, as is the transcript of the interview with Jimmy Carter.

Copies of the correspondence with Punch Sulzberger and Wallace Carroll are at the University of Illinois.

Jonathan Yardley was interviewed by Barbara Gamarekian.

Richard Reston's comments are from the author's interview.

Kate Medina and Arthur Schlesinger Jr. were interviewed by the author.

INDEX

ABOUT THE AUTHOR

JOHN F. STACKS was a reporter and editor for *Time* magazine for more than three decades. He began his career in journalism working for his father, who was the editor of the Lancaster, Pennsylvania, *Intelligencer-Journal*. He was a reporter for the *Washington Evening Star* and then joined *Time*'s Washington bureau in 1967. He reported on the Congress, the White House, and presidential politics, covering the national campaigns from 1968 through 1980. He also directed the bureau's coverage of the Watergate scandals.

Stacks became New York bureau chief in 1983 and chief of correspondents in 1987, managing the magazine's worldwide news bureaus. He was later executive editor and deputy managing editor of the magazine.

This is Stacks's fourth book. He lives in New York.